100 CLASSIC HIKES IN™

OREGON

Oregon Coast / Columbia Gorge / Cascades / Eastern Oregon / Wallowas

SECOND EDITION

Douglas Lorain

THE MOUNTAINEERS BOOKS

THE MOUNTAINEERS BOOKS
is the nonprofit publishing arm of The Mountaineers, an organization founded in 1906 and dedicated to the exploration, preservation, and enjoyment of outdoor and wilderness areas.

1001 SW Klickitat Way, Suite 201, Seattle, WA 98134

First edition, 2004. Second edition: First printing 2011, second printing 2014, third printing with significant updates 2016, fourth printing 2018, fifth printing 2021

Manufactured in China

Copy Editor: Christine Ummel Hosler
Cover and Book Design: The Mountaineers Books
Layout: Ani Rucki
Cartographer: Moore Creative Designs
All photographs by the author

Maps shown in this book were produced using National Geographic's *TOPO!* software. For more information, go to www.nationalgeographic.com/topo.

Cover photograph: *South Sister over Eileen Lake, Three Sisters Wilderness (Hike 52).*
Frontispiece: *Hidden Lake, Wallowa Mountains (Hike 87).*

Library of Congress Cataloging-in-Publication Data
Lorain, Douglas, 1962–

Library of Congress Cataloging-in-Publication Data
   Lorain, Douglas, 1962–
      100 classic hikes in Oregon : Oregon coast, Columbia Gorge. Cascades, eastern Oregon, Wallowas.—2nd ed.
      p. cm.
      ISBN 978-1-59485-492-7 (ppb)
      1. Hiking—Oregon—Guidebooks 2. Trails—Oregon—Guidebooks. 3. Backpacking—Oregon—Guidebooks. 4. Oregon—Guidebooks. I. Title. II. Title: One hundred classic hikes in Oregon.
   GV199.42.O74L67 2011
   796.5109795—dc22
                    2010045518

ISBN (paperback): 978-1-59485-492-7
ISBN (e-book): 978-1-59485-493-4

CONTENTS

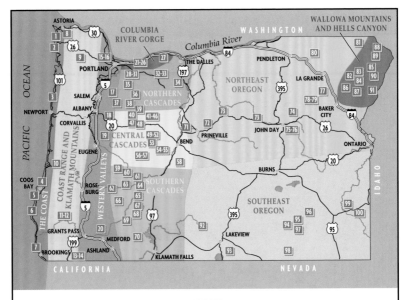

LEGEND

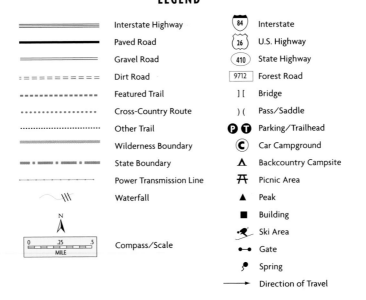

═══════════ Interstate Highway	🛡️84 Interstate
━━━━━━━━━ Paved Road	🛡️26 U.S. Highway
───────── Gravel Road	410 State Highway
= = = = = = = = Dirt Road	9712 Forest Road
▪▪▪▪▪▪▪▪▪▪ Featured Trail	] [Bridge
••••••••••• Cross-Country Route	) (Pass/Saddle
⋯⋯⋯⋯⋯⋯ Other Trail	🅿️ 🆃 Parking/Trailhead
━━━━━━━━━ Wilderness Boundary	Ⓒ Car Campground
━ ▪ ━ ▪ ━ ▪ ━ State Boundary	Λ Backcountry Campsite
─┼─┼─┼─┼─ Power Transmission Line	⛩️ Picnic Area
⌇⌇ \\\ Waterfall	▲ Peak
	■ Building
N ↑ compass	🎿 Ski Area
0 .25 .5 MILE Compass/Scale	●━●● Gate
	🔑 Spring
	⟶ Direction of Travel

HIKE NUMBER AND NAME	DIFFICULTY	SEASON	FEATURES
Half-Day Hikes			
16 Tryon Creek State Park	Easy–Moderate	All year	Woodsy canyon, wildflowers
18 McDowell Creek Falls	Easy	All year	Waterfalls
27 Hood River Mountain Loop	Easy	Mar–Nov	Wildflowers, views
55 Todd Lake Loop	Easy	June–Oct	Mountain lake, meadows
61 Indigo Lake	Easy	June–Oct	Lovely mountain lake
62 Wolf Creek Falls	Easy	All year	Waterfalls, lovely forest
63 Toketee Falls	Easy	All year	Stunning waterfall
73 John Day Fossil Beds Trails	Easy–Moderate	All year	Colorful hills and rock formations
74 Arch Rock	Easy	May–Oct	Unique rock formation
77 Crawfish Meadow	Moderate	June–Oct	Gorgeous mountain meadow, lake
Short Day Hikes			
1 Cannon Beach Trails	Easy–Moderate	All year	Beach, rugged coastline
3 Cascade Head and Harts Cove	Easy–Moderate	July–Dec	Views, grassy headlands
5 Sunset Bay to Shore Acres	Easy	All year	Wildlife, rocky coastline
6 Blacklock Point	Moderate	Apr–June	Coastal cliffs and views
10 Kentucky Falls	Moderate	All year	Waterfalls, old-growth forest
11 Hanging Rock	Easy–Moderate	Apr–Nov	Dramatic rocky overlook
19 Horse Rock Ridge	Moderate	Mar–Dec	Wildflowers, meadows, view
20 Lower Table Rock	Moderate	All year	Wildflowers, basalt rimrock
21 Latourell Falls Loop	Easy	All year	Waterfalls, lush vegetation
23 Horsetail Falls to Triple Falls	Easy	All year	Waterfalls, steep gorge
26 Mitchell Point	Moderate	All year	Rocky viewpoint
31 Eliot Glacier View	Strenuous	Aug–Oct	Up-close views of glacier
32 Barlow Butte	Moderate	June–Oct	Historic trail, viewpoint
34 School Canyon Trail	Moderate	Mar–Dec	Unique botany, wildflowers
35 Clackamas River Trail	Easy	All year	Beautiful river, waterfall
41 Triangulation Peak	Easy	June–Oct	Viewpoint, wildflowers
68 Garfield Peak	Moderate	July–Oct	Crater Lake views
71 Smith Rock State Park Loop	Moderate	All year	Colorful rock formations
72 Steins Pillar	Easy	Apr–Nov	Towering rock pinnacle
75 Baldy Mountain	Moderate	June–Oct	Viewpoint
93 Crane Mountain	Moderate	June–Oct	Viewpoint
95 Wildhorse Lake	Strenuous	July–Oct	Mountain lake, great views
100 Three Forks Trails	Moderate	Apr–Oct	Desert canyon, hot spring
Long Day Hikes			
2 Cape Falcon and Neahkahnie Mountain	Moderate	All year	Dramatic headland, views
4 Umpqua Dunes Scenic Area	Easy–Strenuous	All year	Sand dunes, wildlife

HIKE NUMBER AND NAME	DIFFICULTY	SEASON	FEATURES
Long Day Hikes CONTINUED			
7 Whalehead Cove to Cape Ferrelo	Moderate	All year	Great coastal views, flowers, tide pools
8 Saddle Mountain	Moderate	Mar–Nov	Flowers, high viewpoint
9 Kings Mountain	Strenuous	Mar–Nov	High viewpoint, flowers
13 Sucker Creek Gap and Swan Mountain	Moderate	June–Nov	Diverse plant life, views
15 Forest Park	Easy–Moderate	All year	Quiet forests, flowers
17 Silver Falls State Park Loop	Moderate	All year	Waterfalls, lush canyon
22 Angels Rest– Devils Rest Loop	Strenuous	Mar–Dec	Waterfalls, lush forests, rocky viewpoint
25 Mount Defiance Loop	Very Strenuous	May–Oct	High viewpoint
29 Yocum Ridge	Very Strenuous	July–Sept	Great mountain views
33 Lookout Mountain via Divide Trail	Moderate	June–Oct	Views, rock formations
37 Opal Creek Loop	Moderate	Mar–Dec	Old-growth forests, falls
39 Olallie Lake Scenic Area Loop	Easy	July–Oct	Huckleberries, lakes, fall colors
42 Grizzly Peak	Strenuous	July–Oct	Viewpoint
46 Canyon Creek– First Creek Meadows Loop	Strenuous	July–Oct	Mountain views, wildflowers
47 Iron Mountain Loop	Moderate	June–Nov	Wildflowers, views
48 Browder Ridge	Moderate	June–Oct	Viewpoint, wildlfowers
49 McKenzie Lava Flow and George Lake	Moderate	June–Oct	Huge lava flow, views
50 Black Crater	Strenuous	July–Oct	Viewpoint
51 Soap Creek	Strenuous	July–Oct	Great mountain views
54 Swampy Lakes	Moderate	June–Nov	Mountain meadow, falls
56 Rebel Rock Loop	Very Strenuous	June–Oct	Viewpoint, old-growth forest
58 Paulina Lake Loop	Moderate	June–Oct	Views, volcanic geology
60 Mountain View Lake	Moderate	July–Oct	Lovely mountain lake
64 Tipsoo Peak	Moderate	July–Oct	Viewpoint
66 Rocky Ridge	Moderate	June–Nov	Views, wildflowers
67 Wizard Island	Moderate	July–Oct	Crater Lake views, geology
80 Ninemile Ridge	Strenuous	Apr–Nov	Views, wildflowers
85 Big Sheep Basin and Bonny Lakes	Moderate	July–Oct	Mountain views, wildflowers
88 Imnaha River Trail	Moderate	Mar–Nov	Great canyon scenery
96 Pike Creek Canyon	Moderate–Very Strenuous	Apr–Nov	Great desert canyon
97 Big Sand Gap	Moderate	Apr–Nov	Desert playa, mountain views
98 Pueblo Mountain	Very Strenuous	May–Oct	Great desert views, wildlife
99 Lambert Rocks and Chalk Basin Loop	Strenuous	Apr–Oct	Badlands, canyon scenery

HIKE NUMBER AND NAME	DIFFICULTY	SEASON	FEATURES
Short Backpacks			
12 Lower Rogue River Trail	Easy–Moderate	Mar–Nov	Canyon scenery, wildlife
24 Tanner Butte– Eagle Creek Loop	Strenuous	May–Oct	Waterfalls, lush plant life, high viewpoint
28 East Zigzag Mountain and Burnt Lake	Moderate	June–Oct	Mountain lake, viewpoint
36 Serene Lake Loop	Moderate	June–Oct	Lakes, huckleberries
38 Whetstone Ridge to Twin Lakes	Moderate	June–Oct	Views, quiet lake
40 Jefferson Park	Moderate	July–Oct	Great mountain views
43 Shale Lake Loop	Strenuous	July–Oct	Mountain views, wildflowers
44 Table Lake Loop	Strenuous	July–Oct	Mountain views, lakes
45 Duffy Lake and Santiam Lake	Moderate	June–Oct	Lakes, wildflowers
53 Broken Top Loop	Strenuous	July–Oct	Great mountain scenery, lakes
59 Divide Lake	Moderate	July–Oct	Mountain scenery
65 Thielsen Creek Meadows Loop	Strenuous	July–Oct	Great mountain scenery
70 Mountain Lakes Loop	Strenuous	July–Oct	Lakes, views
76 Strawberry Lakes Loop	Strenuous	July–Oct	Lakes, mountain scenery
79 Rock Creek Lake	Strenuous	July–Oct	Gorgeous mountain lake, solitude, wildlife
81 Wenaha River Trail	Moderate	All year	Canyon scenery
83 Frances Lake	Very Strenuous	July–Oct	High mountain lake
84 Ice Lake	Strenuous	July–Oct	High mountain lake
89 Somers Point	Strenuous	June–Oct	Breathtaking canyon view
91 Summit Trail to Bear Mountain	Moderate	May–Nov	Canyon views, flowers
92 Gearhart Mountain	Moderate	June–Oct	Rock formations, mountain scenery
94 Big Indian Gorge	Strenuous	June–Oct	Huge glacial canyon, fall colors
Extended Backpacks			
14 Red Buttes Loop	Very Strenuous	June–Oct	Diverse geology and botany, views
30 Timberline Trail Loop	Strenuous	July–Oct	Great mountain scenery, flowers
52 Northern Three Sisters Loop	Strenuous	July–Oct	Great mountain scenery, lakes, wildflowers
57 Irish Mountain– Mink Lake Loop	Moderate	July–Oct	Countless mountain lakes
69 Seven Lakes Basin and Sky Lakes	Moderate	July–Oct	Mountain lakes, views
78 Elkhorn Crest Trail	Strenuous	July–Oct	Great mountain scenery
82 West Lostine River Loop	Strenuous	July–Oct	Great mountain scenery, lakes
86 Eagle Creek– West Eagle Loop	Strenuous	July–Oct	Great mountain scenery, lakes
87 Southeast Wallowas Loop	Strenuous	July–Oct	Great mountain scenery
90 Grand Hells Canyon Loop	Very Strenuous	Mar–Nov	Great canyon scenery, wildlife

INTRODUCTION

Not every state can say this (they know who they are), but in Oregon the Great Outdoors really is *great*. Oregon is a state of remarkable geographic diversity. From waterlogged rain forests to arid deserts, from glacier-clad peaks to wave-lapped beaches, from deep river canyons to view-packed ridge crests, Oregon has some-thing to offer every outdoor lover. You could easily spend a lifetime in this beautiful state and never grow tired of its charms.

Carefully selected from more than 2000 hikes in the Beaver State, the trips in this book are, arguably, the 100 best walks in Oregon. Every part of the state is represented, so no matter where you live or where you are visiting, a choice of great hikes is nearby. The hikes also include a mix of difficulty levels, from short, easy strolls suitable for young children and their great-grandparents to extended backpacking trips on which experienced hikers can enjoy a long vaca-tion away from the rat race.

Personal preferences were necessarily a factor in the selection of hikes to include, but under-standing the criteria used will give you a good idea of what kind of hikes you can expect to find in this book. Although no single attribute was required in every hike, the most important criterion was outstanding scenery, especially good views. Water features, such as clear streams, waterfalls, and mountain lakes, were also sig-nificant attractions. Similarly, wildlife sightings enhance any outdoor experience, as do wild-flowers, fall colors, old-growth forests, juicy huckleberries, and interesting geologic features. One factor that is important to many hikers but which played *no* part in the selection criteria for this book is the quality of fishing.

Apart from these subjective judgments, the following *objective* criteria apply to all hikes in this book:
- The trailhead is accessible in a typical pas-senger car. In a few cases the car may get a little banged up in the process, but at least you do not have to drive a high-clearance, four-wheel-drive vehicle.
- The hike follows an established trail or an easy cross-country route (beaches, open ridges, streams, etc.) that any reasonably experienced hiker can follow.

Mount Jefferson from Bear Butte Viewpoint (Hike 44)

• The hike is natural in character. Interesting man-made features such as fire lookouts, historic mines, and old homesteads are acceptable (even welcome), but the bulk of a hike's attributes must be the work of nature rather than human beings.

The best and most intimate way to see the state is at the self-propelled pace that hiking allows. To answer the question of *why* go hiking, simply glance at the photographs and hike overviews in this book to be inspired about what you can experience if you travel on foot. Questions about *where* and *when* to go are answered in the individual hike descriptions. That leaves the question of *how* to do these hikes. Some tips will help you spend more happy hours exploring Oregon's trails.

GETTING STARTED

If you are new to hiking, are new to Oregon, or just want to find new hiking friends, a good place to start is with a local hiking or outdoor club. These groups have a full schedule of hikes suitable for all ability levels. This allows you to save money by carpooling with others, gives you the chance to meet interesting people, and lets you learn from local experts. For a list of the larger hiking clubs in Oregon, see Appendix B at the back of this book.

WHAT TO TAKE

A comprehensive discussion of hiking gear is beyond the scope of this book, but years of experience have shown that no hiker should leave the trailhead without carrying the **Ten Essentials.** In an emergency, these may save your life. The Ten Essentials have evolved from a list of individual items to a list of functional systems to help you respond to an accident or spend an unexpected night outdoors.

1. **Navigation:** map (preferably topographic) and compass or GPS device—and the skills to use them

Clouds above Sky Lakes Basin (Hike 69)

2. **Sun protection:** sunglasses and sunscreen—especially in the desert and high mountains
3. **Insulation:** extra clothing—something waterproof and warm
4. **Illumination:** flashlight or headlamp—and extra batteries
5. **First-aid supplies:** first-aid kit—and the skills to use it
6. **Fire:** firestarter (a candle or equivalent) and matches—in a waterproof container
7. **Repair kit and tools:** knife—for starting fires, first aid, and many other uses
8. **Nutrition:** extra food—have enough so you return with a little left over
9. **Hydration:** extra water—and a means to purify water on longer trips
10. **Emergency shelter:** tent—on day hikes, a trash bag, bivy sack, or reflective emergency blanket

When it comes to equipment for hiking, as with many sports, you can choose to go on a budget (practically zero costs) or spend a fortune on all the latest gear. Day hikes do not require much gear. All you need are a few basic items (see "Ten Essentials" above) thrown into a small pack, and you're ready to go. If you want to be a bit more comfortable, your first purchase should be a pair of lightweight hiking shoes. These will give you better traction and keep your feet dry and free of blisters.

If you plan on backpacking, the least expensive alternative is to borrow gear from friends or to purchase used equipment at army surplus or similar stores. From there, the equipment possibilities range all the way up to a dizzying array of high-tech clothing (made from wonderful new fabrics that keep you warm and dry in the winter and cool in the summer) and rugged hiking boots that will protect your feet from rocks, snow, mud, and any other hazard the trails may have in store. There are also amazingly lightweight nylon tents, wonderfully warm sleeping bags that keep you cozy on the coldest mountain nights, and all kinds of nifty and imaginative accessories. The list is almost endless—and the cost can be frightening. The best approach is to keep it simple and low-cost, at least until you determine whether hiking is something you really enjoy and want to pursue regularly.

PERMITS AND FEES

Unfortunately, no matter how inexpensively you prefer to go, hiking is no longer the "free" activity it once was. Unless you hike only in local city parks, you will probably have to drive to a trailhead and park there. Today, most land management agencies charge a fee for parking at the larger and more developed trailheads. However, so far it is still free to hike on state forest land, in city parks, and on most Bureau of Land Management (BLM) land.

In most, but not all, national forests in Oregon (which includes the majority of hikes in this book), cars parked within 0.25 mile of developed trailheads are required to display a Northwest Forest Pass. These are available at all ranger stations and many sporting goods stores. A daily pass costs $5 as of this writing, but if you hike regularly, it is cheaper and more convenient to purchase an annual pass, which currently costs $30.

Most of the larger state parks in Oregon require a day-use permit (prices vary) or you can purchase an annual state park pass for $30.

Along the Oregon coast, you can buy a single Oregon Pacific Coast Passport, which allows you to enter coastal parks, use trailheads, and visit beaches no matter which state or federal agency manages the land.

At Crater Lake National Park, the National Park Service has charged an entry fee for decades.

HOW TO USE THIS BOOK

The hikes are grouped by region from roughly west to east; within each region, the hikes are listed from north to south. Each region's outstanding features, weather, and other unique characteristics are described in the chapter introductions. The Trails at a Glance chart at the front of this book can help you choose hikes by their duration, difficulty, season, and features.

Every hike begins with an information summary of the most important facts about that outing.

Distance is given for each hike's round-trip.

Only a few specifically identified hikes are recommended as one-way adventures. For hikes that exceed 20 miles or that include any cross-country travel, distances are rounded to the nearest mile or half mile.

Hiking time is a subjective assessment of how long the hike will take, in hours or days.

Elevation gain includes *all* of a hike's ups and downs in cumulative total round-trip elevation gain.

The *Difficulty* rating is a subjective assessment of how strenuous the hike is in comparison to other hikes. This rating takes into account not only a hike's distance and elevation gain but also times when a hike is unusually steep, covers exceptionally rough terrain, or requires cross-country travel. People who are not accustomed to hiking may find that trips rated "moderate" seem pretty darn difficult to them. If so, they probably should not attempt a "strenuous" hike until they have worked up to that level.

The *Season* entry tells you when a trip is usually snow-free enough for hiking, while the following entry indicates when the trail is at its *Best*—when the flowers peak, the huckleberries are ripe, or the mosquitoes have died down, etc.

The weather during an outing, of course, significantly affects the enjoyment of any outdoor adventure. What many hikers do not adequately consider, however, is that the weather during the previous winter will also impact your travel today. Every hike description in this book identifies when the trail is typically snow-free enough for travel—which varies considerably from year to year. But keep in mind that the winter's snowpack also impacts the quantity and blooming season of wildflowers, the difficulty of stream crossings, and the availability of seasonal water sources. The Natural Resources Conservation Service (see Appendix A at the back of this book) collects precipitation and snowfall data and provides this information free of charge to the public. Hikers should check the snowpack about April 1 to see how it compares to normal, then adjust the hike's recommended season accordingly.

This book includes a contour map for each hike, but if you want to carry an additional topographic map, the best available *Map(s)* are listed in the information summary; some are USGS maps, some are U.S. Forest Service (USFS) maps, and some are maps issued by private companies.

The *Information* entry lists the land management agency that administers the area where the hike is located.

Following the information summary for each hike are directions to the trailhead, an overview of the hike's highlights, and a detailed trail description.

At the back of the book are two appendixes to help you locate further information on land management agencies and other information sources as well as conservation and hiking groups in Oregon.

TRAIL ETIQUETTE

As more people hit the trails, we must all work harder to follow some simple, commonsense rules of wilderness etiquette. Fortunately, no one needs to go to finishing school to learn these rules. They are really just a matter of common courtesy and trying to make yourself unobtrusive.

Crowds are incompatible with wilderness, so keep your group as small as possible. In most designated wilderness areas, the maximum allowable party size ranges from twenty down to as few as six people, but even smaller groups are preferable.

One of the attractions of wilderness travel is the chance to enjoy natural peace and quiet. Do not let members of your party yell back and forth, never play a radio in camp at night, and otherwise avoid producing any of the noise pollution that so many of your fellow hikers are trying to escape. If you carry a cell phone, use it only for emergencies rather than carrying on lengthy phone conversations as you hike up the trail.

If at all possible, leave pets at home—even very well-mannered dogs disturb wildlife, which instinctively perceives dogs as predators.

Respect other trail users you encounter. When you meet horse parties, step off on the downhill side of the trail to allow them to pass, and talk in a soft and friendly manner so the horses do not get spooked by this strange creature with an odd-colored hump on its back. Theoretically, hikers have the right-of-way over mountain bikes, but in practice, it is easier to simply step aside and

Wallowa Mountains from Himmelwright Meadow (Hike 91)

let these folks pedal past. As for motorcycles, you will hear these monsters approaching for miles (it is impossible for a motorcycle to be unobtrusive), so go hide someplace until they have passed, then feel free to curse these noisy, erosion-causing, fume-spewing terrors. (And when you return home, write letters of protest to the land managers for allowing the trails to be turned into narrow roads for motor vehicles.)

LEAVE NO TRACE

Hikers today are strongly encouraged and, in some cases, legally required to minimize their impact on the land. For decades the standard advice has been "Take only photographs and leave only footprints"—but in fragile areas, even footprints can be damaging, so be careful about *them* as well. Fortunately, most hikers try their best to follow the familiar "Leave No Trace" principles.

For those who are new to the concept, the idea is to leave the wilderness just as you found it (or, preferably, even better). Never litter, and try to pick up anything left by others (blessedly little these days). Do not pick wildflowers or chop limbs off trees. Never feed wildlife, trample plants, or cut switchbacks. Do not build fires—rely instead on lightweight backpacking stoves for cooking and extra clothes for warmth. Probably most important is to camp only in established sites (preferably on sand or rocks or in deep forests)

well away from fragile meadows and shorelines. Use backcountry toilets when available; when they are not, bury human waste 4 to 6 inches deep at least 200 feet from water sources and trails. Do not bury toilet paper; pack it—and all other garbage—out. Do not wash *anything*—dishes, clothes, or yourself—in natural water sources, even with biodegradable "backpacker's" soap; instead, carry water at least 200 feet away from the lake or stream and wash there.

Your responsibility to the land does not end with the Leave No Trace principles. Important as it is to avoid damaging campsites, trails, and plants, these efforts become irrelevant if the surrounding acreage is despoiled by clearcuts, overrun by all-terrain vehicles (ATVs), scarred by roads, or covered with vacation homes. Hikers must be *at least* as concerned about large-scale conservation issues as they are with smaller-scale ones. Oregon (and the nation as a whole) needs *much* more land set aside as wilderness, as parks, or with other protective means. The land can no longer afford for you to be merely an admirer. It needs you as an *active* supporter. The best advocates for the land are those who have actually been there—camped under the stars, smelled the wildflowers, and been inspired by the beauty. Part of the admission price for taking these hikes is your responsibility to write letters to your elected representatives, to attend public meetings, and to get involved with grassroots organizations that work to protect the land. If you do not know where to start, contact the conservation and hiking groups listed in Appendix B. These groups will be happy to provide information and help you get involved in the good fight.

SAFETY

If you are careful and properly equipped, you are probably in greater danger driving to the trailhead than you are once you get out of the car. Nonetheless, there are some important safety concerns for trail users.

Unless you only travel on busy main trails, you should not hike alone until you are a very experienced wilderness traveler. Always let someone back home know of your destination and when you expect to return, so they can raise the alarm in case you do not arrive home as planned.

At the trailhead, place all valuables out of sight and lock your car. Do not be deceived into believing, however, that this will stop a determined thief. It is better to drive a beat-up old car and leave nothing worth stealing in it. If all hikers did this, the miscreants would soon give up.

Hypothermia is probably the biggest danger to hikers. Generally, it occurs when you lose too much body heat due to being wet and cold for too long. In Oregon's notoriously wet climate, it is important that hikers carry clothing that will keep them warm, dry, and protected from the wind.

Although most wilderness creeks and lakes look clear and drinkable, the best advice is to *not* drink untreated water. Nasty little microorganisms reside there, with the ability to make you sick enough to swear off hiking for the rest of your life. Boil, chemically treat, or filter *all* water, or simply pack in all the water you will need.

Lightning is a potential hazard, especially in the Cascade Range and the mountains of eastern Oregon. If you see thunderheads building, get off the open ridges and head as quickly as possible for lower and preferably forested terrain.

Very few dangerous animals remain in Oregon. Rattlesnakes are a potential hazard in the deserts of eastern Oregon, in Hells Canyon, and in parts of southwestern Oregon. If you watch your step and check the area carefully before sitting down, you should avoid any encounters with these timid creatures. Black bears and mountain lions are present throughout the state, but they are generally so shy that hikers probably will never see them. If either of these animals should attack, fight back.

It is important to hang your food at night, not only to keep it safe from bruins and more common thieves—chipmunks and other small mammals—but to avoid these animals learning to associate campsites with human foodstuffs. Bears especially can become nuisances that then have to be destroyed, all because of hikers' carelessness in storing their food. Hang food 4 feet from tree trunks and 10 feet off the ground, or use a bear-resistant canister.

The biggest wildlife problems come from the insect world, most notably ticks and mosquitoes. A good repellent, a long-sleeved shirt, and long pants are the best preventive measures.

A NOTE ABOUT SAFETY

Safety is an important concern in all outdoor activities. No guidebook can alert you to every hazard or anticipate the limitations of every reader. Therefore, the descriptions of roads, trails, routes, and natural features in this book are not representations that a particular place or excursion will be safe for your party. When you follow any of the routes described in this book, you assume responsibility for your own safety. Under normal conditions, such excursions require the usual attention to traffic, road and trail conditions, weather, terrain, the capabilities of your party, and other factors. Because many of the lands in this book are subject to development and/or change of ownership, conditions may have changed since this book was written that make your use of some of these routes unwise. Always check for current conditions, obey posted private property signs, and avoid confrontations with property owners or managers. Keeping informed on current conditions and exercising common sense are the keys to a safe, enjoyable outing.

— *The Mountaineers Books*

THE COAST

China Beach, Samuel H. Boardman State Park

The Oregon coast is world famous for its rugged beauty, nationally famous for its wildlife, and locally infamous for its weather. The rugged beauty is immediately apparent almost anywhere in this narrow strip of paradise: everything from rolling dunes and sandy beaches to cliff-edged headlands and offshore rocks can be found along the 363-mile coastline. The wildlife takes a bit more effort to see, but it is there in abundance. Patient observers will notice harbor seals, sea lions, migrating whales, colorful tide-pool life, and an incredible number of birds. Until 2008, when a rapidly increasing population of bald eagles started frightening seabirds away from their traditional nesting rocks, an estimated 1.2 million seabirds nested along the Oregon coast—more birds than nest along the much longer coastlines of California and Washington combined.

And that infamous weather? From October to May, a seemingly endless series of storms roll off the Pacific and dump much of their considerable moisture on the Oregon coast. Although rain is rare in the summer months, a thick layer of fog frequently hugs the shore and blocks the view. Spring and fall are the best times to visit. Even during the rainiest of Oregon's notoriously soggy winters, however, there are always a few days that are cloud-free. Locals have learned that these brief winter interludes are the perfect time to hike the coastal trails, because there are fewer visitors and the beaches are blessedly quiet.

Cannon Beach from the north

1 CANNON BEACH TRAILS

Distance: Ecola State Park, 6.2 miles round trip; Cannon/Arcadia beaches, 3.5 miles one way; 9.7 miles total
Hiking time: Ecola State Park, 3 hours; Cannon/Arcadia beaches, 2 hours; 5 hours total
Elevation gain: Ecola State Park, 750 feet; Cannon/Arcadia beaches, 50 feet; 800 feet total
Difficulty: Easy to moderate
Season: All year
Best: All year
Map: USGS Tillamook Head, Arch Cape
Information: Ecola State Park, (503) 436-2844

Directions: From the junction of US 101and US 26 near Seaside, drive 2.9 miles south on US 101, turn right on the access road to Cannon Beach, and drive 1.6 milesto a junction.

To reach Ecola State Park, turn right (north) on the signed park access road and drive 1.7 miles to the park's day-use fee booth where you go left into the Ecola Point Picnic Area.

To hike Cannon and Arcadia beaches, drive US 101 about 1.5 miles south of the Cannon Beach turnoff, then go west to Tolovana Beach State Wayside.You can hike both these areas one way if someone drops you off and picks you up or if you use two vehicles for a shuttle.

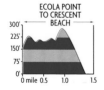

Most Oregonians know that the charming resort town of Cannon Beach has quaint motels, a thriving arts community, and views of one of the state's most distinctive landmarks, Haystack Rock. Not so well known is that the city is the perfect jumping-off point for some of the most scenic hikes on

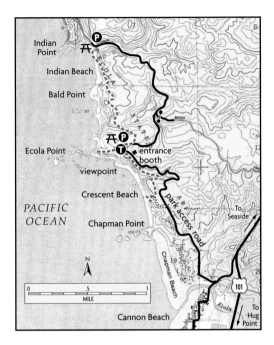

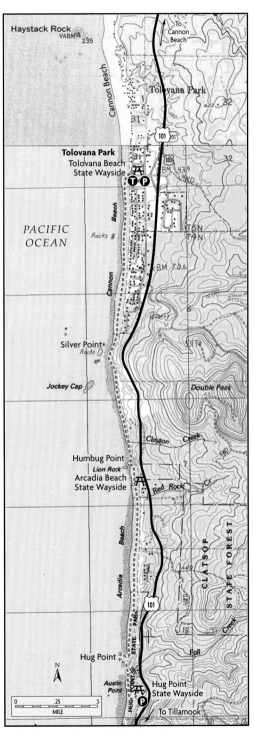

the Oregon coast. Careful timing is important on the beach walk south of town, because a low tide will help you to round three headlands along the way. Remember that winter storms rapidly erode the beach, sometimes leaving it covered with waves and impossible to hike.

Excellent trails radiate from Ecola Point. The most popular route is the 0.2-mile paved trail west to the stunning view at the tip of the point. This route is too well traveled and provides too little exercise for most hikers, however, so plan to also take the spectacular longer trails that go north and south from the picnic area parking lot.

The sometimes muddy southbound trail to Crescent Beach begins near the restroom building, climbs briefly through forest to cross a maintenance road, then goes up and down across a forested hillside with occasional excellent views south to Haystack Rock and down to Crescent Beach. At 1.1 miles you come to a junction. Turn right here and switchback steeply downhill for 0.3 mile to lovely Crescent Beach. Even on busy summer weekends this beautiful stretch of sand, tucked neatly between the rocky headlands of Ecola Point to the north and Chapman Point to the south, is rarely crowded.

The 1.5-mile trail north from Ecola Point starts from the northwest end of the picnic area parking lot and follows a circuitous up-and-down route through Sitka spruce forest with a couple of great views of the Pacific Ocean. The most noteworthy vistas feature the area's many offshore rocks and arches, including the rocky islet off Tillamook Head to the north, on which sits the abandoned Tillamook Rock Lighthouse. The trail ends at Indian Beach Picnic Area.

Another recommended hike goes south from Cannon Beach to Hug Point. The first 2.5 miles of beach south of town are crowded and pass several hotels and vacation homes, so this is the perfect place to let the kids build sand castles and fly kites. A quieter starting point is from Tolovana Beach State Wayside.

From the wayside, hike 1.1 miles south to Silver Point, which marks the southern end of this busy section and the start of wilder terrain. Numerous offshore rocks, including one with a small arch, make Silver Point very scenic. Except at low tide, you will need to crawl over slippery rocks to round the point.

Walk a narrow beach of smooth, hard-packed sand south 0.7 mile to Humbug Point, which requires a below-average tide and perhaps some wading to get around.

The beach south of Humbug Point is more heavily used, due to access from Arcadia Beach State Wayside, but the hiking is easy and attractive. Several small creeks cross the beach, so kids can play in the sand then wash off in fresh water. It is about 1.5 miles to the south end of the beach at Hug Point's line of tan cliffs. An old roadbed is carved into these sandstone cliffs, providing access to the other side of the point. Strong storms often wash away so much of the beach around this point that accessing this old road can be wet and difficult in late winter. For most of the year, however, you should have no problem. The road was built so cars could round the headland while "hugging" the rock face between waves, which gave Hug Point its name. On the other side of this headland are two small coves with interesting caves and a scenic waterfall on Fall Creek. The hike ends with a short uphill spur trail to Hug Point State Wayside.

For the return, if the tide is rising it is prudent to walk the road back to Cannon Beach rather than risk getting trapped behind a flooded headland—or arrange a shuttle with two vehicles.

2 CAPE FALCON AND NEAHKAHNIE MOUNTAIN

Distance: Cape Falcon, 5.2 miles round trip; Neahkahnie Mountain, 5.4 miles round trip; 10.6 miles total
Hiking time: Cape Falcon, 2.5 hours; Neahkahnie Mountain, 3 hours; 5.5 hours total
Elevation gain: Cape Falcon, 200 feet; Neahkahnie Mountain, 1100 feet; 1300 feet total
Difficulty: Moderate
Season: All year
Best: Late May to early June
Maps: USGS Arch Cape, Nehalem
Information: Oswald West State Park, (503) 368-3575

Directions: For Cape Falcon, from the junction of US 101 and US 26 near Seaside, drive US 101 south for 14.8 miles and park in the day-use parking lot. From the south, this pullout is 4.2 miles north of Manzanita. To visit Neahkahnie Mountain, drive 1.2 miles south to a large gravel pullout halfway between mileposts 40 and 41.

In 1913 the governor of Oregon declared that the state's beaches could not be privately owned but would be held in trust for public highways. This action ensured that, unlike the coastlines of almost every other state, the magnificent beaches and rocky shores of Oregon would remain open to the public and free of development. That governor was Oswald West, and in honor of his farsighted action, the state gave his name to a state park that protects a particularly rugged and spectacular stretch of the coast he did so much to preserve. Today, hikers can explore Governor West's legacy on a pair of magnificent trails that lead to two of the coast's most outstanding locations, Cape Falcon and Neahkahnie Mountain.

To visit Cape Falcon, from the day-use parking lot take the well-graded trail that goes west across a hillside covered with a dense coastal rain forest. This lush greenery muffles the sounds of highway traffic but allows you to hear the wind in the trees, the waves on the shore, and the birds all around—a favorable exchange indeed! After 0.4 mile reach a junction; turn right, following signs to Cape Falcon, then go up and down on a trail that winds through an increasingly open forest. The openings provide excellent views south

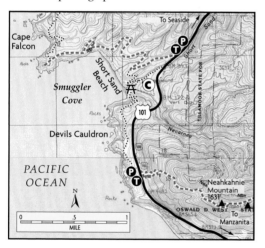

Dramatic cliffs south of Cape Falcon

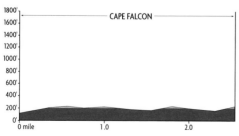

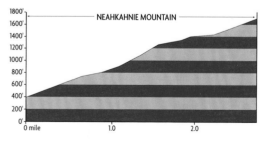

to Short Sand Beach and Neahkahnie Mountain.

At the 2.3-mile point is an unsigned junction. To reach the tip of Cape Falcon, turn left on a trail carved through an otherwise impenetrable tangle of 8-foot-high salal bushes. The winding path leads 0.3 mile to a series of outstanding viewpoints that look both north and south along the rugged shoreline. Bring your binoculars so you can better observe fishing boats bobbing up and down on the waves, look for migrating gray whales, and watch a wide variety of seabirds, including a small colony of pelagic cormorants. Return as you came.

The trail to Neahkahnie Mountain departs from the east side of the highway and switchbacks up an open, brushy slope with excellent views of Cape Falcon to the northwest. The trail soon ducks into the dense coastal forest that drapes this mountain and steadily ascends a series of moderately long switchbacks past partially obstructed viewpoints.

At the 1.4-mile point, you go through a saddle with nice southerly views, then cross a sloping meadow directly below the more westerly of Neahkahnie Mountain's dual summits. In late May and early June, this steep meadow resembles a natural rock garden with a brilliant display of colorful wildflowers. Stay on the trail another 250 yards to a saddle between the two summits at about 2.4 miles, then follow a scramble path to either high point. It is a tough call, but the western summit has better views.

3 CASCADE HEAD AND HARTS COVE

Distance: Cascade Head, 2.4 miles round trip; Harts Cove, 5.4 miles round trip;
7.8 miles total
Hiking time: Cascade Head, 1.5 hours; Harts Cove, 2.5 hours; 4 hours total
Elevation gain: Cascade Head, 200 feet; Harts Cove, 900 feet; 1100 feet total
Difficulty: Easy to moderate
Season: July 16 to December 31
Best: Mid-July to November
Map: USGS Neskowin
Information: The Nature Conservancy, (503) 802-8100; Hebo Ranger District,
(503) 392-5100

Directions: From the junction of US 101 and Oregon Highway 18 near Lincoln City, drive US 101 north 3.8 miles, then turn left (west) onto Forest Road 1861. Follow this narrow gravel road for 3.3 miles to the Cascade Head trailhead. The Harts Cove trailhead is another 0.8 mile west at the road's end. **Note:** To protect threatened species, FR 1861 is closed from January 1 to July 15. During this period, hikers can reach Cascade Head on the longer trail off Three Rocks Road to the south, but Harts Cove has no reasonable access other than FR 1861.

Just north of Lincoln City's gambling casinos, gift shops, fast-food joints, and other "attractions" is a haven for hikers looking to escape the

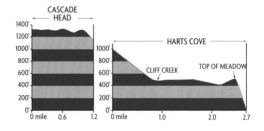

plague of commercialism. From the towering heights of Cascade Head, some 1300 feet above the surf, you can luxuriate in a beautiful grassland filled with wildflowers and enjoy one of the most spectacular views in the state. For a more private slice of paradise, add the hike to Harts Cove. This dramatic spot hides a tall waterfall,

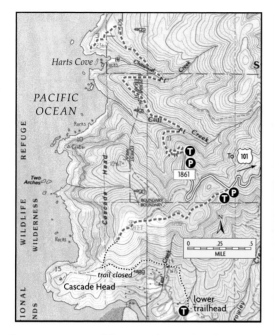

Harts Cove

has numerous offshore rocks, and is home to the occasional bald eagle. It is the perfect place to enjoy the standard hiker's fare of peanut butter and jelly sandwiches instead of the tourist's hamburger and fries.

The short trail to Cascade Head follows an old jeep road through a dense coastal forest of Sitka spruces and Douglas firs. At about the 1-mile point, the forest abruptly opens and the trail enters a glorious grassy headland. You soon reach the first good viewpoint at a windswept knoll, but even better views are found 0.2 mile farther down the trail. To reach them, descend through an open meadow to great views of the Salmon River estuary to the south and the grassy tip of Cascade Head to the west. Beyond this viewpoint the trail descends through brushy meadows and forest; it is better to turn around here. This headland is owned by The Nature Conservancy, a nonprofit organization that works to protect endangered plants and animals. Accordingly, the conservancy prohibits fires, camping, and hunting and has closed the trail to dogs and bicycles. Hikers are required to stay on the trail to keep rare plants untrampled.

From the trailhead at the end of Forest Road 1861, the Harts Cove Trail switchbacks downhill to a footbridge over tiny Cliff Creek. The trail takes you to a partially obstructed viewpoint at 1.5 miles, then heads back inland past a wave-pounded cove filled with barking sea lions to a bridge over Chitwood Creek. From here you turn west, gain a little elevation, then break out of the forest onto a sloping, grassy headland 2.4 miles from the trailhead. The best views are at the base of this headland, overlooking dramatic Harts Cove to the south. A waterfall on Chitwood Creek drops directly into the cove, adding greatly to the beauty of the scene.

4

UMPQUA DUNES SCENIC AREA

Distance: Up to 10.2 miles round trip
Hiking time: 1.5 hours to 2 days (day hike or backpack)
Elevation gain: Up to 300 feet (but dunes shift constantly)
Difficulty: Easy to strenuous
Season: All year
Best: All year
Map: USFS Oregon Dunes National Recreation Area
Information: Oregon Dunes National Recreation Area, (541) 271-6000

Directions: Drive US 101 to 10 miles south of Reedsport or 11 miles north of the Coos Bay bridge, to the John Dellenback trailhead.

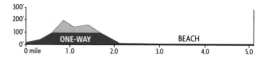

The largest coastal sand dunes in North America are along the central Oregon coast. The unique shifting dunescape here provides a hiking experience unlike anything else in the state. In addition to hundreds of spectacular dunes, some as high as 280 feet, the scenery includes islands of trees untouched by the sand and numerous shallow lakes and ponds that host wintering waterfowl. Although most people associate dunes with a desert environment, that is definitely *not* the case in this seaside Sahara. In fact, heavy winter rains often raise the water level so much that travelers must beware of quicksand developing in low-lying areas. Never camp in these sandy depressions, lest you end up with an unpleasant sinking feeling.

The most spectacular scenery is in the Umpqua Dunes Scenic Area. Fortunately, this is also one of the areas where the Forest Service prohibits motorized travel, so hikers do not have to worry about getting run over by a noisy dune buggy.

Note: Remember that walking through soft sand, especially uphill, is *very* tiring. The energy you have to expend per mile of travel is considerably more than on most hikes.

From the trailhead, the trail immediately crosses a bridge over Eel Creek, a good-sized stream that somehow escaped the attention of the USGS, which failed to include it on its maps. The route then winds through forests and dense shrubbery for 0.2 mile to a junction with a spur

trail to a loop road in Eel Creek Campground. Turn left, climb a short distance, then cross the edge of an isolated dune area. After another short traverse through forest, the formal tread ends at 0.5 mile at a junction on the edge of the massive Umpqua Dunes.

Immediately to the west rises an enormous sand pile that cries out to be climbed. From the top, you can enjoy a magnificent panorama of shifting sand, small ponds, and isolated tree islands between you and the endless Pacific Ocean. This dune is a fine goal for hikers with children.

Those who prefer a wilder experience should

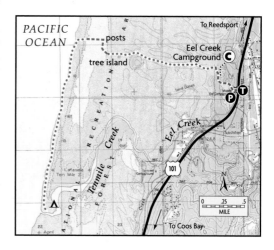

Amid the Umpqua Dunes

head west across the dunes for a little over 1 mile, then go around the north side of a large tree island. The dunes end a little west of this island at a nearly level plain covered with marshes and stunted shore pines, a coastal subspecies of lodgepole pine. To reach the ocean, go north along a line of posts for 0.2 mile, then pick up a trail through the deflation plain to the beach at about 2.7 miles. Since this beach is far from any road, you will probably have this long strip of sand to yourself. Before heading along the shore, however, be sure to carefully note where the trail meets the beach, so you can find it on the way back.

Backpackers and adventurous day hikers can turn south and walk another 2.4 miles to the mouth of Tenmile Creek. Remember that fog often rolls in off the ocean, especially in the summer, which makes finding your way back across the trackless sand nearly impossible. On clear days you will need sunglasses, because the light-colored sand reflects so much sunlight.

5   SUNSET BAY TO SHORE ACRES

Distance: 4.8 miles round trip
Hiking time: 2.5 hours
Elevation gain: 200 feet
Difficulty: Easy
Season: All year
Best: All year
Map: USGS Cape Arago, Charleston
Information: Shore Acres State Park, (541) 888-3732

Directions: From US 101 in downtown North Bend, turn west onto Virginia Avenue, following signs to state parks, and drive 0.8 mile to a traffic light. Turn left on Broadway Street, proceed 1 mile, then turn right on Newmark Street. Stay on this paved road to the day-use parking lot at Sunset Bay State Park, 11.7 miles from US 101.

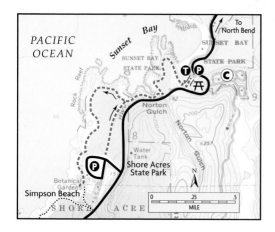

The rugged coastline immediately south of Coos Bay is one of the most diverse and scenic sections of the Oregon coast. Here, onshore humans can look offshore to large rocky reefs where hundreds of lounging sea lions bark at one another. Closer at hand are densely forested hillsides, rocky headlands, and several coves with tide pools and sandy beaches perfect for a quiet lunch near the waves. When those waves are *really* big, the turbulent waters crash into this coastline's many oddly tilted rocks. You can even add a visit to a unique man-made feature, a lovely garden with acres of colorful flowers and manicured hedgerows similar to the gardens of England. Best of all, these varied attractions are all connected by a magnificently scenic segment of the Oregon Coast Trail, which makes for a highly enjoyable and surprisingly easy hike. Dogs are not allowed on the trails in Shore Acres State Park.

Gardens in Shore Acres State Park

Immediately south of the parking lot, the trail crosses a bridge over Big Creek and comes to an unsigned junction. Turn right, climb two moderately long switchbacks, and reach a forested plateau. The wood-chip–covered trail then loops around a group camping area and past several short side paths that lead to stunning ocean viewpoints. The trail returns to the road at 0.8 mile on the south side of the plateau above the wave-pounded cove at Norton Gulch. A nice side trail drops to this rocky cove, where at low tide you can examine a colorful assortment of mussels, crabs, sea snails, and other tide-pool life.

The main trail follows the road shoulder for 120 yards, then veers right onto a foot trail that goes past a pair of excellent viewpoints of the reefs and rocks just offshore. To the north is the flashing beacon of Cape Arago Lighthouse. The trail nearly touches the road again, then curves right and soon reaches an unsigned junction, 1.1 miles from the trailhead. Veer right and hike past several cliff-top viewpoints framed by wind-whipped Sitka spruce trees. At 1.9 miles you meet the paved pathways of Shore Acres State Park.

In about 0.4 mile, at a dramatic overlook west of the large parking lot, a circular observation building is ideal for storm watching. Trails wander through the formal gardens south of the parking lot. For a wilder experience, take the trail around the west side of the gardens; it winds down 0.3 mile to Simpson Beach, a small cove hemmed in by cliffs. Another option: The Oregon Coast Trail goes south to a grassy headland that features excellent ocean vistas.

To take a shorter inland trail on the way back, return to the Shore Acres parking lot and walk east to a trailhead beside the park's entrance booth. Turn left (north) and walk about 0.4 mile through a viewless forest back to the junction near Norton Gulch, where you turn right to return to Sunset Bay.

6   BLACKLOCK POINT

Distance: 5.2 miles round trip
Hiking time: 3 hours
Elevation gain: 120 feet
Difficulty: Moderate
Season: All year (but trails are very muddy and may be flooded in winter)
Best: April to June
Maps: USGS Cape Blanco, Floras Lake
Information: Floras Lake State Natural Area, (541) 888-8867, ext. 26

Directions: From Port Orford, drive 7 miles north on US 101 to a signed junction where you turn left (west) on Airport Road. Follow this paved road for 2.7 miles to its end, where there is a small gravel parking area just before a gate blocking access to the airport runway. Park here.

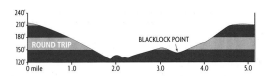

In the previous edition of this guidebook, the hike to the spectacular wildflower meadows and wave-carved sandstone cliffs of Blacklock Point was described from the north, starting from Floras Lake. Unfortunately, that hike, while still feasible, has been made less enjoyable by severe erosion that has wiped out several sections of trail and by seasonal beach closures imposed to protect the nesting sites of the threatened snowy plover. It is now better to start this trip from the east, at the tiny Cape Blanco State Airport. This shorter approach avoids the beach and features fewer views

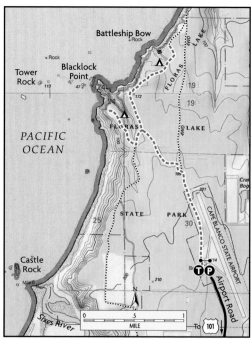

Cliffs north of Battleship Bow, near Blacklock Point

along the way, but it includes a fun forest hike and the destination remains outstanding. Many past visitors consider little-known Blacklock Point the best-kept secret on the Oregon coast. With its tall, orange sandstone cliffs, dozens of off-shore rocks, bright May-blooming wildflowers, and hidden waterfall, you'll find it easy to agree with that opinion.

Starting from the west side of the gravel parking lot, ignore a gravel road that goes left (southwest) and instead take a wide trail that begins near the trailhead sign and goes to the right (northwest). This trail, like many of the hiking routes in this area, is actually a long-abandoned jeep road that has been converted to a trail. The path is lined by tall brush and takes you almost straight in a north-northwest direction as you parallel the mostly unseen airport runway.

After 0.9 mile you reach a signed junction. Turn left, following signs to Blacklock Point, and keep generally northwest on a winding trail with a lot of mud and standing water for much of the year. Boardwalks and narrow "detour" trails are usually available at the worst locations.

At 1.4 miles the trail forks. The shortest route to the tip of Blacklock Point goes to the left, but for a fuller exploration of this area you should first go right on the Coast Trail toward Floras Lake. Just 0.3 mile later you break out of the trees where a very short side trail goes left to a superb

cliff-top overlook with colorful red soil. The ocean and many offshore rocks provide exceptional scenic beauty from this location, which makes an ideal lunch stop. To see the spectacular cliffs of Battleship Bow and its waterfall, keep hiking north on the main trail for another 0.4 mile, crossing two seasonal creeks and a larger permanent stream along the way. The sheltering canopy of trees and the abundant flat ground around these creeks makes camping here very inviting.

Just 0.1 mile after you cross the last and largest creek, turn left and bushwhack through the salal and manzanita for about 50 yards to Battleship Bow, a windswept overlook atop sheer cliffs about 150 feet above the beach and crashing surf. The waterfall is at the south end of the beach beneath some of the highest cliffs. The falls is less impressive than it was just a few years ago, as erosion has changed the course of the creek away from its previous sheer 150-foot drop. Now more of a twisting, multi-stage waterfall, it is still worth seeing. Views to the north along the line of cliffs are impressive. This dramatically wild, little-visited landscape is excellent wildlife habitat, in particular for a pair of nesting peregrine falcons, which you have a good chance of seeing.

To visit Blacklock Point, return 0.7 mile to the junction at 1.4 miles from the trailhead and turn right (west). Follow this winding route for about 0.5 mile through viewless forest and tall thickets of salal to a large, waterless campsite. Immediately beyond this camp the forest ends in favor of lovely meadows atop a view-packed headland overlooking miles of rocky coastline. To the south you can see Cape Blanco and its working lighthouse. In May the headland meadows host many colorful wildflowers, including gorse, violets, buttercups, lupines, and wild strawberries. Return the way you came.

7 WHALEHEAD COVE TO CAPE FERRELO

Distance: 5 miles round trip to House Rock; 5.1 miles one way to Lone Ranch Wayside
Hiking time: House Rock, 2.5 hours; Lone Ranch Wayside, 3 hours one way
Elevation gain: House Rock, 500 feet; Lone Ranch Wayside, 700 feet one way
Difficulty: Moderate
Season: All year
Best: April to June
Map: USGS Brookings, Carpenterville
Information: Samuel H. Boardman State Park, (541) 469-2021

Directions: Drive US 101 to 19.5 miles south of Gold Beach or 10 miles north of Brookings, then turn west on the short, steep access road to Whalehead Picnic Area. If you have two cars, drive the second one 3 miles south on US 101 and park it at Lone Ranch Wayside.

The most spectacular section of the Oregon coast is its final 25 miles before the California border. The grassy headlands, offshore rocks, and pocket beaches here are as good (or better) than anywhere else in Oregon—and that's saying something! Most of this shoreline is protected in Samuel H. Boardman State Park. Boardman served as superintendent of Oregon State Parks from 1929 to 1950; his tireless efforts to preserve more parkland gave him the title "Father of Oregon State Parks." The magnificent namesake preserve has dozens of great short hikes. The most satisfying longer trip—arguably the best coastal hike in the state—is the outstanding section of the Oregon Coast Trail between Whalehead Cove and Cape Ferrelo.

From the picnic area parking lot, the trail quickly descends to the beach and crosses Whalehead Creek on drift logs. Although several sea stacks and small islands just offshore make Whalehead Cove one of the most scenic beaches in Oregon, relatively few people visit this beach, as the undisturbed tracks of raccoons and deer attest.

Follow the beach south, generally on hard-packed sand, hopping over several small creeks and passing numerous barnacle- and mussel-covered rocks along the way. After 0.7 mile you cross Bowman Creek a little below an attractive waterfall, then walk another 0.5 mile to a rocky area at the south end of the beach. At low tide this rocky area provides some of the best tidepooling on the Oregon coast. Feel free to observe the crabs, sea stars, and other animals, but do not disturb this fragile environment.

About 50 yards before the end of the beach and immediately south of a small creek, the trail leaves the sand and switchbacks steeply up an open

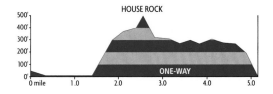

Whalehead Cove

hillside. Views are excellent here, but also impressive are the colorful assortment of horsetails, thistles, foxgloves, iris, cow parsnips, and yellow monkeyflowers. The steep switchbacks take you into a Sitka spruce forest through which you traverse uphill to a junction a little below US 101 at about 1.7 miles. Veer right, still in deep forest, and follow the winding path as it makes numerous, often steep ups and downs. Occasional breaks in the tree cover provide dramatic viewpoints.

The highest viewpoint is at House Rock, where you reach a parking lot at the end of a short spur road off US 101 at 2.5 miles. Those with only one car should turn back here, more than satisfied with their efforts.

But even better scenery lies ahead, so if you have the energy or a vehicle shuttle, pick up the Oregon Coast Trail from the southwestern corner of the parking lot and go gradually downhill through forest. In 0.3 mile an unsigned side trail angles right and downhill. Bear left on the main trail, continuing up and down for 0.6 mile, then leave the forest for a gorgeous rolling grassland with terrific ocean views at 3.4 miles. The prominent grassy hump a short distance south is Cape Ferrelo.

After a short climb through the grassland, you meet the end of another viewpoint spur road at 3.9 miles. Turn right (west) here and go 0.1 mile directly toward Cape Ferrelo to a fork. Bear right and walk along the top of the headland, enjoying great views and an abundance of May wildflowers. Side trails drop to the left, but the best route is the wildly scenic upper trail that goes to the dramatic tip of Cape Ferrelo at 4.4 miles. Views north and south along the extremely rugged coastline are superb.

If you left a car at Lone Ranch Wayside, it is an easy switchbacking 0.7-mile descent from Cape Ferrelo to the picnic area parking lot.

COAST RANGE AND KLAMATH MOUNTAINS

Hanging Rock from the west, Wild Rogue Wilderness (Hike 11)

The Coast Range rises like a crumpled green rug between the crashing surf of the Pacific Ocean and the gentle valleys of western Oregon. Although never very high, the mountains are quite rugged, with steep slopes leading up from densely forested river valleys to ridges thickly mantled with trees. Most Oregon hikers ignore the Coast Range, but those willing to look beyond the checkerboard of clearcuts soon discover a wonderland of spectacular waterfalls, lush rain forests, and some of Oregon's most beautiful rivers.

In the extreme southwestern corner of Oregon, the mountains rise higher in elevation, made up of an unusual assortment of uplifted rocks and rare serpentine soils. No longer considered part of the Coast Range, this area is actually a northern extension of the Klamath Mountains, a complex mountain system that Oregon shares with northern California. In addition to impressive scenery, the Klamath Mountains—especially the Siskiyou Range—hide dozens of unique plants that live nowhere else in the world.

In the drought-plagued summer of 2002, Oregon's Klamath Mountains, centered on the Kalmiopsis Wilderness Area, were scorched by one of the largest forest fires in Oregon history. The 500,000-acre Biscuit Fire burned for weeks and was not entirely put out until winter rains arrived months after the fire began. The blaze effectively destroyed several trails in this area, which will be decades in recovering before they are once again "classic" hikes.

8   SADDLE MOUNTAIN

Distance: 6.1 miles round trip (including 0.5-mile side trip)
Hiking time: 3.5 hours
Elevation gain: 1700 feet
Difficulty: Moderate
Season: March to November
Best: Late May to mid-June
Map: USGS Saddle Mountain
Information: Saddle Mountain State Natural Area, (503) 368-5943

Directions: Take US 26 to 64 miles northwest of Portland or 12 miles southeast of Seaside, to a junction near milepost 10. Turn north on the narrow paved road to Saddle Mountain State Park and drive 7 miles to the road-end parking lot.

Saddle Mountain is the highest peak in the northern Coast Range, and the trail to the panoramic summit is justifiably the most popular hike in the region. Views extend from the endless Pacific Ocean to the west to the snowy summits of the Cascade Range to the east. Closer at hand is a wealth of colorful wildflowers, including a handful of beautiful species found nowhere else in the world.

The trail departs from the southeast side of the parking lot and gradually ascends through a living tunnel of 6-foot-high salmonberry bushes beneath a canopy of red alder and bigleaf maple. After 300 yards, you come to a junction. The not-to-be-missed 0.25-mile side trail to the right climbs to an open knoll with excellent views of the park's namesake mountain.

The main trail climbs irregularly spaced switchbacks through a mixed forest of stately conifers and spreading deciduous trees. About

1 mile from the trailhead, the steady uphill takes you past a large basalt dike that juts out of the hillside west of the trail. This section of rock cooled at a different rate than the basalt flows that compose the rest of the mountain, which caused this harder rock to fracture and be less susceptible to erosion.

At about 2 miles the trail climbs out of the forest and into the wildflower meadows that cover the upper third of the mountain. The floral displays are some of the best in the state, providing color from March to September. The best show comes in early June, when iris, larkspur, paintbrush, buckwheat, and dozens of other varieties create a rainbow of color.

The trail soon tops a rounded ridge, where an unsigned boot path drops left to some great viewpoints of Saddle Mountain's rounded summit. To reach that summit, the trail crosses a

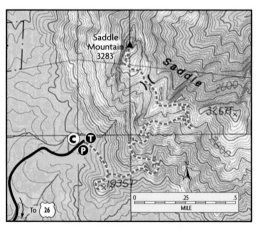

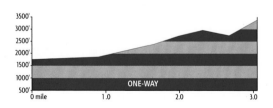

Saddle Mountain summit

walkway in the low point of the mountain's "saddle" at 2.4 miles, then steeply ascends a rocky hillside, where a cable handrail provides security for unsteady pedestrians all the way to the top at 2.8 miles. On a clear day you can see not only every high point in the northern Coast Range but snowy Cascade peaks from Mount Rainier to the Three Sisters. Sharp-eyed hikers can even pick out the 125-foot-high Astoria Column on a hill to the northwest.

9 KINGS MOUNTAIN

Distance: 5.5 miles round trip
Hiking time: 4 hours
Elevation gain: 2800 feet
Difficulty: Strenuous
Season: Late March to November
Best: Mid-May to mid-June
Map: Tillamook State Forest map
Information: Tillamook State Forest—Forest Grove District, (503) 357-2191

Directions: Drive Oregon Highway 6 west from Hillsboro or east from Tillamook to a trailhead parking lot near milepost 25.

Rising impressively above the Wilson River canyon, Kings Mountain is the star attraction along a growing network of trails in Tillamook State Forest. The challenging hike to the top rises

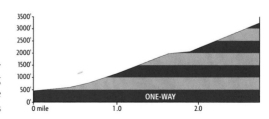

View north from the summit of Kings Mountain

quickly from dense rain forests near the river to view-packed wildflower meadows at the summit. It is an experience that will thrill not only hikers who enjoy the intense greenery of Oregon's famous forests but those who prefer to look down on that greenery from above.

The trail begins in a lush forest of moss-draped Douglas firs, western hemlocks, and red alders that shade a forest floor carpeted with sword ferns, white-blooming oxalis, and candy-flowers. After 0.2 mile reach a junction; bear left and gently climb between two gullies, each of which holds a small creek. The grade increases noticeably around the 1-mile point, where the vegetation changes to a somewhat drier forest.

At about 2 miles, after gaining 1500 feet from the trailhead, your thighs get a break where the trail follows portions of an old road that mysteriously appears from nowhere on the forested hillside. More steep climbing leads to a rickety picnic table, a good place to rest even though it has only obstructed views.

For a more exhilarating panorama, trudge up a final section of dangerously loose gravel to the open summit. In early June the meadow here comes alive with grand displays of wildflowers. Regardless of the season, the vista looks down the Wilson River canyon and across the vast Tillamook State Forest. This remarkably unblemished sea of green shows no clearcut scars because logging has yet to begin after the area was replanted following the Tillamook Burns of the 1930s and 1940s. A few silvery snags, evidence of those colossal blazes, can still be seen.

A rugged scramble trail goes east from the summit to nearby Elk Mountain, but most hikers are satisfied with Kings Mountain and head back the way they came.

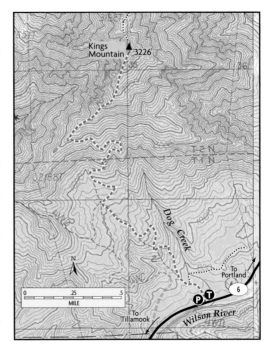

10   KENTUCKY FALLS

Distance: 4.4 miles round trip to viewing platform; 8.5 miles one way to lower trailhead
Hiking time: 2 hours to viewing platform; 4 hours to lower trailhead
Elevation gain: 700 feet to viewing platform; 800 feet to lower trailhead
Difficulty: Moderate
Season: All year
Best: April to June
Map: USGS Baldy Mountain
Information: Siuslaw National Forest—Central Coast Ranger District/Waldport Office, (541) 563-8400

Directions: On US 101 near Reedsport, from just north of the Umpqua River bridge, turn east on paved Smith River Road (County Road 48) and drive 15.3 miles to a junction immediately before a bridge over North Fork Smith River. Turn left on Forest Road 48, proceed 7.7 miles to the end of pavement, then dodge potholes for 3.3 miles to a fork. Turn right, drive 0.6 mile, then turn right again onto Forest Road 23, a single-lane paved road that goes 4.1 miles to the North Fork Smith trailhead, the recommended exit point (leave a shuttle vehicle here for a one-way hike). To reach the upper trailhead, continue on FR 23 another 5.7 miles to a junction, veer left, then proceed 2.6 miles to the Kentucky Falls trailhead, the recommended starting point.

Secreted away in an isolated canyon deep in the Coast Range is a hidden wonderland of waterfalls, clear streams, and old-growth forests. The Kentucky Falls Special Interest Area is a magnificent getaway that hikers readily agree is both special and extremely interesting. Although the area's three 100-foot waterfalls are the main attractions, the dense vegetation and forest

wildflowers provide plenty to enjoy before you reach these highlights. The hike is marvelous at any time of year, but it is most impressive in the spring when the vegetation bursts with new greenery and the falls are full of water. The trip is better as a one-way, downhill hike, but if you have only one car, make it a shorter out-and-back hike from the upper trailhead.

From the upper trailhead, the well-graded route descends through a lush rain forest of massive Douglas firs with a tangle of ferns, mosses, shrubs, and small wildflowers covering almost every inch of the forest floor. At a little less than 0.5 mile, the trail descends a series of switchbacks to a viewpoint of Upper Kentucky Falls, a sliding waterfall on Kentucky Creek. From here, the trail goes steadily downhill to a bridge over Kentucky Creek at about 1.4 miles, then switchbacks down a steep hillside to a wooden observation platform at 2.2 miles. This is the ideal location to observe North Fork and Lower Kentucky Falls, both outstandingly beautiful 100- to 120-foot-tall waterfalls that thunder over cliffs to the north and east. Turn around here for a short out-and-back hike.

To make the joyous walk to the lower trailhead, from a junction near the platform follow

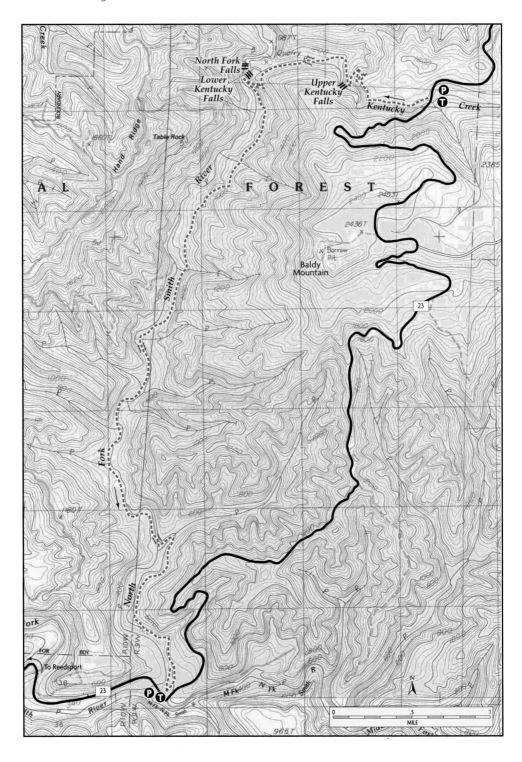

the scenic North Fork Smith Trail, which heads downstream. Most of the way is through a forest that has naturally regrown after fires in the late 1800s. Wildlife has returned with the trees, as the numerous elk prints in the middle of the trail attest. Lucky hikers sometimes spot the majestic creatures that made these prints.

The trail climbs away from the river, then goes in and out of small side canyons on a densely forested hillside. For the next few miles you pass numerous seasonal waterfalls on tiny side creeks, but the river remains well below you. About 3 miles below North Fork Falls, the trail descends to the river and crosses it on a bridge.

Below this crossing, the trail hugs the riverbank for 1.5 miles, then crosses the river on a wooden bridge at 7.1 miles. From here, the trail climbs again, then crosses the heavily forested hillside above the river and comes to a junction with a nature trail loop at 8.2 miles. Go straight and finish the hike with a short walk past grand old-growth trees that are up to 8 feet in diameter and more than 200 feet tall.

Lower Kentucky Falls

11 HANGING ROCK

Distance: 2 miles round trip from south; 4 miles round trip from north
Hiking time: 1 hour from south; 3 hours from north
Elevation gain: 300 feet from south; 1300 feet from north
Difficulty: Easy from south; moderate from north
Season: Mid-April to November
Best: Late May and June
Map: USFS Rogue River Wilderness
Information: Rouge River–Siskiyou National Forest—Powers Ranger District, (541) 439-6200

Directions: You can approach both trailheads from either the southeast near Grants Pass or from the northwest near Coos Bay. From the southeast, leave Interstate 5 at Glendale exit 80 and drive 2.5 miles west into town. At a junction directly across from a lumber mill, turn right, following signs to the high school, and drive 0.2 mile to a second junction. Turn left, go 0.1 mile, then turn left again on Rueben Road, which you follow into a maze of often confusing BLM roads. Stay on the main road at several unsigned intersections. Exactly 15.3 miles west of Glendale, turn left on West Fork Cow Creek Road and go 4 miles to a junction with Bobby Creek Access Road. Turn left, following signs for Marial, and climb 6.5 miles to a fork. Bear right and proceed 5.2 miles to a six-way junction at Anaktuvuk Saddle. Go straight and drive 13.9 miles to a junction beside Buck Creek Campground.

From the northwest, take Oregon Highway 42 to a major junction about 2 miles east of Myrtle Point, then County Road 219 south to Powers. From Powers follow Forest Road 33 south to a junction with FR 3348. Turn left (east), following signs for Glendale, and drive 9.1 miles to the junction beside Buck Creek Campground.

From the junction at the campground, turn south on gravel FR 5520 and go 1.3 miles to a junction. To reach the north trailhead, turn left on FR 230 and proceed 0.8 mile to the trailhead; to reach the south trailhead, bear right, still on FR 5520, go 4.5 miles, then turn left on FR 140 and proceed 1.1 miles to the Panther Ridge trailhead.

Hanging Rock is a little-known overlook perched on the rim of the Rogue River canyon. The breathtaking view from this grandstand looks 3600 feet down steep forested slopes to the wild rapids of the Rogue River. With binoculars, you can even pick out white-water rafters zipping through the rapids. Even more impressive than the view, however, is Hanging Rock itself. Perhaps a better name for this landmark would be *Over*hanging Rock, because this huge formation juts several feet over the lip of a towering cliff, creating a downright frightening viewing platform for awestruck hikers. All this makes Hanging Rock one of the most dramatic day-hike destinations in the state, but for some reason few Oregonians come here. There is no good

Hanging Rock

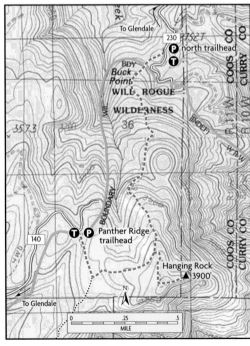

explanation for this, but don't complain. Just thank your lucky stars and enjoy the solitude.

Two similar trails lead to Hanging Rock. Your choice of route depends on how far you want to hike and how much elevation gain you can take.

The shorter trail starts from the Panther Ridge trailhead and goes south through a stately old-growth forest of lichen-draped Douglas firs that shade a mostly open forest floor. You almost immediately enter the Wild Rogue Wilderness, then steadily ascend for 0.25 mile to a T-junction. Turn left and walk at a gentle uphill grade through forest and past patches of beargrass and Pacific rhododendrons to a second junction, at about 0.7 mile, this time with the longer approach trail from FR 230.

Hikers who elect to take the longer approach trail pass through similar forest scenery but must gain an additional 1000 feet on a somewhat steeper route. On the other hand, they get a better workout and pass through superior displays of June-blooming rhododendrons. From the north trailhead, at 0.1 mile you enter the Wild Rogue Wilderness, then climb for another 1.5 miles to the junction with the shorter approach trail.

From the intersection of the two approach trails, turn south, climb a bit, then descend through increasingly open but brushy terrain to trail's end in 0.3 mile beside the obvious hump of Hanging Rock. It is reasonably easy to scramble to the top of the rock, although acrophobes probably should forgo this pleasure. The views both of the rock itself and from the top are superb.

12 LOWER ROGUE RIVER TRAIL

Distance: 1.6 miles round trip to Inspiration Point; 12.4 miles round trip to Brushy Bar; 15 miles one way to Foster Bar
Hiking time: 1 hour to Inspiration Point; 6 hours to Brushy Bar; 7 hours to Foster Bar
Elevation gain: 100 feet to Inspiration Point; 300 feet to Brushy Bar; 700 feet to Foster Bar
Difficulty: Easy to moderate
Season: March to November
Best: Late April and May; mid-September to early November
Map: USFS Rogue River Wilderness
Information: Rogue River–Siskiyou National Forest—Gold Beach Ranger District, (541) 247-3600; Paradise Lodge, (888) 667-6483

Directions: Leave Interstate 5 at Glendale exit 80 and drive 2.5 miles west into town. At a junction directly across from a lumber mill, turn right, following signs to the high school, and drive 0.2 mile to a second junction. Turn left, go 0.1 mile, then turn left again on Rueben Road, which you follow into a maze of often confusing Bureau of Land Management (BLM) roads. Stay on the main road at several unsigned intersections.

Exactly 15.3 miles west of Glendale, turn left on West Fork Cow Creek Road and go 4 miles to a junction with Bobby Creek Access Road. Turn left, following signs for Marial, and climb 6.5 miles to a fork. Bear left on BLM Road 32-9-14.2, still following signs for Marial, and proceed 13.5 miles on this winding downhill road, which turns to gravel after 4 miles, to the turnoff for Rogue River Ranch. Go straight and drive 2 rather rough miles to the road-end trailhead.

If you are leaving a second car at the Foster Bar trailhead, retrace Road 32-9-14.2 for 15.5 miles to the fork, then turn sharply left (west) and drive 28 miles to a junction with Forest Road 33. Turn left and go 16.4 miles

Rogue River at Mule Creek Canyon

on this paved then gravel road to a junction at the bottom of the canyon. Turn sharply left and proceed 3.6 miles to the trailhead.

The Rogue River Trail traces a 40-mile course along the river's wilderness section between Grave Creek, west of Grants Pass, and Foster Bar, upstream from Gold Beach. The complete trail is an outstanding backpacking trip, but most hikers do not have time to do the entire distance. For a sampling of the trail's best scenery, try this shorter version that starts from Marial, a remote trailhead in the heart of the canyon. Although the scenery is breathtaking, the hike has drawbacks. Chief among these is summer heat, which can be unbearable. Other major problems include poison oak, abundant in the canyon; black bears, which raid hikers' and boaters' camps; and rattlesnakes, common enough to make squeamish hikers a bit nervous. Another potential problem is landslides, which occur frequently on these steep slopes and sometimes close the trail. Call ahead about the latest conditions.

From Marial, the trail gradually descends through a dense old-growth forest, then travels across an open hillside, where the path has been blasted into the rock face. Directly below the trail, the Rogue River churns through Mule Creek Canyon, a rocky chute so narrow that larger rafts sometimes get turned the wrong way and bridge the river. At about 0.8 mile is aptly named Inspiration Point, a dramatic viewpoint where you can watch rafters float past or look across the river to impressive Stair Creek Falls.

The trail follows the curving river for another 1.4 miles to good campsites near Blossom Bar Creek and a mandatory side trip to Blossom Bar Rapids. This roaring maelstrom of boulders and white water is considered the most difficult rapid on the Rogue River. Just beyond, the trail detours around a flat meadow that hosts Paradise Lodge at 3.1 miles, a comfortable guest facility that serves meals to passing hikers but requires reservations to spend the night. Look for wild turkeys in the forest rimming the meadow.

The up-and-down trail continues downstream past stunning canyon viewpoints to a small guard station and good camps at woodsy Brushy Bar at 6.2 miles, a notorious hangout for the local black bears. Next is a nice viewpoint at Solitude Bar and at 8.2 miles a quaint bridge over Tate Creek, which drops over a pretty little

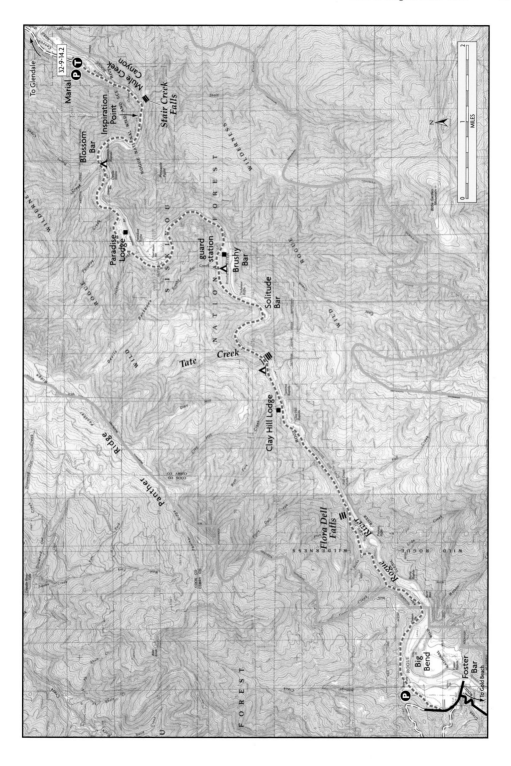

waterfall just below the bridge. Just beyond Tate Creek you pass a good campsite, then come to Clay Hill Lodge, another nice guest facility, at 9 miles. From here, you traverse a steep, mostly open slope to the charming, fern-lined grotto holding Flora Dell Falls at 10.7 miles. On a hot summer day, the pool at the falls' base is one of the nicest swimming holes in the state.

Any of these highlights makes a good turn-around point, but hikers with a second car can keep going to trail's end at Foster Bar. The final 4.3 miles take you through forests, around a wide curve in the river called Big Bend, then through an old orchard to the lower trailhead at 15 miles.

13 SUCKER CREEK GAP AND SWAN MOUNTAIN

Distance: 10 miles round trip
Hiking time: 5 hours (day hike or backpack)
Elevation gain: 2400 feet
Difficulty: Moderate
Season: June to early November
Best: Mid-June to mid-July
Map: USFS Red Buttes Wilderness
Information: Rogue River–Siskiyou National Forest—Siskiyou Mountains Ranger District, (541) 899-3800; Illinois Valley Visitor Information, (541) 592-2631

Directions: From Grants Pass, go 18 miles southeast on Oregon Highway 238 to a junction immediately before a bridge over the Applegate River. Turn right (south) on Thompson Creek Road, drive 12 miles to the end of pavement, then continue 2.7 miles to a junction. Turn right on Forest Road 1030, following signs to Steve Fork Trail, and proceed 11 miles to the road-end trailhead.

This fun trail provides a nice sampling of the western Siskiyou Mountains. The route takes you through varied forests with plenty of wild-life to a shelter in a pretty wildflower meadow. From there, a rewarding climb to the top of Swan Mountain leads to a superb viewpoint from which you can see practically every summit

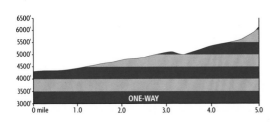

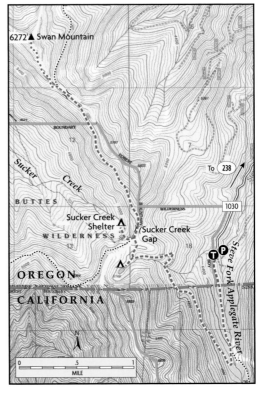

within 100 miles, including Craggy Peak and Grayback Mountain to the north; orange-tinted Pearsoll Peak to the northwest; Preston Peak to the southwest; the Marble and Russian mountains to the south; Mount Shasta and the double humps of Red Buttes (Hike 14) to the southeast; and the pyramid of Mount McLoughlin to the east. One special feature of this area that may or may not be welcome is black bears. Your chances of seeing one are good, which some consider a rare treat and others think of as a troubling prospect. Backpackers should hang their food and anything else a bruin might find interesting.

The trail begins as a wide, rocky track, but it soon changes to a narrow trail that makes a gentle up-and-down traverse on a woodsy hillside. At 0.8 mile is a junction with the Sucker Creek Trail. Go straight, staying on the west side of trickling Steve Fork Applegate River, and soon switchback to the right. From here, the rocky trail begins a long, gradual ascent across a hillside covered with a mix of incense cedars; Jeffrey, sugar, and ponderosa pines; Douglas firs; canyon live oaks; and Pacific madrones.

Shortly after crossing two seasonal creeks, you make one switchback and come to a meadow at 2.8 miles. The trail makes a sharp right turn here, but it is worth your time to go straight on an unsigned use path that travels 200 yards to a small, scenic lake covered with lily pads. There are nice campsites here, but the lake has no fish.

The main trail climbs over a rounded ridge to a four-way junction in grassy Sucker Creek Gap at 3.1 miles. To reach Sucker Creek Shelter, veer slightly left and, 150 yards later, turn right on a steep trail that goes down to a meadow and the shake-covered shelter. The lush meadow is rimmed by huge incense cedars, has a small spring, and features nice views north to rounded Swan Mountain.

To reach that mountain, from Sucker Creek Gap go north on the Boundary Trail and begin a gradual uphill traverse of a brushy hillside. In addition to nice westerly views, this hillside has plenty of wildflowers in June and July. The trail returns to the ridge crest at a wide saddle at 4.3 miles, just south of Swan Mountain.

View of Swan Mountain from Sucker Creek Gap

To reach the top, leave the trail at the northwest end of the saddle and scramble up the open, brushy slopes on the south side of the peak. The thick brush can be difficult, so wear long pants to protect your legs. The summit's panoramic views include some roads and clearcuts, but these do not significantly detract from the scene. Hikers familiar with this area can pick out dozens of prominent peaks. Although you will want to spend many hours enjoying this view, you will eventually be forced back down by the flies, carried here by the wind in large numbers.

14 RED BUTTES LOOP

Distance: 25-mile loop
Hiking time: 3 days
Elevation gain: 5800 feet
Difficulty: Very strenuous
Season: Late June to October
Best: July
Map: USFS Red Buttes Wilderness
Information: Rogue River–Siskiyou National Forest—Siskiyou Mountains Ranger District, (541) 899-3800

Directions: From Jacksonville, just west of Medford, go 8 miles southwest on Oregon Highway 238 to a junction at Ruch. Turn left (south), following signs to Applegate Reservoir, and drive 19 miles to a junction at the south end of the reservoir. Go straight and, 0.9 mile later, turn sharply right at an unsigned intersection. This gravel road (Forest Road 1040) crosses a bridge, then goes 3.6 miles to the Horse Camp trailhead, immediately after a bridge over Cook & Green Creek.

Trails in the Siskiyou Mountains, of which this loop is arguably the best, typically feature outstanding views, unusual geology, and diverse botany. This trail has all of those attributes, plus an exceptional abundance of wildlife. Although this loop is technically in California, by any logical geography it is really an *Oregon* hike. From the south, this is one of those you-can't-get-there-from-here places, so Californians are forced to drive north into Oregon, then turn back south to reach the trailhead. Beaver Staters, on the other hand, have much easier access and are happy to claim this area as their own.

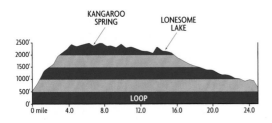

From the Horse Camp trailhead, the trail climbs through a forest of Douglas firs and red-barked Pacific madrones for 0.6 mile to a junction with Butte Fork Trail and the start of your loop. Go straight and ascend unrelenting switchbacks through an open forest that gradually becomes more varied with the addition of western white and Jeffrey pines, grand firs, and incense cedars. One of the more interesting views along the way is of Butte Fork Slide, a large gash in the hillside west of the trail. The ascent eases once you get above the slide, where a spur trail leads to Horse Camp.

The main trail charges up a steep hillside to a sloping meadow bisected by a small creek, then climbs to a junction at 3.3 miles with the short spur trail to Echo Lake. This small lake boasts an impressive setting surrounded by red and black cliffs and has a couple of decent campsites above its northeast shore. In addition to small brook trout, the lake teems with rough-skinned newts, brown salamanders with bright orange bellies.

The main trail climbs a steep, view-packed hillside above Echo Lake to a junction at 3.9 miles at a low point in the ridge east of aptly named Red Buttes. Turn right on the Pacific Crest Trail (PCT) and follow this well-graded route as it gradually descends to a crossing of a jeep road. The trail soon comes to Bee Camp at 4.4 miles, in a pretty basin with good views back to Red Buttes, then rounds a ridge and contours above shallow Lily Pad Lake. (Actually, cattle and frogs are both more abundant than lily pads.) You meet the end of a jeep road just above this lake, then

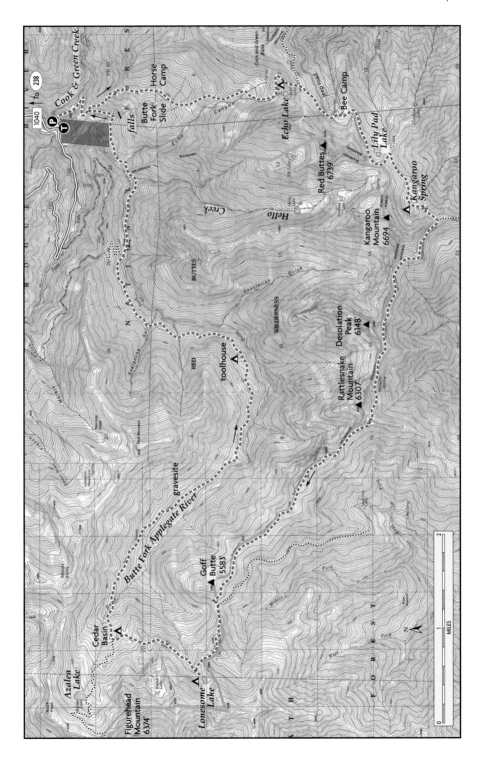

Kangaroo Mountain

briefly follow a stone fence before going around a ridge to the west. On the open hillside here you will see a few Brewer's "weeping" spruces, a rare, droopy-limbed tree found only in these mountains and a few other nearby ranges.

At Kangaroo Spring at 6.5 miles is a lush meadow with two small ponds, good campsites, and excellent views of the striking reddish orange slopes of Kangaroo Mountain. Stock up on water here, because this is the last reliable source for several miles. A series of gentle switchbacks take you out of this basin and past a scenic intrusion of white marble poking out of the orange peridotite rock. At the top of the next ridge, the PCT turns sharply left, but you go straight on the Boundary Trail, which crosses open slopes dotted with fire-scarred snags and features great views southwest to the rugged summits in California's Siskiyou Wilderness Area.

The next few miles are gentle as you travel beneath the cliffs of Desolation Peak and contour around the south side of Rattlesnake Mountain. Things get a bit more challenging when you descend a series of short switchbacks to a saddle at about 10 miles with a photogenic rock pinnacle, then follow an up-and-down course along the top of the scenic ridge to the northwest. The trail eventually rounds the southwest side of Goff Butte, then drops to a junction with the Fort Goff Trail at 13 miles. Go straight, climb an open ridge, then drop to the outlet creek of unseen Lonesome Lake at 14 miles. This is your first water source since Kangaroo Spring, 7.5 miles back. A little before you cross this creek, look for an unsigned junction with the 0.1-mile spur trail to Lonesome Lake. This small, scenic pool sitting in a rocky basin has good campsites on its north shore.

The main trail crosses the creek, then makes a rolling traverse to a small marsh with a nice view of craggy Figurehead Mountain. A short walk past this is the lush meadow at Cedar Basin at about 15.5 miles. There are good campsites here among the huge incense cedars that gave the basin its name. On the north side of this two-tiered meadow is a junction with the trail to Azalea Lake. Turn right and drop through forest to a crossing of the trickling headwaters of Butte Fork Applegate River.

From here, the trail is almost all downhill. Although generally viewless, the hike is consistently pleasant, because the trail's grade remains gentle and the forests are diverse and attractive. The first major landmark is a gravesite, not quite 2 miles from Cedar Basin, where three people died in an airplane crash in 1945. Another 2.5 miles takes you to a good campsite beside a picturesque wooden toolhouse at 20 miles. Beyond this structure, the canyon curves north and the forest becomes more varied with Pacific yews, Pacific madrones, canyon live oaks, Pacific dogwoods, bigleaf maples, and massive old sugar and ponderosa pines adding their shades of green to those of the ubiquitous grand firs and Douglas firs.

At the junction with Shoo Fly Trail at about 22 miles, keep straight; then 0.1 mile later, cross the flow of Butte Fork on a large wooden bridge. The trail follows the stream for 0.7 mile, makes a switchback up a forested slope, then comes to an easy ford of Hello Creek. After this you leave the wilderness, splash across Echo Creek, and ascend a forested hillside to a rocky gorge just below an impressive, twisting waterfall. The loop ends with a short additional climb to the junction with Horse Camp Trail at about 24.5 miles.

WESTERN VALLEYS

Middle North Falls (Hike 17), Silver Falls State Park

The vast majority of Oregonians live in one of three fertile lowlands that lie between the Coast Range to the west and the Cascade Mountains to the east. The two southern valleys, centered on the Umpqua and Rogue rivers, are both pleasant landscapes with rolling hills, stately oak woodlands, and attractive farms. Farther north is the larger and much better-known Willamette Valley, the center of commerce and home to most of the state's residents for at least 150 years. In the 1840s, the mild climate and rich soil of this valley made it the principal destination of pioneers on the Oregon Trail. In addition to establishing farms, these settlers founded the state's largest cities—Salem, Eugene, and Portland. Some of those migrants later made their way south along the Applegate Trail to settle in the Rogue and Umpqua valleys. The settlers rapidly staked out farms on almost every acre of cultivable land, so there is now very little under public ownership. As a result, hikers are restricted to a few isolated parks, which take on added importance because of their relative scarcity and proximity to major population centers.

15   FOREST PARK

Distance: 1.8 miles round trip to Wildwood Trail; 4.8-mile loop on Wild Cherry
    Trail; 20 miles one way to NW Germantown Road
Hiking time: 1–10 hours
Elevation gain: 150 feet to Wildwood Trail; 600 feet to Wild Cherry Trail; 800 feet
    to NW Germantown Road
Difficulty: Easy to moderate
Season: All year
Best: Late March to mid-April (for wildflowers)
Maps: Art of Geography—Forest Park (available from www.artofgeography.com
    /maps/fp)
Information: Portland Parks and Recreation, (503) 823-7529

Directions: Leave Interstate 405 at exit 3, following signs to St. Helens, and proceed 0.3 mile to the traffic light at 26th Street. Turn left, go less than one block, then turn right on Northwest Upshur Street and drive 0.5 mile to a road-end parking lot beneath a tall bridge.

If the sole criterion for including hikes in this book was scenery, then the trails in Forest Park probably would not make the cut. The dense forests that the park's name correctly advertises restrict views and limit the scenery to delicate ferns, forest wildflowers, and splashing creeks— all very attractive, but hardly spectacular. What makes Forest Park unique is that this 5000-acre wilderness is just a short walk from the sky-scrapers of a major American city. Excellent trails explore almost every corner of the park. One of the best is the Lower Macleay Trail, which fol-lows Balch Creek, a lovely urban stream, to a junction with the Wildwood Trail; you can fol-low this for as long as you like. Numerous side trails intersect the route, allowing you to fashion hikes of almost any length, depending on when you elect to turn right, descend to Northwest Leif Erikson Drive, and follow this closed road back to your starting point. Or use a vehicle shuttle to hike the entire 20 miles one way.

From the parking lot on Northwest Upshur Street, the paved trail goes under the bridge, then up the surprisingly wild canyon of Balch Creek. The trail crosses the creek twice on wooden bridges, passing lovely cascades and enchanting little waterfalls along the way. The surrounding forest features droopy western red cedars and towering Douglas firs above a green carpet of mosses, sword ferns, Oregon grape, and trillium. At the 0.9-mile point is a moss-covered stone ruin and a junction with the Wildwood Trail. Those seeking a short hike can turn back here, refreshed by the sounds of falling water and singing birds.

For a longer trip, turn sharply right and climb a hillside covered with English ivy, an intro-duced species that park officials and volunteers work hard to keep under control. The trail soon begins zigzagging out to minor ridges and into small gullies that continue for the remainder of the hike. Another constant is the shade of a thick mantle of Douglas firs, western hemlocks, and Pacific yews. In April, wildflowers such as tril-lium, wood violet, and false solomon's seal add other colors to the green forest.

The Wildwood Trail takes you past Holman Lane to a junction with Aspen Trail at 1.7 miles. This is followed by the trail's only significant climb, a switchbacking, 300-foot ascent of a sword fern-covered hillside. Next are junc-tions with Birch Trail and Wild Cherry Trail at 3.2 miles, the latter a good return route for a

ONE-WAY

| 0 mile | 4.0 | 8.0 | 12.0 | 16.0 | 20.0 |

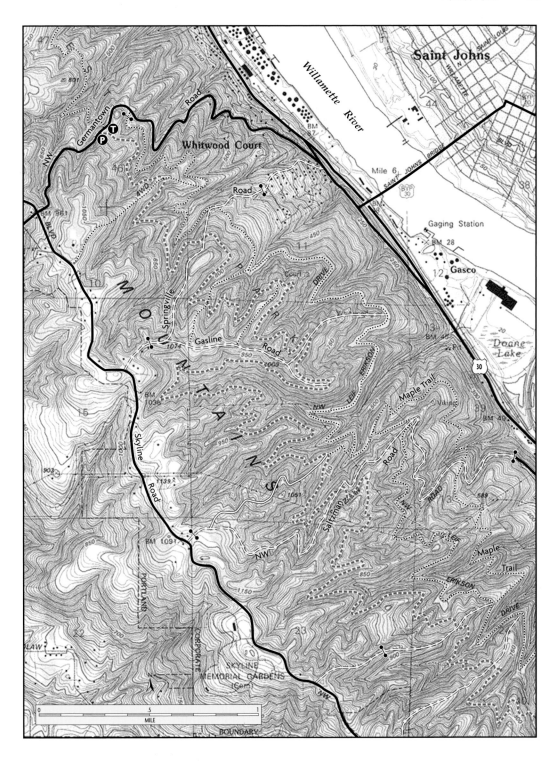

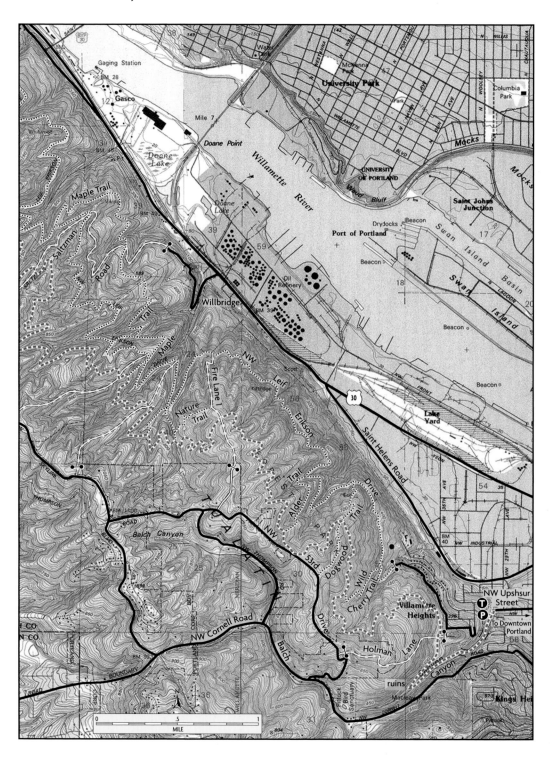

4.8-mile loop that follows Thurman Road through quiet neighborhoods to the bridge above the trailhead.

But the Wildwood Trail keeps going (and going, and going), zigzagging through dense forest, over countless little creeks, and past a dizzying array of junctions. The route is never strenuous, since the trail rarely does much up or down, and the scenery remains pleasantly green throughout. In such natural surroundings, it is easy to forget that you have never left the city limits and are just a short distance from busy railroad yards, highways, and factories.

Only a few of the trail junctions are mentioned here. At 4.8 miles is Alder Trail, followed by Fire Lane 1 at 6.5 miles and the Maple Trail at 8.2 miles. You reach closed Saltzman Road at 11.4 miles, Springville Road at 17.8 miles, and finally the trailhead at Northwest Germantown Road at 20 miles. Although the Wildwood Trail goes another 5.1 miles to Newberry Road, German-

Stone ruins along Balch Creek

town Road is a better stopping point, because the trailhead is easier to reach and has better parking.

16 TRYON CREEK STATE PARK

Distance: 1–7 miles round trip; 2.1-mile loop recommended
Hiking time: 1–3 hours
Elevation gain: 100–400 feet; recommended loop, 300 feet
Difficulty: Easy to moderate
Season: All year
Best: Early to mid-April
Map: USGS Lake Oswego
Information: Tryon Creek State Natural Area, (503) 636-9886

Directions: From downtown Portland, go 2 miles south on Interstate 5, then leave the freeway at exit 297. Go 2.2 miles south on Terwilliger Boulevard, through numerous traffic lights and junctions, to the parking lot for Tryon Creek State Park.

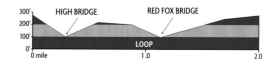

Hidden amid the busy streets and housing complexes of Portland and Lake Oswego, Tryon Creek State Park is a wilderness treasure. The park's 645 acres protect a forested canyon, a lovely urban stream, and crucial habitat for a wide range of wildlife. All of this provides an amazingly wild hiking

experience just a few minutes from downtown Portland. Although these low-elevation trails are open all year, the best time to visit is the first two weeks of April when the forest floor is brightened by thousands of trillium, a lovely white-blooming lily that is the symbol of this urban preserve. A

Trillium in Tryon Creek State Park

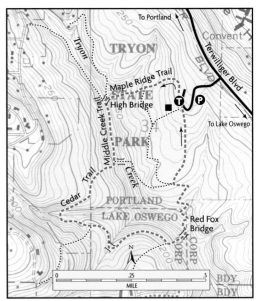

complex network of trails winds through the park, making possible hundreds of imaginative loops. With so many trails and junctions it is easy to become confused, but it really does not matter where you go, because every trail is attractive and worth exploring. Although some trails are gravel and others travel over boardwalks, most paths have no such amenities. Expect plenty of mud during western Oregon's seemingly endless rainy season.

The recommended tour starts on the Maple Ridge Trail, which leaves from the north end of the parking lot. This trail goes past Jackson Shelter, then descends through an attractive forest of western red cedar, western hemlock, red alder, and the omnipresent Douglas fir. The trunks and branches of these trees are handsomely decorated with an assortment of mosses, lichens, and licorice ferns.

At (not so) High Bridge at 0.4 mile the trail crosses Tryon Creek, a remarkably wild urban stream that is home to wildlife such as beavers, western pond turtles, and river otters. Numerous trails converge near this bridge, giving you plenty of choices. The recommended route takes you across the bridge, then turns left (downstream) on the Middle Creek Trail. The trail soon takes you through a bog filled with skunk cabbage, a plant that chokes marshy areas like this with large, shiny, dark green leaves and big yellow flowers in April. Although the unpleasant aroma that gave this plant its name will never be made into a perfume, it is a lot better than the exhaust fumes so prevalent along the interstate freeway just a couple of miles away.

At the next junction, at 0.6 mile, your best bet is to turn right on the Cedar Trail, which climbs through some of the park's best displays of trillium to a junction on the canyon rim. The most attractive choice here is to go straight, following signs to Red Fox Bridge, and wander through lovely forest, over small side creeks, and past various junctions back down to Tryon Creek. The trail crosses the creek on the scenic wooden span of Red Fox Bridge at 1.5 miles, then climbs four short switchbacks to a junction on the canyon's east rim at about 1.9 miles. Turn right and you will soon walk past the park's Nature Center to your car.

17 SILVER FALLS STATE PARK LOOP

Distance: 0.6 mile round trip to Upper North Falls; 7.1-mile loop; 7.7 miles total
Hiking time: 4 hours total
Elevation gain: 700 feet total
Difficulty: Moderate
Season: All year
Best: All year
Maps: USGS Drake Crossing, Elk Prairie
Information: Silver Falls State Park, (503) 873-8681

Directions: From the junction of Oregon Highways 213 and 214 at Silverton, go 14 miles southeast on Hwy 214 to Silver Falls State Park. You can also reach the park from Oregon Highway 22 east of Salem by driving 17 miles east on Hwy 214.

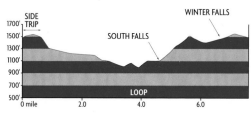

It's hardly surprising that the trails in Silver Falls State Park, in a beautiful forested canyon hosting ten spectacular waterfalls, are popular. In fact, this 8700-acre crown jewel of one of the finest state park systems in the country is visited by thousands of hikers and car-bound tourists every year. But don't be put off by the crowds, because the popularity is well deserved. Just try to visit on a weekday. There are two possible starting points for this loop. South Falls is the more popular, with a campground, a picnic area, a gift shop, and an enormous parking lot, but as described here, begin at quieter North Falls, where a much smaller parking lot provides access to the northeast part of the loop. At either location, you must have a day-use parking permit, which you can buy either at the South Falls entrance station or the self-serve pay station at North Falls.

From the North Falls parking lot, the trail immediately drops to a footbridge over North Fork Silver Creek and comes to a junction. Before starting the loop, take time for a 0.3-mile side trip that goes under the highway bridge and travels upstream to quiet Upper North Falls. This lovely, 65-foot drop is a perfect appetizer for this trip.

To reach spectacular North Falls, go west (downstream) from the junction below the North

Falls parking lot and immediately come to a fork at the start of the loop. Bear right and soon reach the lip of the cliff-lined grotto holding 136-foot North Falls, a narrow tube of water that explodes over a basalt cliff. Like many other waterfalls in the park, the spray at the base of this falls has eroded the softer rock below the basalt, leaving a large cavern behind the falls.

Upper North Falls

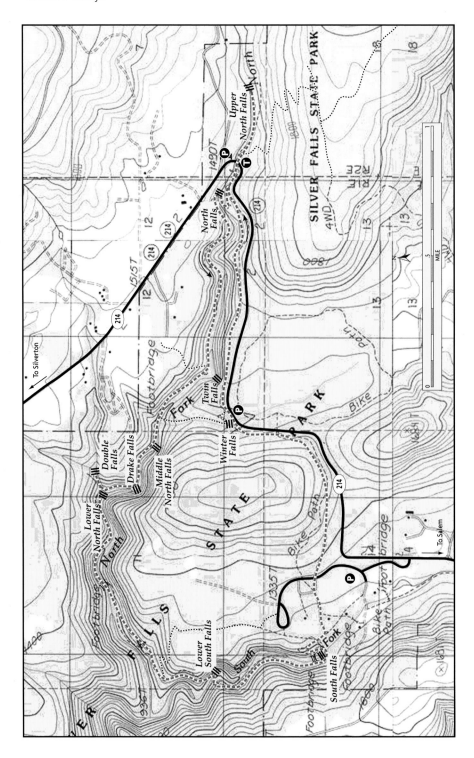

The trail descends a series of switchbacks on the south side of the creek, then takes you on an exciting course through the amazingly dry cavern behind the falls to the other side of the canyon. Visitors who have never had the pleasure of walking behind a waterfall love it! Continue downstream through a lush forest to a junction near Twin Falls, a roaring 31-foot drop. Bear left and at 2 miles reach a junction with the trail to Winter Falls (less-ambitious hikers can go left on this trail to make a 2.9-mile loop).

Go straight and soon come to the broad drop of 106-foot Middle North Falls, where a fun side trail turns left off the main route and travels through the grotto behind this falls. Next in line is Drake Falls, in a narrow chasm on your left, then a junction at 2.5 miles with the not-to-be-missed 0.1-mile side trail to the delicate drop of 120-foot Double Falls. Immediately below this junction is Lower North Falls, a nearly perfect sliding cascade with a lovely pool at its base.

It is almost 2 miles to the next waterfall, but the scenery is no less attractive. The canyon becomes narrower here, with tall basalt cliffs covered with moss and maidenhair ferns. Several seasonal side creeks drop over these cliffs in wispy, unnamed waterfalls. Cross North Fork Silver Creek on a wooden bridge, then ascend the south canyon wall to a junction at 3.6 miles. Go straight and gradually descend into the canyon of South Fork Silver Creek to the spectacular bowl holding 93-foot Lower South Falls. The trail goes behind this falls in yet another eroded grotto, climbs a series of stairs, then follows the beautiful creek upstream. After 0.3 mile you come to a bridge at 4.7 miles just below South Falls, a 177-foot sheet of water that is the park's most famous and crowded attraction. A paved trail goes through the cavernous grotto behind South Falls, then makes an uphill traverse to the fenced canyon rim.

With the confusing network of roads, parking lots, and trails around South Falls, it can be difficult to locate the proper course to continue the loop. In general, head east following trail signs that direct you to North Falls. Eventually you leave the congestion and follow a dirt hiker's trail that parallels the highway for 1.6 miles to the tiny parking lot above Winter Falls at 6.9 miles.

To close the loop, the trail traverses a heavily forested hillside not far below the highway. Along the way you pass an excellent viewpoint of North Falls before returning to the junction beside the North Falls parking lot at 7.7 miles.

18 MCDOWELL CREEK FALLS

Distance: 1.7-mile loop
Hiking time: 1 hour
Elevation gain: 200 feet
Difficulty: Easy
Season: All year
Best: April and May
Map: USGS Sweet Home
Information: Linn County Parks, (541) 967-3917

Directions: Drive US 20 to 4 miles southeast of Lebanon or 8 miles northwest of Sweet Home to a junction with Fairview Road. Turn east, following signs to McDowell Creek Park, drive 1 mile, then turn left on McDowell Creek Road and stay on this paved road for 7.7 miles to the picnic area at the west end of the park.

Western Oregon's rugged topography and wet climate combine to make it a waterfall-lover's paradise. Thousands of falls mean hikers have a wide range of possibilities to choose from. Some falls are hidden in remote wilderness canyons inaccessible to all but the most determined explorers. Other falls plunge over cliffs right next to

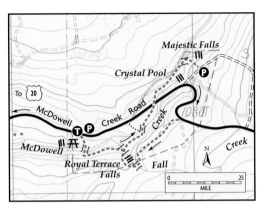

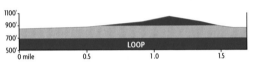

Royal Terrace Falls

interstate freeways. The ones in between—the hundreds of cascades accessible only by trail—are now popular destinations for local hikers. One excellent destination on the easier end of the hiking scale is McDowell Creek Park, a small county park that protects a group of impressive waterfalls in the hills southeast of Lebanon. The park's trails are open all year and are easy enough for hikers of all ages.

From the southeast corner of the parking lot, the gravel trail immediately crosses a bridge over McDowell Creek just above a wide, cascading falls. From here, the trail winds gradually through a mossy rain forest where the ground is covered with forest wildflowers such as bleeding heart, false lily of the valley, salmonberry, and twisted stalk. The first big waterfall is 119-foot Royal Terrace Falls, a two-tiered cataract on Fall Creek, a major tributary of McDowell Creek. The trail crosses Fall Creek on a tall bridge at 0.3 mile, just below the falls.

Shortly after Royal Terrace Falls, the trail crosses a bridge over McDowell Creek and comes to an unsigned junction. Turn right on a lovely creekside path and keep right at a second unsigned junction just 150 yards later. The trail soon crosses McDowell Creek Road at 0.5 mile

and goes upstream to the roaring cascade at Crystal Pool. Climb away from this falls on two short switchbacks, then continue upstream to an elaborate wooden boardwalk and bridge over McDowell Creek just below aptly titled Majestic Falls at 0.8 mile. A platform provides excellent views of this thunderous waterfall and its mossy grotto.

A series of wooden and stone stairs climb a short way out of this grotto to an upper parking lot. From here, walk 0.1 mile downhill on the parking lot's access road to a junction with McDowell Creek Road. You can return to your car by walking back along McDowell Creek Road 0.4 mile, but for more exercise, turn left (uphill) and follow the road's shoulder around a large bend. After about 250 yards, turn right on a trail that traces a woodsy course along the forested rim of the canyon. This gently graded route takes you to a bridge over Fall Creek at 1.3 miles just above Royal Terrace Falls. The trail then very steeply descends the hillside beside the falls to an unsigned junction beside the second bridge over Fall Creek. Turn left here to return to the trailhead. **Note:** In wet conditions the steep downhill section beside Royal Terrace Falls is slippery and dangerous, so park officials sometimes close the trail to hikers.

19 HORSE ROCK RIDGE

Distance: 3 miles round trip
Hiking time: 1.5 hours
Elevation gain: 900 feet
Difficulty: Moderate
Season: March to early December
Best: Mid-April and early May
Maps: USGS Crawfordsville, Union Point
Information: Bureau of Land Management—Eugene District, (541) 683-6600

Directions: From Interstate 5 just north of Eugene, take exit 194A, go east on Highway 126 for 3.9 miles, then take the exit for Marcola and 42nd Street. Drive northeast on Marcola Road through the pleasantly rural Mohawk River Valley for 14.3 miles, then turn left on paved Shotgun Creek Road. After 1.1 miles you bear right at a fork and proceed 2.1 miles to another fork beside a parking area for OHVs (Off-Highway Vehicles, a.k.a. All-Terrain Vehicles). There you go right. After 0.3 mile you turn right onto Seeley Creek Road, a narrow paved route that passes several minor intersections as it climbs into the clearcut-strewn Mohawk Hills. After 2.4 miles you bear right (staying on pavement) at a ridge-top junction, then drive another 0.7 mile to a confusing multi-way junction. Veer right here and drive a final 0.2 mile before parking where an unmarked gravel road angles uphill to the left.

Despite its close proximity to Eugene, Horse Rock Ridge remains a semi-secret hideout for local botanists and only a handful of knowledge-able hikers. The trail here is not maintained, but it is in good shape and generally easy to follow. Best of all, the scenery is wonderful, featuring steeply sloping meadows, a lot of interesting volcanic rock formations, excellent spring wild-

flowers, and extensive views. Even though the area's highest elevation is only 2864 feet, the open terrain provides the look and feel of much higher mountains. Since the trails here open as early as March, this hike is a great way to smell the flowers and get a taste of the High Cascades early in the hiking season. To protect the unusual botany of Horse Rock Ridge, one of the last remaining grassy "balds" on the west margin of the Cascade Range, the Bureau of Land Management (BLM) has set aside this place as a research

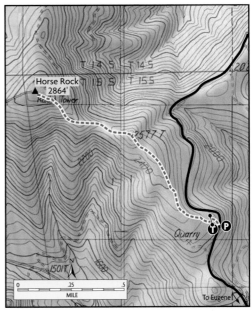

Horse Rock Ridge from the southeast end of the meadows

natural area. The agency does not promote or manage the area for recreation, and visitors are strongly encouraged to tread lightly and to faithfully remain on the trail. Larger groups are asked to coordinate their visit with the BLM office in Eugene.

Begin by walking through a pedestrian access in a fenceline, then follow the old road as it travels gradually uphill through a dense forest of Douglas fir, western hemlock, and western red cedar. Along the way, you must crawl over several downed logs across the road, many of which were deliberately placed here to keep machines out of this sensitive area. Shortly after the old road peters out, near 0.6 mile, the forest ends at

the base of a huge and dramatically scenic sloping meadow. This south-facing meadow gets a lot of sun and hosts most of the remainder of the trail to the summit of Horse Rock.

As the trail makes its way up this lovely meadow, you enjoy excellent views, mostly of the Willamette Valley and distant Coast Range to the west. Unfortunately, several nearby clearcuts mar the view, but it's still very good. Wildflowers put on an impressive show from mid-April to early May. The many rare and colorful varieties include saxifrage, yellow monkeyflower, blue-eyed Mary, shooting star, and countless others. Although the trail is faint at times, the route up the ridge is never difficult to follow; simply remain near the spine of the up-and-down ridge and you will be fine.

The trail goes over a knoll at 0.8 mile, then at 1.3 miles things become quite steep as the trail climbs beside a narrow rim of exposed basalt. To compensate for the extra sweat, there are excellent views to the east of distant Mount Jefferson and the Three Sisters. The trail's last 150 yards are a bit overgrown as you leave the steep meadow and travel through forest to the actual summit of Horse Rock. For most hikers it is usually better to simply skip this final section, because the summit has no meadows or much in the way of views and it features the man-made intrusion of a fenced microwave tower. The meadows below are much prettier.

20 LOWER TABLE ROCK

Distance: 3.8 miles round trip
Hiking time: 2 hours
Elevation gain: 800 feet
Difficulty: Moderate
Season: All year
Best: April and May
Map: USGS Sams Valley
Information: The Nature Conservancy, (503) 802-8100

Directions: Leave Interstate 5 at Central Point exit 33, north of Medford, and go 1 mile east to a four-way junction. Turn left (north) on Table Rock Road and drive 7.5 miles to a junction with Wheeler Road. Turn left and drive 0.9 mile to the spacious trailhead parking lot.

A springtime display of wildflowers atop Lower Table Rock

The Table Rocks are a pair of misplaced monoliths that rise above the Rogue Valley northwest of Medford. For itchy-footed hikers zipping by on Interstate 5, these cliff-edged basalt mesas stir an almost irresistible desire to climb to the top and take in the view. Fortunately, good trails lead to the top of each rock. And once you get there, you can not only enjoy the expected view but also marvel at the many unusual plants that call these rocks home. Both trails are worthwhile, but the one up Lower Table Rock, owned by The Nature Conservancy, is marginally more scenic and has better wildflower displays. Dogs are not allowed on the trail.

From the parking lot, the well-graded trail goes under a powerline, then gradually ascends through a lovely oak woodland where many of the larger oak trees sprout clumps of parasitic mis-

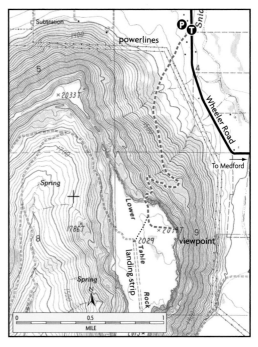

tletoe. In April and May this grassy environment is filled with wildflowers, especially common camas, death camas, cats ear (a fuzzy mariposa lily), lupine, desert parsley, and dandelion. Also everywhere (and that means everywhere) are thickets of poison oak, so stay on the trail. As you gain elevation, the terrain gets more brushy and you enter a chaparral ecosystem that is more typical of central California. Still farther up, the oaks are joined by Pacific madrones, ponderosa pines, and Douglas firs in a denser forest environment. Numerous interpretive signs keep you informed about the changes in your surroundings.

After 0.7 mile the steady, uphill trail reaches a small, woodsy flat spot and makes a rounded right turn. From here, steadily climb five switchbacks, then go through a small gap in the rock's cliffs to the flat top of Lower Table Rock at 1.6 miles. Continue south, then east over the summit to a viewpoint at 1.9 miles.

The open summit supports a unique ecosystem of rock-strewn grasslands, ephemeral lakes, and scattered oaks with a wide range of rare and beautiful wildflowers. Botanists will love it, but even if you don't know the first thing about plants, it is hard not to be impressed. You could easily spend several hours exploring this landscape, taking various unmarked trails, following an old landing strip to the south end of the rock, and seeking out cliff-top viewpoints. Let your imagination be your guide, but stick to the trails to avoid trampling the plants.

COLUMBIA RIVER GORGE

Angels Rest (Hike 22)

One of the things that makes Portland unique is that no other major American city has a backyard comparable to the Columbia River Gorge. Here one of North America's largest rivers forgoes the sensible course of going *around* a major mountain range and decides instead to simply plow right through it. The result is a remarkable, nearly sea-level passage between forest-draped peaks that are up to 5000 feet high. This rapid elevation change, in conjunction with the wet climate, leads to an incredible concentration of waterfalls. The best known is 542-foot Multnomah Falls, one of the highest in North America. But tucked away in hidden canyons throughout the gorge are hundreds of other cascades that are just as beautiful and much less crowded.

Despite its proximity to a major urban area and its status as a vital transportation corridor, much of the Columbia Gorge remains as wild today as when Lewis and Clark led their band of explorers through in 1805. That wild character is preserved by the Mark O. Hatfield Wilderness (significantly expanded in 2009), numerous state parks, and the zoning restrictions of the Columbia River Gorge National Scenic Area. But what really keeps this remarkable region out of the hands of developers is a cadre of dedicated people who work to protect this treasure for future generations. If you are interested in helping this grassroots effort, contact the Friends of the Columbia Gorge (see Appendix B, Selected Conservation and Hiking Groups, at the back of this book).

21 LATOURELL FALLS LOOP

Distance: 2.4-mile loop
Hiking time: 2 hours
Elevation gain: 600 feet
Difficulty: Easy
Season: All year (except during winter storms)
Best: April and May
Map: Green Trails No. 428 Bridal Veil
Information: Guy W. Talbot State Park, (503) 695-2261

Directions: From Interstate 84 east of Portland, take exit 28 and drive the 0.4-mile exit road to a junction with the Old Columbia River Highway. Turn right (west) and drive 2.9 miles to the Latourell Falls parking lot.

The first major waterfall visitors see along the Old Columbia River Highway is Lower Latourell Falls, and if you were expecting to gradually work your way up to the best scenery, forget it! With its 249-foot plunge over a sheer, lichen-covered cliff, this falls' beauty rivals any other in the gorge. For hikers, the only downside to Lower Latourell Falls is that to see it, you barely have to leave your car. Fortunately, those who want to get a little exercise can take a very scenic loop trail that goes from the lower falls to rarely visited Upper Latourell Falls.

The trail starts as a paved walkway that goes up a steep hill to a jaw-dropping viewpoint of Lower Latourell Falls. This viewpoint is far enough for most visitors, but hikers inspired by the scenery will want to go much farther. Bear left and take a dirt trail up a hillside that bursts with new greenery in April and May. The trail soon takes you to a second viewpoint of the falls, then reaches a junction with a shortcut trail at 0.3 mile. The main loop trail goes left up a woodsy canyon

where several small wooden bridges span trickling side creeks.

At the south end of the loop is a bridge across Latourell Creek at 0.8 mile, immediately below Upper Latourell Falls. This scenic, twisting cataract is a great place for a relaxing lunch stop, especially appealing to photographers.

The loop's return route traces the west side of the canyon to a junction with the shortcut trail mentioned above at 1.3 miles. Bear left, ascend

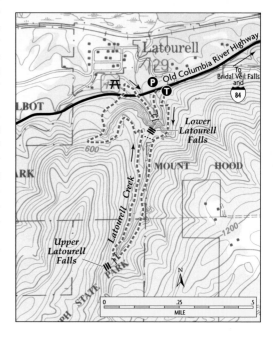

two quick switchbacks to a nice viewpoint of the Columbia River, then lazily descend back to the road at 1.8 miles. The trail crosses the road, descends a set of stairs, then goes through a picnic area and travels under a tall highway bridge. Cross the creek a final time at 2.3 miles, then come to a wonderful viewpoint at the base of the amphitheater of Lower Latourell Falls. From here, a paved trail takes you back to the trailhead.

If you have the time, check out nearby Bridal Veil Falls. From the Latourell Falls parking lot, drive 2 miles east on the Old Columbia River Highway to the signed parking lot and pick up a trail that leaves from the east end of the lot. The gravel, 0.3-mile trail travels through lush vegetation down to a bridge over cascading Bridal Veil Creek, then heads upstream to a wooden platform with a stunning view of this two-tiered falls.

Camas blooming in Bridal Veil State Park

22 ANGELS REST–DEVILS REST LOOP

Distance: 9.3 miles round trip
Hiking time: 5.5 hours
Elevation gain: 2800 feet
Difficulty: Strenuous
Season: Late March to December
Best: April to June
Map: Green Trails No. 428 Bridal Veil (some trails not shown)
Information: Columbia River Gorge National Scenic Area, (541) 308-1700

Directions: From Interstate 84 east of Portland, take exit 28 and drive the 0.4-mile exit road to a junction with the Old Columbia River Highway. Bear left (east) and proceed 2.6 miles to the Wahkeena Falls parking lot.

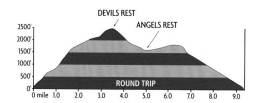

As their names suggest, Devils Rest and Angels Rest are dramatically different in character. While our heavenly patrons take their leisure atop a dramatic rock formation with spectacular views up and down the Columbia River, Satan relaxes on an unassuming hill where heavy forest blocks nearly every potential vista. Hikers can sample both heaven and hell on a single outing that also includes a nice sampling of wildflowers, impressive waterfalls, and some of the most verdant greenery in the gorge.

A paved trail leaves from the south side of the road and immediately crosses a bridge

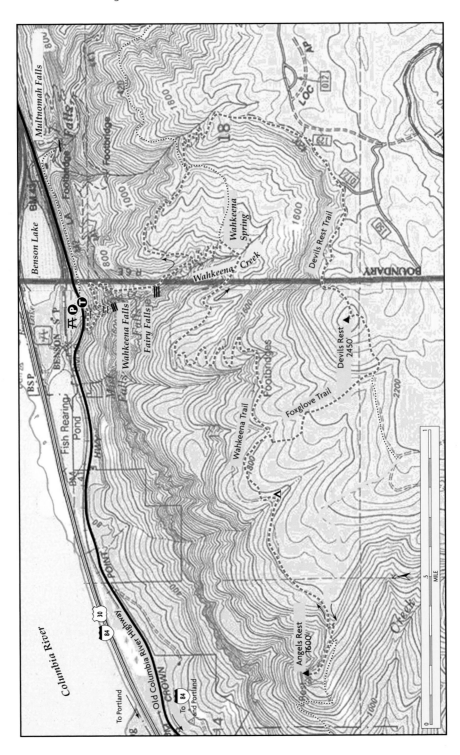

over cascading Wahkeena Creek. In one long switchback the trail ascends to a second bridge at 0.3 mile, which crosses the creek directly under the spray of Wahkeena Falls. On a hot summer day this is a welcome interlude, but in the winter it can be a bone-chilling experience. Most car-bound tourists turn back here, still within sight of their vehicles. But hikers keep going on a gravel trail that switchbacks up a hillside covered with luxuriantly green vegetation. After passing a short spur trail to Lemmon's Viewpoint, head upstream beside cascading Wahkeena Creek to a bench beside lovely Fairy Falls. A few more uphill switchbacks take you to a junction at 1.3 miles and the start of the loop.

Turn left, ascend to a ridge-crest junction with another viewpoint trail, then climb to a junction with the Wahkeena Trail at 1.9 miles. Turn left and, 50 feet later, bear right (uphill) on Devils Rest Trail. This moderately graded path switchbacks up to a ridgeline, then curves right and gradually climbs past viewpoint spur trails to a junction just below the summit of Devils Rest at 3.6 miles. Although there are no views here, the mossy boulders comprising the Devil's "easy chair" are surprisingly comfortable.

To go from resting with devils to kicking back with angels, go west on Foxglove Trail and steeply descend for 0.4 mile through head-high shrubbery to a junction. Turn right and descend 0.5 mile through forest and some brushy areas to another junction.

The return route of the loop goes right, but to visit Angels Rest, turn left and stroll through a brush-covered burn area to a creekside campsite, then through forest to a junction at 5 miles. Go straight and scramble 0.3 mile out to this massive outcropping, which reminds many visitors of a castle battlement with the Columbia River as a huge moat. Views up and down the river are magnificent. The flower displays are equally impressive, made all the more so by a fire that swept the area clear of trees in 1991. Unfortunately, this exposed location is particularly vulnerable to the gorge's legend-

Trail bridge below Wahkeena Falls

ary winds, which can blow so hard it may be impossible to stand up to enjoy the view.

To complete the loop, retrace your steps 0.8 mile, go straight at the junction and switchback downhill through old-growth forest to gushing Wahkeena Spring and a trail junction at 7.6 miles. Turn left and descend a series of switchbacks back to the junction above Fairy Falls and the close of the loop at 8 miles.

23 HORSETAIL FALLS TO TRIPLE FALLS

Distance: 4.5 miles round trip
Hiking time: 2.5 hours
Elevation gain: 700 feet
Difficulty: Easy
Season: All year (except during winter storms)
Best: April to June; late October to early November
Map: USFS Trails of the Columbia Gorge
Information: Columbia River Gorge National Scenic Area, (541) 308-1700

Directions: From Interstate 84 east of Portland, take exit 28 and drive the 0.4-mile exit road to a junction with the Old Columbia River Highway. Bear left (east) and drive 5.5 miles to the Horsetail Falls parking lot.

If you had to choose a single hike in the Columbia Gorge to showcase the charms of this region to an out-of-town visitor, this would be it. Of course, that decision would only come after loud protests that there are dozens of *other* great trails you would want to take them on as well, but in the end you would settle on this one, confident that your visitor would enjoy a great trip with a good sampling of the lush forests, breathtaking viewpoints, deep canyons, and spectacular waterfalls that make the gorge such a hiker's paradise. Unfortunately, you would have to share the trail with a lot of fellow admirers, because word of the treasures here has gotten out. But the scenery is so good it is impossible to complain. Try to visit on a weekday.

The well-graded trail starts a few yards east of 176-foot Horsetail Falls and switchbacks up a densely vegetated hillside to a switchback and a junction with the Gorge Trail at 0.2 mile. Turn sharply right, cross the base of a basalt cliff, then curve into the canyon above Horsetail Falls, where

Ponytail Falls shoots over an overhanging ledge into a mossy grotto. The trail takes an exciting course under the ledge behind this plunging falls, then contours across a mossy rockslide and past a junction with a short side trail at 0.8 mile that leads to a dramatic viewpoint. The main trail curves left (south) and switchbacks down to a breathtaking view of the fern-lined slot canyon of Oneonta Gorge. This 200-foot-deep chasm is so narrow that fallen trees often bridge the 20-foot-wide opening at the top. The trail then descends more switchbacks to a bridge over Oneonta Creek at 1.2 miles, immediately below a pretty 60-foot-high falls and just above an unseen 100-foot plunge, where the creek drops into the abyss of Oneonta Gorge.

On the other side of the bridge, a short uphill walk leads to a junction. To reach Triple Falls,

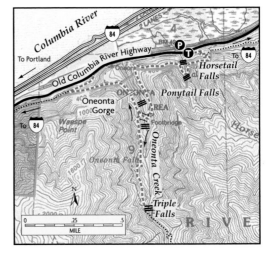

Triple Falls

turn sharply left and make a gradual uphill traverse across the nearly vertical slopes above Oneonta Creek. After 0.9 mile you reach an unsigned junction at 2.1 miles with a short spur trail to a stunning viewpoint of Triple Falls. This remarkable cascade, with its three nearly perfect branches, is one of the gorge's most outstanding waterfalls. Any season is beautiful, but perhaps the best is early November, when yellowing big-leaf maple leaves frame this dramatic scene.

Return 0.9 mile to the junction just west of the bridge over Oneonta Creek, and for variety go straight (north), then climb a short distance to a junction with another viewpoint spur trail. From here, descend through dense forest, turn sharply right at a junction at 3.8 miles, and soon return to the highway at 4 miles. Walk 0.5 mile along this narrow road back to Horsetail Falls.

24 TANNER BUTTE–EAGLE CREEK LOOP

Distance: 25-mile loop
Hiking time: 3 days
Elevation gain: 4300 feet
Difficulty: Strenuous
Season: May to October
Best: Late May and June
Map: Green Trails No. 429 Bonneville Dam
Information: Columbia River Gorge National Scenic Area, (541) 308-1700

Directions: From Interstate 84 east of Portland, take Eagle Creek exit 41, turn right (south), and drive 0.1 mile to a small parking lot 50 yards before a prominent hiker's bridge over Eagle Creek. Parking is very limited on summer weekends, so arrive early in the morning.

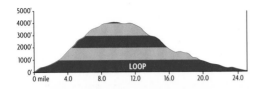

Lower Punch Bowl Falls

Eagle Creek is certainly no secret. With a string of breathtaking waterfalls, a beautiful canyon, several dramatic viewpoints, and glorious creek-side campsites, it was probably inevitable that this would become a popular hike—and it certainly is. On a typical summer weekend, hundreds of admiring pedestrians crowd the trailhead. Although day hikers dominate the trail, it is more satisfying to make this a back-packing trip. An up-and-back overnighter is the usual itinerary, but if you have time, make a three-day loop that includes not only Eagle Creek but the glorious ridge-top meadows around Tanner Butte.

Cross the arcing wooden bridge over Eagle Creek, then turn right on a gently graded trail that climbs to a fenced viewpoint overlooking Bonneville Dam. The trail switchbacks uphill to a brushy opening choked with thimbleberry and a junction at 0.9 mile with the dead-end trail to Wauna Point. Go straight and soon meet Tanner Creek Road, a narrow dirt road closed to motor vehicles.

Veer left (uphill) and walk 1.3 miles to the Tanner Butte trailhead just before the road crosses a small creek. Take this trail past a pair of small waterfalls in a lush little canyon, then cross under a powerline and switchback up a heavily forested hillside. A long uphill traverse takes you to a ridge-top junction with the unsigned Wauna Point Trail at 5 miles. Turn right and steadily climb a wide ridge, eventually entering a higher-elevation environment dominated by Pacific silver firs with huckleberries and beargrass covering the forest floor. Pass the junction with the Tanner Cutoff Trail at 7 miles; then, 150 yards later, reach the steep, 0.4-mile trail downhill to Dublin Lake. This tiny, forest-rimmed lake has good campsites above its southwest shore.

At the Dublin Lake junction, the Tanner Butte Trail goes straight and soon meets an overgrown jeep road, which you follow for the next several miles. The abandoned road leaves the forest after a mile and enters the glorious meadows around Tanner Butte. Views are superb here, including the green depths of Eagle Creek Canyon to the east and the hulking summit of Tanner Butte to the south. In late May and early June, these meadows

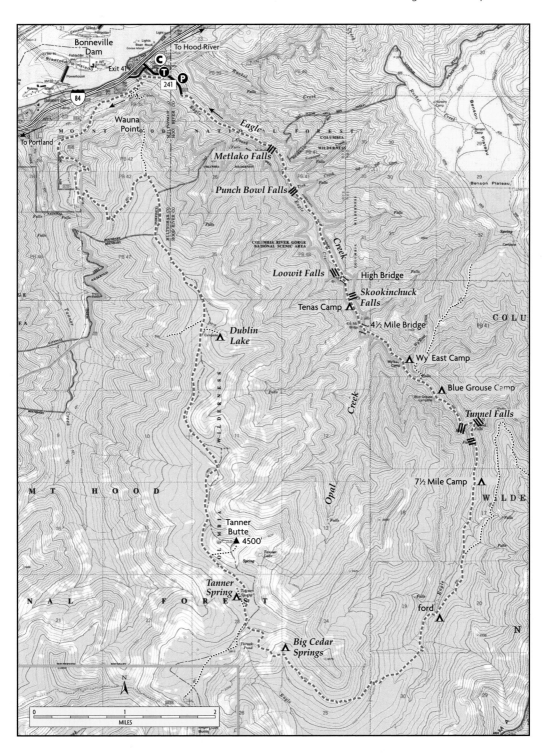

Bonneville Dam

To Hood River

Exit 41

241

P

C

T

84

To Portland

Wauna Point

Eagle

Creek

Metlako Falls

Punch Bowl Falls

COLUMBIA RIVER GORGE NATIONAL SCENIC AREA

Loowit Falls

High Bridge

Skookinchuck Falls

Tenas Camp

4½ Mile Bridge

COLU

Wy East Camp

Blue Grouse Camp

Dublin Lake

Tunnel Falls

WILDERNESS

Opal

Creek

7½ Mile Camp

WILDE

MT HOOD

Tanner Butte ▲ 4500'

Tanner Spring

ford

NAL FOREST

Big Cedar Springs

N

0   1   2
MILES

are carpeted with wildflowers, especially lupine, paintbrush, larkspur, and beargrass.

The old road goes up and down along the scenic ridge, eventually taking you around the brushy west side of Tanner Butte, whose summit is accessible by a short side trip at 10.5 miles. The detour is worthwhile, because the butte has some of the best views in the Columbia Gorge, including towering peaks from Mount Rainier to Mount Hood and hundreds of lesser summits that hikers familiar with this area can spend hours identifying.

A little south of Tanner Butte you pass the short side trail to Tanner Spring (with nice campsites), then turn left onto the Eagle–Tanner Cutoff Trail. This path rapidly descends past marshy Thrush Pond to a lovely campsite at 12.5 miles under the huge evergreens that gave nearby Big Cedar Springs its name. From here, several often-steep switchbacks take you down to Eagle Creek and an excellent campsite at about 14.5 miles, just after a knee-deep ford of the creek. Not quite 1 mile beyond this campsite is a junction with the Eagle Creek Trail.

The scenic highlights come in rapid succession along this well-engineered trail as it heads down the canyon. Not surprisingly, there are also increasing numbers of day hikers the farther you go. The first highlights are grouped around the confluence of Eagle Creek and East Fork Eagle Creek. First is a twisting, unnamed waterfall on the main creek. Rounding a cliff where the trail has been blasted into the vertical rock face, you come face-to-face with 120-foot Tunnel Falls on East Fork Eagle Creek. This impressive falls got its name because the trail goes through a tunnel dynamited into the rock behind the falls.

Just below Tunnel Falls you pass a smaller falls on Eagle Creek and reach Blue Grouse Camp at 18 miles. The trail crosses Eagle Creek at 4½ Mile Bridge, then reaches popular Tenas Camp at 20 miles near Skookinchuck Falls. Next up is High Bridge, spanning a narrow chasm on Eagle Creek, and Loowit Falls on a tributary on the west side of the canyon. Perhaps the most impressive highlight comes at Punch Bowl Falls at 22.5 miles, where a 0.1-mile side trail leads to the famous calendar spot at the base of this 30-foot drop. In 0.6 mile, you pass an unsigned side trail to a viewpoint of 100-foot Metlako Falls. The final section traverses a woodsy hillside to the end of the Eagle Creek Road. Your car is a 0.5-mile walk down this narrow road.

25   MOUNT DEFIANCE LOOP

Distance: 11.8 miles round trip (including summit)
Hiking time: 9 hours (tough day hike or backpack)
Elevation gain: 4900 feet
Difficulty: Very strenuous
Season: Late May to October
Best: June
Map: Green Trails No. 430 Hood River
Information: Columbia River Gorge National Scenic Area, (541) 308-1700

Directions: From eastbound Interstate 84 east of Portland, take Starvation Creek exit 54 and immediately park in the small trailhead parking lot. Exit 54 has access to and from only the eastbound lanes, so from westbound Interstate 84 west of Hood River, take Wyeth exit 51 to get on the eastbound lanes, then follow the eastbound directions above.

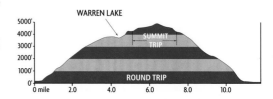

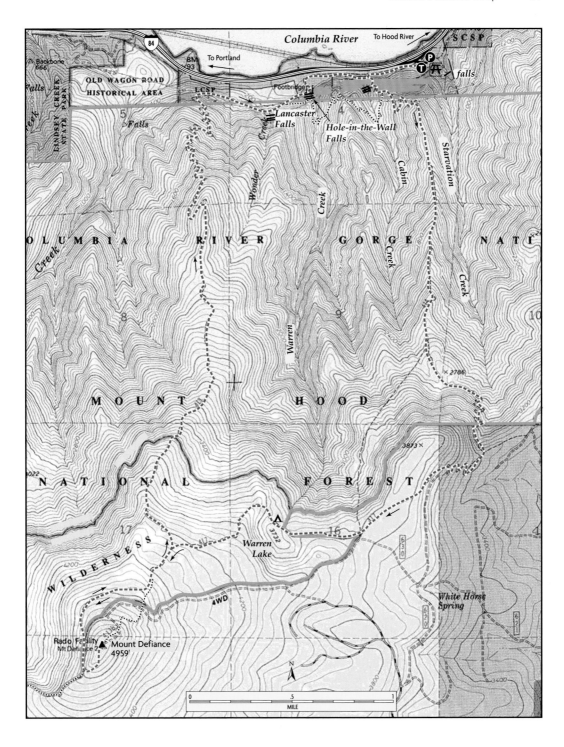

A view of Mount Hood from Mount Defiance Trail

Mount Defiance is the highest point in the Columbia River Gorge, and the trail from the river (near sea level) to the top (almost 5000 feet) is a major challenge. But nothing worthwhile ever comes easily—just keep telling yourself this as your thighs and lungs loudly dispute the point on the way up and your knees and toes continue the debate on the way down. The impressive scenery, especially the outstanding views from the top, make the effort worthwhile.

The level trail heads 0.3 mile west along the freeway shoulder to a junction with the Starvation Cutoff Trail at the start of the loop. Turn left and climb a series of short, steep switchbacks through dense forest to a junction with the Starvation Ridge Trail at 0.6 mile. Turn left and ascend ten more switchbacks to a viewpoint under a powerline tower.

The next section is steep and tiring as the trail rapidly climbs a narrow ridge for 2 miles before the grade eases and you cross a brushy slope with nice views of Mount Adams to the northeast. More switchbacks and an uphill traverse then lead to the edge of an old clearcut. The trail curves right and goes through a higher-elevation forest dominated by Pacific silver firs and June-blooming beargrass to an unsigned junction. Turn right and descend to Warren Lake at 4.3 miles, a beautiful mountain pool at the base of a scenic rockslide with good campsites and enticing swimming spots.

After a well-deserved rest, climb the view-packed ridge west of Warren Lake to a junction with the Mount Defiance Trail at 5.1 miles. This slightly better-graded trail is the return route of your loop, but the summit still beckons, so turn left and climb 0.2 mile to a possibly unsigned junction. Either route takes you to the summit. The more scenic trail goes right across a talus slope on the west side of the peak. At a junction on the south side of the mountain, turn left and make the final short climb to the top at 6.3 miles.

A closed jeep road and several microwave towers detract from the scene, but the views are still outstanding. In a basin to the west is shimmering Bear Lake and beyond that are Green Point Mountain and a host of other Columbia Gorge high points. Most of your attention, however, will be drawn south to Mount Hood's dramatic, horn-shaped spire.

Once you have had your fill of views (which may take several hours), return 1.2 miles to the junction west of Warren Lake and go straight (north) on the Mount Defiance Trail. This path heads downhill past some nice viewpoints above a talus slope, then switchbacks down the spine

of a wooded ridge. Several grassy viewpoints provide welcome rest stops. The last part of this waterless, 4800-foot descent switchbacks down the east side of the forested ridge. The downhill ends rather abruptly where the path levels and makes a sharp right turn at 10.7 miles.

The going is easy now as you pass joyful Lancaster Falls, then veer left at a junction with the Starvation Ridge Trail. Soon thereafter a bridge crosses Warren Creek a little below 100-foot Hole-in-the-Wall Falls. This is one of the more interesting waterfalls in the gorge, because engineers ingeniously altered the flow by diverting the water into a tunnel, so cars driving the old Columbia River Highway would not get wet. Past this falls the trail goes over Cabin Creek, then completes the loop at the junction with the Starvation Cutoff Trail at 11.5 miles. Turn left, and hike 0.3 mile to the trailhead.

26 MITCHELL POINT

Distance: 2.4 miles round trip
Hiking time: 2 hours
Elevation gain: 1200 feet
Difficulty: Moderate
Season: All year
Best: Late March through April
Map: Green Trails No. 430 Hood River (trail not shown)
Information: Vinzenz Lausmann Memorial State Natural Area, (541) 374-8811

Directions: From eastbound Interstate 84 east of Portland, take Mitchell Point Overlook exit 58 and drive the short access road to a parking lot. Exit 58 has access to and from only the eastbound lanes, so from westbound Interstate 84 west of Hood River, drive to Viento Park exit 56 to get on the eastbound lanes, then follow the eastbound directions above.

The craggy edifice of Mitchell Point is a familiar landmark that rises directly above Interstate 84 west of Hood River. Many people drive past this promontory on their way to other hikes and are tantalized by the prospect of finding a way to the top. But those hikers are usually disappointed, because few guidebooks discuss the peak and no map shows a trail to the summit. More determined individuals who vow to find a way regardless of the difficulties discover a good trail all the way to the view-packed summit.

From the southeast corner of the parking lot, walk 25 yards down the paved walkway

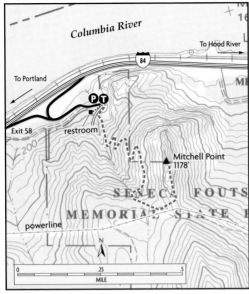

toward the restroom, then bear left onto an old gravel road. After 100 yards, turn left onto an unsigned foot trail. This pleasant trail begins with a moderately steep climb through a lush forest of Douglas firs and bigleaf maples above a trickling creek. At 0.2 mile the path switchbacks away from the creek and steeply climbs across a rockslide beneath the tall cliffs of Mitchell Point. Picturesquely twisted Oregon white oaks rim the edges of this slide, but the abundance of poison oak will keep your attention focused more on the dangers near your feet than the glories above. On the plus side, while looking down you will also notice a wide variety of wildflowers such as larkspur, Oregon grape, prairie star, and lomatium.

Above this rocky area, the trail climbs through dense forest to a junction in a brushy saddle beneath a set of powerlines at 1 mile. Turn left

Mitchell Point from just below the summit

and follow an open ridge past colorful displays of late-April-blooming wildflowers to the exposed summit of Mitchell Point. Views from this narrow, rocky spine are outstanding, including the distinctive summits of Dog and Wind mountains in Washington and higher peaks such as Table Mountain and Oregon's Mount Defiance (Hike 25) to the west. The sheer cliffs and serrated ridgeline make acrophobes a bit nervous and preclude any travel beyond the end of the trail.

27 HOOD RIVER MOUNTAIN LOOP

Distance: 2.9-mile loop
Hiking time: 2 hours
Elevation gain: 600 feet
Difficulty: Easy
Season: March to November
Best: Late April to mid-May
Map: USGS White Salmon (trail not shown)
Contact: SDS Lumber Company, (509) 493-2155

Directions: From Hood River, drive south on Oregon Highway 35 for 0.4 mile, then turn left (southeast) onto East Side Road. Follow this paved road for 1.9 miles, then turn left on paved Old Dalles Road, which climbs 2.1 miles to the unsigned trailhead at a ridge-top saddle. When you park, be sure you do not block the gated road that goes north.

Hood River Mountain almost seems like cheating. You just should not be able to obtain such grand vistas and colorful wildflower meadows with so little effort. But it's hard to complain as you sit back on this windswept ridge and enjoy breathtaking views over the orchards of the Hood River Valley to the distinctive horn-shaped spire of Mount Hood. Prime time for a visit is early May, when the mountain is covered with millions of wildflowers, including yellow lomatium and balsamroot, blue larkspur and lupine, and red paintbrush. The property is owned by the SDS Lumber Company, which allows public access but prohibits motorized travel—a rule that hikers greatly appreciate. Since this is private property, it is especially important that visitors be respectful so that public access is not denied in the future.

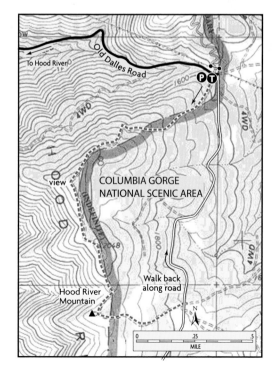

Mount Hood from Hood River Mountain

The trail begins beside a low berm south of the road and climbs gradually through a second-growth woodland of Douglas firs, ponderosa pines, and Oregon white oaks. Flowering shrubs are abundant; white-blooming serviceberry and red-flowering currant put on an especially fine show in early May. The irregular climb ends after 1 mile when the path rather suddenly emerges from the brush at the grassy summit of Hood River Mountain.

Convenient flat-topped rocks that provide a place to sit without trampling the flowers are ideal for taking in the view. In addition to a grand perspective of Mount Hood, you can look north to the bulky mass of Mount Adams and northwest to Mount St. Helens, just barely visible over the intervening ridges. The Columbia River and several of the higher peaks in the eastern gorge can also be seen. Be sure to bring a wildflower identification guide and a camera. A windbreaker will also come in handy, because the almost constant winds here range from gentle breezes to near hurricane force.

You could return the way you came, but for more exercise continue 0.6 mile south along the scenic ridge, then bear left and descend through meadows to a gravel road. Turn left and walk 1.3 miles along this little-traveled road back to your car.

NORTHERN CASCADES

Picturesque Mount Hood dominates the scenery of many northern Cascade hikes.

The Cascade Range is the most important geographic feature in Oregon. This rugged, north–south line of uplifted hills and volcanic peaks effectively separates the state's heavily populated and very wet west side from its rural and relatively dry east side. Residents on either side of this geographic and cultural divide generally disagree on political questions but have come together on at least one issue: this beautiful range is the top recreational playground in the state.

For convenience, this book separates the range into three subregions. Everything north of Mount Jefferson is classified as the Northern Cascades (not to be confused with the North Cascades, an entirely different geographic region in Washington State). The Central Cascades extend from Mount Jefferson to Willamette Pass, and the Southern Cascades stretch from there to the California border.

At 11,235 feet, Mount Hood dominates the first subregion, towering several thousand feet above everything else in the neighborhood. Portlanders have an understandable affection for this mountain that dominates the city's skyline, and they have made it their prime destination for escaping the rat race. Permanent snowfields and glaciers provide a base for year-round skiing, while in the summer spectacular trails open routes to every corner of the mountain. Less well-known are the hundreds of miles of trails that explore the lower terrain of the nearby hills. Here you will discover old-growth forests, towering waterfalls, subalpine meadows, and views of Mount Hood that cannot be obtained when walking on its slopes.

28 EAST ZIGZAG MOUNTAIN AND BURNT LAKE

Distance: 10.5 miles round trip
Hiking time: 5 hours (day hike or backpack)
Elevation gain: 1900 feet
Difficulty: Moderate
Season: Mid-June to October
Best: Mid-July (flowers); mid-August (huckleberries)
Map: Green Trails No. 461 Government Camp
Information: Mount Hood Information Center, (503) 622-4822

Directions: Drive US 26 to 1.5 miles east of Rhododendron, turn north onto Forest Road 27, and proceed 0.6 mile to the end of the pavement. The road immediately switchbacks left, goes steeply uphill, and becomes miserably rocky with deep mud holes. The trailhead is 5.2 miles from US 26 at a small road-end parking area.

The Mount Hood Wilderness contains almost no mountain lakes, so it is not surprising that the few that *do* exist are popular. But even if there were hundreds of lakes to choose from, many

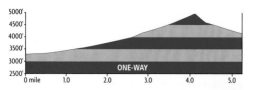

Mount Hood over Burnt Lake

hikers would still opt for Burnt Lake because it is so strikingly beautiful. The excellent swimming lake features a picture-postcard view of snow-clad Mount Hood. The most crowded trail to the lake starts from Lost Creek to the north. For a quieter approach, start from the south on a trail that goes through better wildflower meadows and takes you near a superior viewpoint missed by the northerly approach.

The trail goes northeast on an abandoned jeep road that gently climbs through dense forest with a lush understory that includes many relatively unusual wildflowers such as tiger lily, devil's club, goatsbeard, beardtongue, and goldenrod. At 2 miles the old jeep road ends where a spur trail goes to the old car campground at Devils Meadow. Veer left and ascend a foot trail that crosses a trickling creek and comes to a junction with the Devils Tie Trail. Go straight and steadily switchback up a hillside covered with huckleberries.

At the ridge-top junction at 3.7 miles is an excellent view of Mount Hood, but for an even better one, turn left and climb a steep, rocky trail 0.3 mile to the open summit of East Zigzag Mountain. Mount Hood is the principal attraction, but there are also fine views of Burnt Lake some 800 feet below and Mount Jefferson in the distance to the south.

To visit Burnt Lake, return to the ridge-top junction and descend 0.3 mile to a second junction. Turn left and switchback down a well-graded route on a shady, north-facing slope 0.8 mile to Burnt Lake. A trail around the lake takes you to several designated campsites that invite an overnight stay. Return the way you came.

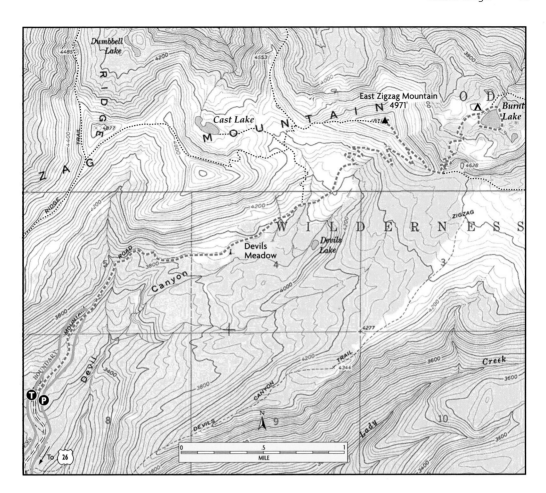

29 YOCUM RIDGE

Distance: 18.4 miles round trip
Hiking time: 10 hours (day hike or backpack)
Elevation gain: 3800 feet
Difficulty: Very strenuous
Season: Mid-July to September
Best: Late July and August
Maps: Green Trails No. 461 Government Camp, No. 462 Mount Hood
Information: Mount Hood Information Center, (503) 622-4822

Directions: Drive US 26 to Zigzag and turn north on East Lolo Pass Road (Forest Road 18). Drive 4.3 miles, turn right onto paved FR 1825, and proceed 1.2 miles to a fork. Bear left and, 1.5 miles later, bear left again, then pull into the large Ramona Falls parking lot.

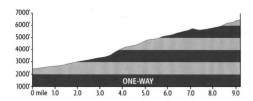

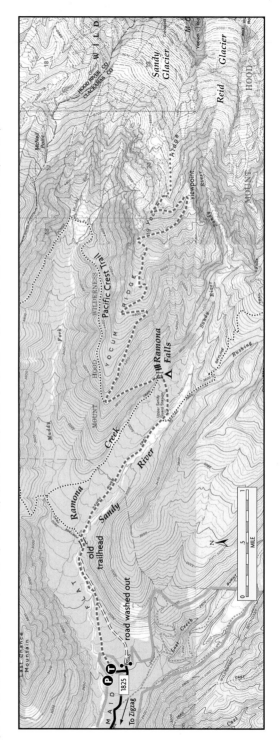

How's this for the perfect hiking fantasy? A magnificent alpine ridge that protrudes from the slopes of a towering, snow-clad peak, where visitors can enjoy unequaled views not only of the bulky peak but also a sea of forested mountains, distant volcanoes, and deep river valleys. Wildflowers grow in incredible abundance, adding color and an intoxicating aroma to the gentle breezes that waft over your grandstand seats. On a hot summer day, those breezes are naturally air-conditioned by nearby glaciers. And from those glaciers, loud cracking resonates, alerting you to the movement of these great rivers of ice. Yocum Ridge is this fantasy come to life. But get in shape first, because the trail is no Sunday stroll in the park.

The trail takes you through loose, riverbed material as it slowly ascends the Sandy River's wide valley to a junction with a washed-out road. Parallel this road to an abandoned trailhead, then cross the Sandy River on a metal bridge and come to a junction at 1.3 miles. Turn right and walk 1.5 miles up the rather desolate glacial valley to a junction with the Pacific Crest Trail. Bear left and walk 0.5 mile through open forest to Ramona Falls at 3.3 miles. This lovely 120-foot falls fanning out over a moss-covered basalt cliff is the destination of most day hikers.

Yocum Ridge is still a long way away, however, so cross the bridge below the falls, bear right (uphill) at a junction, and climb 0.6 mile to a ridge-top junction with the Yocum Ridge Trail. Turn right and steadily ascend a woodsy, south-facing hillside covered with head-high Pacific rhododendrons. The trail snakes up the ridge, passing rocky slopes, dense forests, and a shallow pond along the way as the terrain gradually becomes more open and the meadows larger and more attractive. Through July and August, these meadows are a wildflower bonanza, with acres of glacier lilies, avalanche lilies, western anemones, bistorts, columbines, beargrass, larkspurs,

Mount Hood from Yocum Ridge

lupines, wallflowers . . . the list is almost endless.

The grandest views begin at a stunning overlook at the edge of a steep-walled canyon at 7.4 miles, where the melting ice of Reid Glacier feeds the headwaters of the Sandy River. Impressive as this is, do not turn around yet. Instead, stick with the trail as it makes one switchback, climbs to a ridge crest, then travels above timberline where nothing obstructs the views north to Mount Rainier and south to Mount Jefferson. More flowers, more views, and more glaciers lie higher on the ridge, enough to fulfill any hiker's fantasy. Just keep going uphill on the rapidly diminishing trail over snowfields and rocky slopes to an alpine plateau. From there, you can explore to the base of the Sandy and Reid glaciers. This is the side of Mount Hood that is familiar to every Portland resident, but it is much more dramatic up close and personal. Those willing to haul a sleeping bag to these heights can enjoy glorious sunsets, but set up camp on either rocks or snow to preserve the fragile meadows. Melt snow for water.

30 TIMBERLINE TRAIL LOOP

Distance: 41-mile loop
Hiking time: 4–6 days
Elevation gain: 8600 feet
Difficulty: Strenuous
Season: Mid-July to October
Best: Early to mid-August
Maps: Green Trails No. 461 Government Camp, No. 462 Mount Hood
Information: Mount Hood Information Center, (503) 622-4822; Hood River Ranger District (541) 352-6002

Directions: Drive US 26 to a junction just east of Government Camp. Turn north onto Timberline Lodge Road and climb 5.5 miles to the enormous parking lot for the historic lodge.

The Timberline Trail is arguably the best, and is certainly the most famous, extended backpacking trip in Oregon. The up-and-down trail circles Mount Hood, generally near timberline (as the name suggests), allowing hikers to appreciate the state's highest mountain in a way that drive-by tourists miss.

With outstanding wildflower displays, idyllic campsites, and ever-changing views of the mountain, it is easy to understand why this trail is so popular. Still, the trip is quite physically demanding. Be prepared to ford glacial streams, cross large snowfields, and travel well above timberline, where snow can fall in any season. **Note:** Due to a debris flow in 2006, the Timberline Trail's crossing of Eliot Creek is officially "closed" and requires often-difficult detours to bypass. A long-awaited rerouting is scheduled for completion by late 2017. Call the Hood River

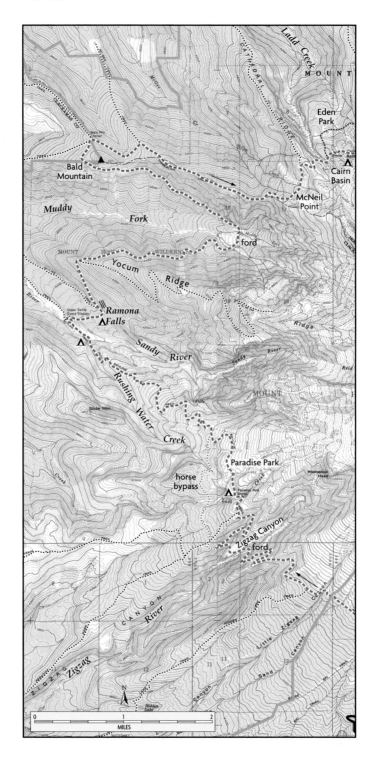

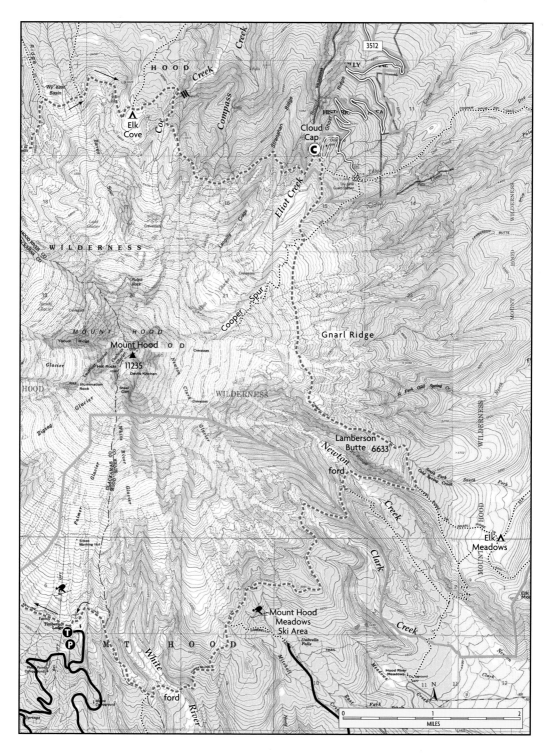

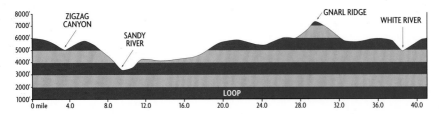

Ranger District for the latest conditions.

So how much time should you take to complete the hike? Well, a few people of the "because it's there" mentality have run around the mountain in a single day, but to enjoy the scenery at a more reasonable pace, allow at least four days. The loop is great in either direction, but a clockwise tour is the usual itinerary.

From the back of the lodge, follow a paved trail to a junction with the Pacific Crest Trail (PCT). Turn left and slowly descend through sloping meadows and open forests of wind-whipped mountain hemlocks and whitebark pines. Views south to Mount Jefferson are outstanding. Pass a junction with the Hidden Lake Trail at 1.5 miles, then come to a great viewpoint at the edge of Zigzag Canyon. From there, the trail descends to the bottom of the canyon at 3.5 miles, where you make a potentially tricky ford of the Zigzag River. Like all glacial stream crossings, the ford is easier in the morning before the melt increases in the afternoon.

The trail climbs out of Zigzag Canyon to a fork. A horse bypass trail goes left, but the hiker's trail goes right and climbs to Paradise Park at 5.5 miles. This famous wildflower mecca boasts a clear creek and the trip's first good campsites. The trail loops through a sloping meadow above Paradise Park, reconnects with the horse bypass, then begins a long, toe-jamming descent into the Sandy River canyon. Near the bottom is a nice campsite at 10 miles beside Rushing Water Creek, shortly before you cross the aptly named Sandy River. The PCT then makes a sharp right turn at a junction with the popular Ramona Falls Trail and soon reaches this lovely curtain of water at 11 miles. There is a designated camping area a little south of the falls.

From Ramona Falls, the trail ascends 0.6 mile to a junction with the Yocum Ridge Trail, then traverses the north side of Yocum Ridge to a cold ford of the two branches of the Muddy Fork Sandy River. This is followed by a gradual uphill traverse to Bald Mountain, where there are outstanding views over the Muddy Fork canyon to Sandy Glacier and Mount Hood. On the northwest side of Bald Mountain is a junction at 16.5 miles, where the Pacific Crest and Timberline trails diverge.

The Timberline Trail goes east and begins its course around the north side of Mount Hood. The views, glaciers, and wildflower meadows are all at their best on this less-crowded side of the peak. The first highlight is McNeil Point, an exposed location with a stone shelter reached by a 0.5-mile side trip up a very steep scramble path. Cairn Basin at 20 miles is the next great spot, with excellent campsites amid millions of glacier lilies and western anemones that bloom in mid-July. Superb side trips from here lead down to appropriately titled Eden Park and up to trailless Barrett Spur.

The next highlight is Elk Cove at 23 miles, one of the mountain's classic beauty spots with campsites, outstanding views of Coe Glacier, and millions of flowers. A bit more climbing takes you past a hidden waterfall on Coe Creek, then a more easily viewed falls on Compass Creek. The northern traverse ends after you cross rampaging Eliot Creek (hopefully) on a bridge, if it has been rebuilt, and reach Cloud Cap at 27 miles.

The trail turns south here and climbs above timberline, with constantly great views. Pass the side trail to Cooper Spur (yet another great side trip), then make your way over icy snowfields to Gnarl Ridge and the 7300-foot high point of the circuit at 29.5 miles. From here, descend past Lamberson Butte, which has a terrific view of enormous Newton Clark Glacier, then return to a gentler landscape of forests and meadows.

At 32 miles is a junction with the side trail to Elk Meadows, which has superb views and excellent (but popular) campsites 1.2 miles off the main trail. From the junction, the Timberline

Elk Cove offers excellent views of Coe Glacier.

Trail then fords the glacial flow of Newton Creek and passes under the ski lifts of Mount Hood Meadows. Another downhill section takes you to the potentially difficult crossing of White River at 38 miles amid a wasteland of rubbly glacial material. A final climb leads to a reunion with the PCT in a beautiful meadow, then up a sandy, view-packed ridge to Timberline Lodge.

31 ELIOT GLACIER VIEW

Distance: 5 miles round trip
Hiking time: 3 hours
Elevation gain: 2600 feet
Difficulty: Strenuous
Season: Mid-August to early October
Best: Late August and September
Map: Green Trails No. 462 Mount Hood
Information: Mount Hood National Forest—Hood River Ranger District, (541) 352-6002

Directions: From Hood River, drive south on Highway 35 for 22.5 miles, then turn right (west) on the road to the Cooper Spur Mountain Resort. After 2.4 miles, turn left on the road to Tilly Jane Campground and proceed 1.5 miles to Cooper Spur Ski Area. The road (now Forest Road 3512) turns to bumpy gravel here and climbs 8.3 miles to a T-junction. Turn right and proceed 0.6 mile to the trailhead.

Massive Eliot Glacier, the largest on Mount Hood, tumbles down the northeast slopes of the mountain in a wildly contorted mass of icy crevasses. An unofficial trail traces a scenic course up the rocky moraine beside the glacier, giving you the chance to take a trip in time back to the Ice Age. The goal is one of Mount Hood's most dramatic viewpoints, directly above the rumbling blue and white mass of moving ice. **Note:** Due to a debris flow in 2006, the Timberline Trail's crossing of Eliot Creek is officially "closed" and requires often-difficult detours to bypass. A long-awaited rerouting is scheduled for completion by late 2017. Call the Hood River

Ranger District for the latest conditions.

Walk a short distance through primitive Cloud Cap Saddle Campground, then turn right (west) on Timberline Trail No. 600, which drops to a bridge (if it has been rebuilt) across the silty waters of Eliot Creek, then switchbacks up a ridge to the west. A few feet before reaching the top of this ridge, look for an unsigned but obvious trail that goes left at about 0.6 mile. Turn onto

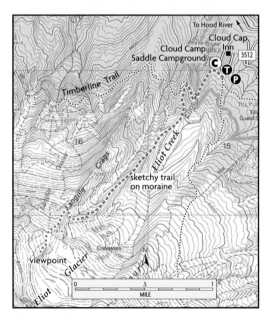

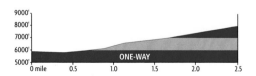

this path and follow it through alpine meadows and past stunted trees, which soon disappear once you get above timberline.

For most of the rest of the hike you follow a steep, rocky moraine on the west side of Eliot Glacier. For the first mile there is no ice, so only the rampaging torrent of Eliot Creek flows at the bottom of the canyon. Above that point, you parallel an ever-larger sheet of ice that gets more rugged and impressive the higher you go. For safety, it is important that you stay well back from the unstable rocks overlooking the ice and, of course, never scramble out on the glacier itself without proper equipment and training.

When the path starts to peter out at about 2 miles, detour to the right around a rocky buttress, then scramble up rocks and snowfields to a dramatic overlook directly above the glacier's crevasses. This viewpoint is about 8000 feet above sea level, no place to be if bad weather is approaching.

Eliot Glacier view

32   BARLOW BUTTE

Distance: 3.7 miles round trip
Hiking time: 2 hours
Elevation gain: 1100 feet
Difficulty: Moderate
Season: Mid-June to October
Best: July
Map: Green Trails No. 462 Mount Hood
Information: Mount Hood Information Center, (503) 622-4822

Directions: From the intersection of US 26 and Oregon Highway 35, drive Hwy 35 northeast 2.7 miles, then turn right (south) on Forest Road 3531 and go 0.2 mile on this single-lane, paved road to the Pacific Crest trailhead.

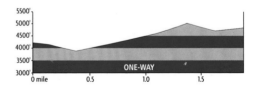

In the 1840s, thousands of families loaded their worldly possessions into wagons and walked 2000 miles from Missouri to The Dalles at the eastern gates of the Columbia River Gorge, a tantalizingly close 60 miles from their goal: the Willamette Valley. But a significant obstacle still stood between them and that goal, and these tired travelers faced a difficult decision. Some chose to get on wooden rafts and run the dangerous rapids of the Columbia River, risking the loss of their possessions or even their lives in the process. Others decided to stay on land and make a long, slow, and potentially snowy loop on the Barlow Trail through a gap in the Cascade Range south

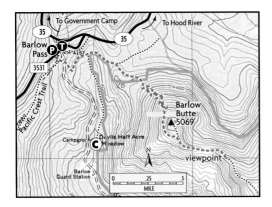

of Mount Hood. Parts of that old wagon route still exist, and today's history buffs can explore it with a degree of comfort undreamed of by those early travelers. This little-known hike takes you along a short section of that historic route and throws in a great viewpoint at trail's end.

From a sign identifying the Oregon Trail, walk a few yards east to a four-way junction with a more modern travel corridor, the Pacific Crest Trail. Go straight, still on the Barlow Trail, cross a dirt road, then travel gradually downhill, literally in the tracks of pioneers, to a junction at 0.3 mile. The Barlow Trail goes right, but to reach the viewpoint atop Barlow Butte, turn left.

This trail climbs a heavily forested hillside to a saddle and a junction with Mineral Jane Ski Trail at 0.5 mile. Turn right, gradually climb past a small clearcut, then ascend a series of short, very steep switchbacks to an unsigned junction in a small clearing at about 1.3 miles. The trail to the left goes a short distance to the rocky summit of Barlow Butte, where trees block the view. A more satisfying objective lies down the trail to the right.

This route descends 0.5 mile or so through a subalpine rock garden, then climbs to a ridge-top opening with outstanding views of Mount Hood and the glacial valley of White River. With a map and a little imagination, you can trace the old pioneer route, which went down the valleys of Barlow Creek and White River to The Dalles. This viewpoint is the best turnaround spot, because the trail south of here gets little or no maintenance and has very few views.

Mount Hood from a ridge south of Barlow Butte

33

LOOKOUT MOUNTAIN VIA DIVIDE TRAIL

Distance: 7 miles round trip
Hiking time: 4 hours
Elevation gain: 2000 feet
Difficulty: Moderate
Season: Late June to October
Best: July
Maps: Green Trails No. 462 Mount Hood, No. 463 Flag Point
Information: Mount Hood National Forest—Barlow Ranger District, (541) 467-2291

Directions: Drive Oregon Highway 35 south from Hood River or north from US 26 to a junction between mileposts 70 and 71. Turn east onto Forest Road 44, following signs for Dufur, and stay on the paved road for 8.6 miles to a junction with one-lane paved FR 4420. Turn right, following signs for Flag Point Lookout, and drive 4.4 miles to a small pullout for the Fret Creek trailhead just past Fifteenmile Campground.

Surveyors Ridge rises like a long green wall east of Mount Hood, forming the last major bastion of the Cascade Range before the mountains slope down to the semi-arid grasslands of northcentral Oregon. From high points along this ridge, hikers take in outstanding views of Mount Hood, Oregon's highest mountain, just 6 miles to the west. Not surprisingly, the best viewpoint comes at the ridge's highest point, Lookout Mountain. The shortest trail to this vista is from a logging road to the north, but if you want a bit more exercise, consider this longer and more scenic approach past a tiny mountain lake and a string of impressive cliff-edge viewpoints.

The trail departs from the south side of the road and ascends rather steeply through dense

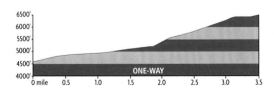

forest with huckleberries, grouse whortleberries, and wildflowers such as Sitka valerian, lupine, Oregon anemone, and an unusual abundance of Jacob's ladder covering the forest floor. Splashing Fret Creek provides pleasant background music as you hike. The steep grade soon eases; then, in the next mile, you cross Fret Creek three times on wooden bridges or easy rock-hops. The trail then climbs steeply once again, reaching tiny Oval Lake at 2 miles, with a good campsite above its northeast shore.

The trail continues 0.1 mile to a junction with the Divide Trail. The nearest viewpoint is Palisade Point, a dramatic rock outcropping 0.3 mile east (left) along the Divide Trail. If Lookout Mountain is your goal, however, turn right and follow this up-and-down (mostly up) trail past a series of rock formations with many rock-garden wildflowers and southerly views over the Badger Creek valley to distant Mount Jefferson. But Mount Hood remains hidden, so keep going west mixing level spots with short climbs, to a junction with an abandoned road at 3.4 miles. Turn right, and walk 100 yards to the rocky summit of Lookout Mountain.

Although at least eleven summits in Oregon carry the uninspired name of Lookout Mountain, none has a better view than this one. To the east stretch the rolling plains of eastern Oregon, while to the north and south rise the heavily forested hills of the Cascade Range. But your attention will mostly be drawn to the west, over the deep chasm of East Fork Hood River to the glacier-clad slopes of Mount Hood.

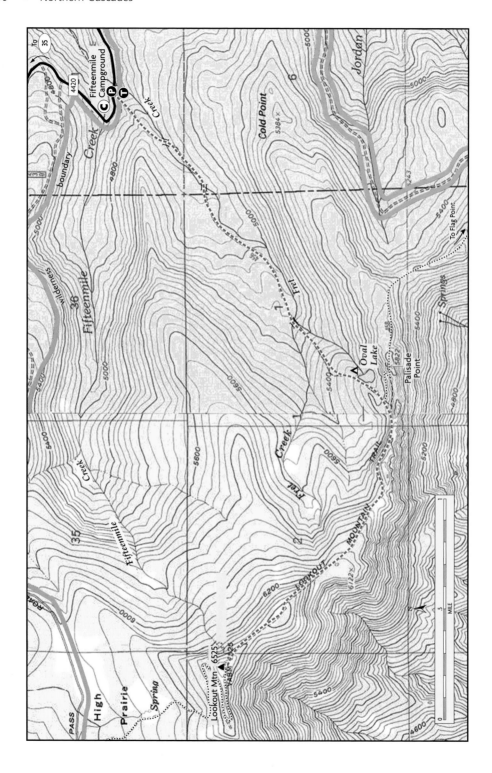

Mount Hood from Lookout Mountain

34   SCHOOL CANYON TRAIL

Distance: 7.2 miles round trip
Hiking time: 4 hours
Elevation gain: 1400 feet
Difficulty: Moderate
Season: Mid-March to early December
Best: Mid- to late May
Map: Green Trails No. 463 Flag Point
Information: Mount Hood National Forest—Barlow Ranger District, (541) 467-2291

Directions: Drive US 197 south from The Dalles to a junction near milepost 33, north of Tygh Valley. Turn right (west) on Shadybrook Road, drive 1.1 miles, then turn left onto Fairgrounds Road. After 0.7 mile, turn right on gravel Badger Creek Road and drive 6.6 miles to a prominent junction. Turn right on single-lane, paved Forest Road 27 and go 2.1 miles to the School Canyon trailhead.

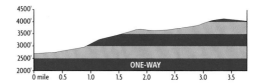

As the Cascade Mountains slope downward on their eastern "rain-shadow" side, the climate gets progressively drier and the forests become more open. In the transition zone between forested mountains and semi-arid grasslands is a unique pine-oak ecosystem filled with outstanding wildflower displays and surprisingly good scenery. The School Canyon Trail, perhaps the best way to sample this beautiful environment, is a particularly good option for west-side hikers tired of the waterlogged paths closer to home. In addition to the scenery, you will get a kick out of the place names in this area. Elsewhere the map of Oregon is filled with uninspired names

Along the School Canyon Trail

such as "Deer Creek" and "Lost Lake," but here it is a pleasant surprise to see how someone with a little imagination put some thought into the naming process. Three particularly inspired examples are the low summits dubbed Felt Tip, Ball Point, and Pen Point. All that is missing is an Ink Creek for a complete set.

The gently graded trail immediately enters the Badger Creek Wilderness and goes west along an old jeep road through dry grasslands, over shallow gullies, and past open forests of ponderosa pines. This rich mix of habitats supports large numbers of birds, including wild turkeys, various warblers, and several species of woodpeckers. Wildflowers are even more common, as a visit in late May demonstrates, when the open areas are covered with colorful balsamroot, lupine, prairie star, lomatium, and paintbrush. When the jeep road ends, the foot trail turns right and goes up a steep, rocky hillside where gnarled Oregon white oaks provide picturesque contrasts to the ponderosa pines and wildflowers.

The narrow trail temporarily leaves the dry environment and travels through dense coniferous forest on the north side of Ball Point to a saddle at 2.1 miles. From here, you traverse the more open, south-facing slopes of Felt Tip to a junction at 3.4 miles with Little Badger Trail in a lovely meadow. Just southwest of this junction is

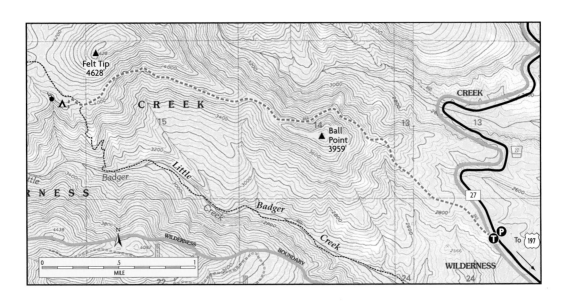

a nice viewpoint and some impressive rock pinnacles. A good trail continues west to Flag Point Lookout and another route goes southeast down Little Badger Creek. Most hikers, however, simply head back the way they came. **Note:** In August 2007, fire heavily damaged this trail from Ball Point west to the junction with Little Badger Trail. You can expect blackened snags in this area for the next several years.

35 CLACKAMAS RIVER TRAIL

Distance: 7.4 miles round trip to Pup Creek Falls; 10 miles round trip to The Narrows; 8.1 miles one way to Indian Henry trailhead
Hiking time: 3.5 hours to Pup Creek Falls; 5 hours to The Narrows; 4 hours to Indian Henry trailhead (day hike or backpack)
Elevation gain: 600 feet to Pup Creek Falls; 1100 feet to The Narrows; 1300 feet to Indian Henry trailhead
Difficulty: Easy
Season: All year (except during winter storms)
Best: All year
Map: Green Trails No. 492 Fish Creek Mountain
Information: Mount Hood National Forest—Clackamas River Ranger District, (503) 630-6861

Directions: From Estacada drive southeast on Oregon Highway 224 for 15 miles to a junction with Fish Creek Road. Turn right, cross a bridge, and almost immediately reach the trailhead parking lot. To leave a shuttle vehicle at the upper trailhead, continue southeast on Hwy 224 another 7 miles, turn right at a junction just before a bridge over the Clackamas River, and drive 0.6 mile to the Indian Henry trailhead.

The Clackamas River, which rises in the densely forested highlands south of Mount Hood, is one of the most strikingly beautiful rivers in Oregon. The stream's incredibly clear waters cascade over rollicking rapids and swirl in glassy eddies through a scenic canyon of steep, wooded slopes and basalt cliffs. A stroll along the Clackamas River Trail is the best way to

appreciate this enchanting stream in all of its many moods.

From the Fish Creek trailhead, the wide trail goes upstream through an old-growth forest of western hemlocks and western red cedars that shade a forest floor covered with sword fern, moss, salal, and oxalis. You can sometimes see cars barreling along the highway on the other side of the river, but their sounds are drowned out by the river's rushing water and the amazingly loud songs of tiny winter wrens. Adding to the scenery are several seasonal tributary creeks, which are more impressive in the winter when they drop over small waterfalls beside the trail.

The trail negotiates several small ups and downs as it travels over and around mossy, riverlevel cliffs, then descends two short switchbacks to a possible campsite at 1.3 miles. From here,

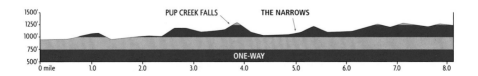

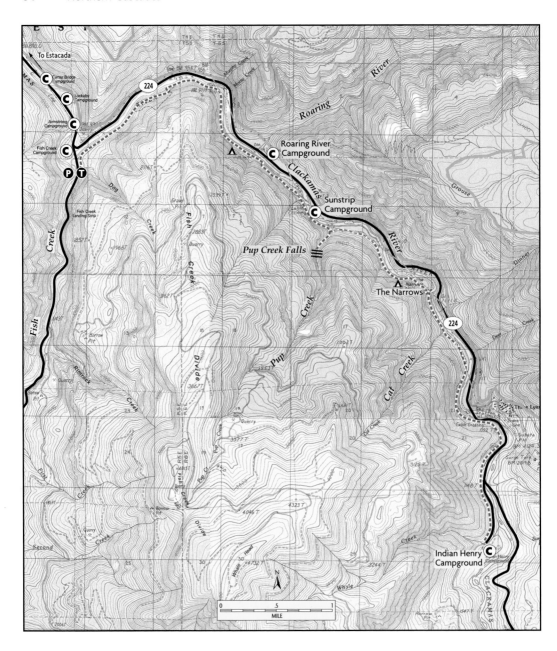

you gradually travel through more forest to a campsite in a grove of giant cedars at about 2.3 miles. A short climb leads to a viewpoint of Roaring River's canyon on the other side of the Clackamas River and your first meeting with a set of powerlines. Unfortunately, you have frequent contact with this eyesore for much of the rest of the hike. At the second powerline crossing at 3.6 miles is a junction with a not-to-be-missed, 0.1-mile side trail to Pup Creek Falls. This very impressive falls drops 100 feet into a shady, lichen-covered grotto. The falls makes an excellent turnaround point for those seeking an easy hike.

For more exercise, continue upstream 0.8 mile through a cleared area under the powerlines to a nice riverside beach ideal for a rest stop. For an even better lunch spot, stick with the trail as it climbs over a small knoll, then switchbacks down to an unsigned junction at 5 miles. The short, dead-end trail to the left leads to The Narrows, where the Clackamas River squeezes through a 20-foot-wide chasm between large mossy boulders. A bonus for spending time here is the chance to watch rafters and kayakers pass through the narrow chute.

If you have only one car, turn around here. But if you left a car at the upper trailhead, stay on the Clackamas River Trail for another mile to a man-made cavern where the trail has been carved out of a cliff face, then parallel Highway 224 for a couple of miles to the Indian Henry trailhead.

Pup Creek Falls

36   SERENE LAKE LOOP

Distance: 11 miles round trip
Hiking time: 6 hours (day hike or backpack)
Elevation gain: 1800 feet
Difficulty: Moderate
Season: Mid-June to October
Best: Late August to September
Maps: Green Trails No. 492 Fish Creek Mountain, No. 493 High Rock
Contact: Mount Hood National Forest—Clackamas River Ranger District, (503) 630-6861

Directions: Drive 25.5 miles southeast of Estacada on Oregon Highway 224 to a junction just past the Ripplebrook Guard Station. Turn left on Forest Road 4631 and drive 3 miles on pavement then gravel to a fork. Bear left onto FR 4635 and go 9.8 miles to a fork. Bear right on FR 140, drive 1.8 miles, then park in a small pullout just before a culvert over Cripple Creek.

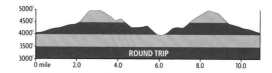

At the headwaters of the Roaring River, a major tributary of the Clackamas River, lies a lake-dotted mountain wonderland that appeals to hikers of all ages. Youngsters enjoy swimming in the lakes and getting a purple tongue from munching on yummy huckleberries. Older travelers appreciate the viewpoints, the rugged scenery, and the fields of wildflowers. What persons of all ages *hate* are the mosquitoes, which are also drawn to the area's lakes. Visit in late August or September, when most of the bugs are gone and the berries are at their delicious best. This loop has several possible starting points. The most popular is Frazier Campground, but the access road there is too rough for most passenger cars. Another option is Hideaway Lake, but that follows a much more crowded trail. The recommended starting point is Cripple Creek.

The unsigned trail goes 50 yards upstream to a junction. Go straight and gradually climb through an attractive forest of Pacific silver firs and mountain hemlocks with a dense understory of beargrass and huckleberries. The trail is a bit

sketchy, but prominent yellow paint marks on the trees keep you on course. At the 1-mile point is a campsite beside tranquil Cripple Creek Lake. The trail then rounds the north lakeshore and follows the inlet creek upstream. In about 0.3 mile you reach soggy Cache Meadow, a haven for mosquitoes, frogs, and June-blooming marsh marigolds.

The trail disappears here. To relocate it, hop over a seasonal creek and walk a few feet into the forest on the north side of the meadow to a campsite at the former site of Cache Meadow

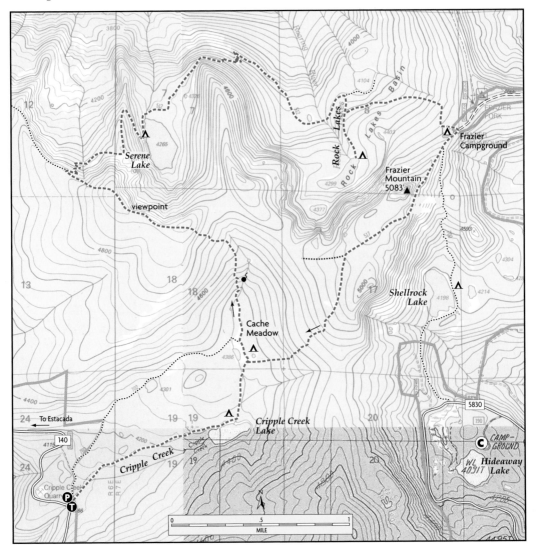

A quiet pond in Cache Meadow

Shelter at 1.5 miles. Turn left on a trail that passes this shelter and walk 200 yards to a junction. Turn right, pass a spring, then climb to a superb viewpoint at 2.7 miles featuring the Serene Lake basin and distant Mount Hood.

To reach large and inviting Serene Lake, descend a forested slope 0.8 mile to a junction in a saddle, turn right, then switchback downhill to a popular camping area on the northwest shore of the deep lake at 4.2 miles. The trail curves around the north side of the lake, then goes up and down for 2 miles to a pair of junctions shortly beyond the crossing of the headwaters of South Fork Roaring River at 6.2 miles. Forest-rimmed Lower

Rock Lake sits in the basin 0.1 mile to the left, while more spectacular Middle Rock Lake fills an impressive cirque on a steep 0.2-mile trail to the right. Both lakes have good campsites.

The loop trail climbs to primitive Frazier Campground in 0.8 mile, then turns right and follows an old jeep road 0.2 mile to a junction. The trail to the left leads past lovely Shellrock Lake (a worthy 1.2-mile side trip) to Hideaway Lake (a mile farther). Your route sticks with the jeep road, crosses a view-packed rockslide, then climbs to a junction on a forested plateau. Veer left off the road and steeply descend back to Cache Meadow to close the loop.

37 OPAL CREEK LOOP

Distance: 10.5 miles round trip
Hiking time: 5 hours (day hike or backpack)
Elevation gain: 500 feet
Difficulty: Moderate
Season: March to December
Best: April and May
Map: Green Trails No. 524 Battle Ax
Information: Willamette National Forest—Detroit Ranger District, (503) 854-3366

Directions: From Salem drive east on Oregon Highway 22 for 22.5 miles to Mehama. Turn left on North Fork Road, following signs to Little North Santiam Recreation Area, and drive 15.6 miles to the end of the pavement. From there, proceed 5.6 miles on bumpy gravel Forest Road 2209 to the trailhead parking lot.

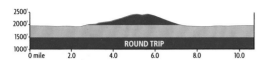

Although this hike follows a clear stream, passes several small waterfalls, and visits an interesting old mining settlement, the real stars of the show are the trees. But not just *any* trees. These are big trees, *old* trees, *magnificent* trees! The kind of trees that make hikers look up in awe and loggers look up and drool. It was those competing views that led to one of Oregon's fiercest environmental battles during the 1980s and 1990s. The issue was resolved in 1996, when parts of the Opal Creek drainage were designated as wilderness and others as a scenic area. Both classifications provided enough protection to save the trees for future generations.

Walk around a gate and follow a narrow dirt road past stands of impressive Douglas firs and western red cedars that tower over an understory of salal and sword fern. You soon cross a bridge over the narrow gorge of Gold Creek,

Sawmill Falls or "Cascada Ninos"

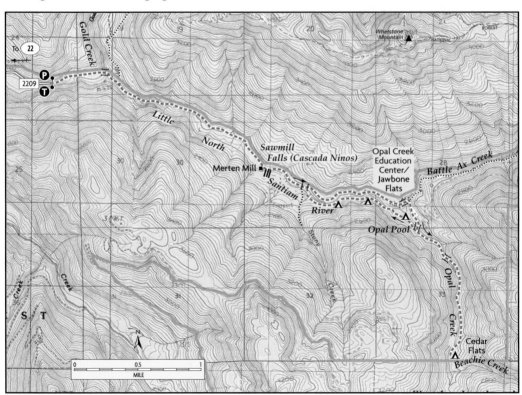

then come to a junction with the Whetstone Mountain Trail at 0.5 mile. Go straight, still on the road, and walk past more giant trees, some as much as 8 feet in diameter, to an old mine shaft at the 1-mile point. From there, the road crosses a series of wooden half-bridges suspended over a rocky cliff face, then continues to the site of Merten Mill at 2.1 miles. Take some time here to check out the old building and to follow a use path behind the mill to a fine viewpoint of what was traditionally called Sawmill Falls, although a sign now identifies it as "Cascada Ninos." Regardless of what you call it, this wide sheet of falling water along the Little North Santiam River is worth some time to appreciate.

Just 0.2 mile past Merten Mill a footbridge across the cascading stream provides access to the Opal Creek/Mike Kopetski Trail. This is the return route. For now, remain with the road on the north bank of the river and go upstream to the old mining settlement of Jawbone Flats at 3.5 miles. A sign informs you that this collection of quaint wooden buildings is inhabited by eleven permanent residents and serves as the Opal Creek Ancient Forest Scientific and Education Center. The public is welcome to walk through, but most of the buildings are private residences, so do not trespass. Signs also direct that you must walk your bicycle through town and keep your dog on a leash. At the east end of town is a (really) tiny company store, where you can purchase maps, t-shirts, and postcards of Opal Creek.

Just past the store, cross a bridge over Battle Ax Creek and come to a junction with another jeep road. Turn right, walk 0.3 mile, then bear right onto a foot trail, following signs to Opal Pool. This path takes you across a bridge over an impressively narrow, rocky gorge on Opal Creek. It is wonderful to see how remarkably clear the water is—ah, the joys of an unlogged watershed!

Just past the bridge is a junction with the Opal Creek/Mike Kopetski Trail at 4.2 miles. Before heading back that way, turn left and walk a rugged, up-and-down path frequently blocked by large roots and downed logs that require some athleticism to circumvent. You soon cross Opal Creek on a flat-topped log bridge, then pass several cascades and small waterfalls to Cedar Flats at 5.4 miles, where a group of massive, 10-foot-thick western red cedars provide shade for a great lunch or camp spot beside the tumbling creek. This is the recommended turnaround point.

For variety on the return leg of your journey, skip Jawbone Flats and follow the Opal Creek/Mike Kopetski Trail past several potential creekside campsites for 1.6 miles. This sometimes rugged trail goes through impressive old-growth forest beside the cascading Little North Santiam River to a junction with the signed but little used and unofficial trail up Stony Creek just before the bridge near Merten Mill at 8.2 miles. Keep right, cross the bridge, and retrace your route along the road back to the trailhead.

38 WHETSTONE RIDGE TO TWIN LAKES

Distance: 9.2 miles round trip to Silver King Lake junction; 14.2 miles round trip to Upper Twin Lake
Hiking time: 4.5 hours to Silver King Lake junction; 2 days to Upper Twin Lake
Elevation gain: 1200 feet to Silver King Lake junction; 1700 feet to Upper Twin Lake
Difficulty: Moderate
Season: Late June to October
Best: Mid-July
Map: Green Trails No. 524 Battle Ax
Information: Mount Hood National Forest—Clackamas River Ranger District, (503) 630-6861

Directions: Drive 26 miles southeast of Estacada on Oregon Highway 224 to a junction just after a bridge over Oak Grove Fork Clackamas River. Go straight on Forest

Road 46, proceed 3.7 miles, then turn right on FR 63. Follow this winding road for 3.6 miles, then bear right on FR 70, following signs to Bagby Hot Springs. After 7.6 miles, this road turns to gravel, then proceeds 1.6 miles to a fork. Bear right on FR 7030, following signs to Whetstone Mountain Trail. Drive 6.4 miles, then turn right on short spur FR 7020 to the trailhead in an old clearcut.

The Bull of the Woods Wilderness protects a precious remnant of what the western Cascades used to look like. While the surrounding terrain is scarred by logging roads and an epidemic of clearcuts, the densely forested canyons, small lakes, clear streams, and scenic ridges of this preserve take the visitor back to a time before rampant commercialism radically altered the landscape. Only a couple of lakes are crowded, leaving the rest of this fairly large wilderness a haven for hikers searching for solitude. This route

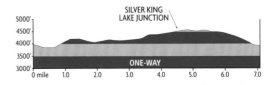

gives you the option of a day hike along an exceptionally scenic ridge in the western part of the wilderness or an overnight trip to a pair of small, attractive lakes near the heart of the preserve.

From the trailhead, the trail soon leaves the clearcut and wanders through a lovely old-growth forest, past a small pond, and up to a ridge-crest junction at 1.3 miles. Turn left and go through a long saddle where the forest is crowded with junglelike thickets of Pacific rhododendrons that turn this area into a sea of pink in mid-July. After 0.7 mile, reach a junction; go straight, then gradually climb along a beautiful, open ridge crest with lovely meadows, countless

View south over Bull of the Woods Wilderness

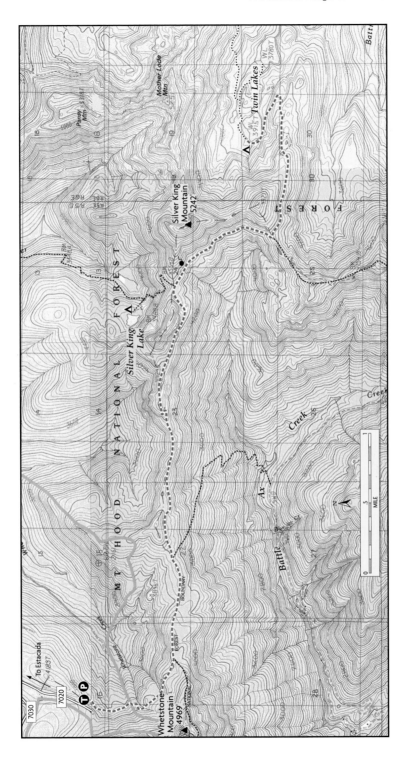

wildflowers, and fine views east to Mount Jefferson. The trail follows this scenic ridge for 2.5 miles to a junction at 4.6 miles in a small meadow on the west side of Silver King Mountain. This is a good turnaround point for day hikers.

Overnight visitors can turn left and switchback steeply down to tiny Silver King Lake, but a longer and more attractive route leads to better campsites at Twin Lakes. To reach these lakes, bear right and traverse the steep southwest side of Silver King Mountain to a junction in a high saddle at 5.3 miles. Turn left, walk along a scenic ridge to the east, then make a long, well-graded switchback to a good campsite at the west end of Upper Twin Lake at 7.1 miles. Lower Twin Lake is less scenic and has poorer campsites but is still worth a look. To reach it, hike 0.2 mile past Upper Twin Lake, then turn right at a junction and follow a short, dead-end path to the lower lake. Return the way you came.

39 OLALLIE LAKE SCENIC AREA LOOP

Distance: 6.5-mile loop; 1.8-mile side trip to Double Peaks; 0.8-mile side trip to Upper Lake; 9.1 miles total
Hiking time: 3 hours for loop (plus side trips)
Elevation gain: Loop, 900 feet; Double Peaks, 700 feet; 1600 feet total
Difficulty: Easy
Season: July to October
Best: Late August to mid-September; mid-October
Map: Green Trails No. 525 Breitenbush
Information: Mount Hood National Forest—Clackamas River Ranger District, (503) 630-6861

Directions: From Salem, drive east on Oregon Highway 22 for 50 miles to Detroit. Turn left (northeast) onto paved Forest Road 46, following signs to Breitenbush, and drive 23.5 miles to a junction with FR 4690. (From Portland, you can reach this junction more quickly by driving 48 miles southeast of Estacada on Hwy 224 and FR 46.) Turn east, following signs to Olallie Lake, and proceed 8.3 miles on this paved, then good gravel road to a T-junction. Turn right on FR 4220, drive 4.7 miles to Lower Lake Campground, then park at the west end of the campground loop road.

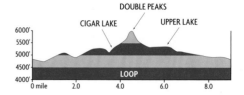

The gentle subalpine landscape of the Olallie Lake Scenic Area is well suited to families, because the area's many lakes and ponds have numerous joyous campsites that provide easy destinations where the kids can go fishing and swimming. Millions of wildflowers bloom in July, but this is also when mosquitoes are most abundant. Although day hikers can outrun the little vampires and retreat before the evening bug rush commences, backpackers should wait for better conditions later in the year. Late August is an excellent choice, with relatively comfortable water temperatures for swimming and acres of ripe huckleberries. Another excellent season is mid-October, when the huckleberry leaves turn orange and red, the bugs are gone, and, other than a few hunters, the trails are deserted.

From the campground, the nearly level trail wanders through a forest of Pacific silver firs, lodgepole pines, western white pines, and mountain hemlocks above a forest floor covered with huckleberries, grouse whortleberries, and pinemat manzanitas. After less than 0.5 mile, you

Fall color in the Olallie Lake Scenic Area

reach sparkling 15-acre Lower Lake, with good campsites near its northwest shore.

At a junction at 0.7 mile just past Lower Lake, veer left and gradually climb to rock-rimmed Middle Lake. Although it is a stretch to call this small pond a "lake," it was probably inevitable that something be called "Middle" Lake when there is a "Lower" Lake nearby and an "Upper" Lake a few miles away. Descend to a junction at 2.1 miles beside meadow-rimmed Fork Lake, turn left, and climb steadily past several small ponds to a four-way junction with the Pacific Crest Trail (PCT) at 3.3 miles. Turn right (south-bound) on the PCT and, 0.5 mile later, reach an unsigned junction just below Cigar Lake at 3.8 miles. This narrow, rock-lined pool features scenic campsites and good views of Double Peaks rising above its west shore.

Before making the return leg of the loop, take some time for two excellent side trips. The first goes 0.9 mile to the area's best viewpoint, atop 5998-foot Double Peaks. To reach it, walk 50 yards along the east shore of Cigar Lake, then bear right on an unmaintained trail marked with a low cairn. This path skirts the south side of Cigar Lake, then climbs steeply to the rocky summit of Double Peaks. Views feature pointed Mount Jefferson, smooth-sided Olallie Butte, and the tarn-studded Olallie Lake Scenic Area.

From Cigar Lake, a second good side trip takes you to Upper Lake, 0.4 mile south along the PCT. The good campsites on the shore of this beautiful lake have great views of Double Peaks to the northwest and a scenic talus slope on Peak 5960 to the south.

To complete the loop, return to the unsigned

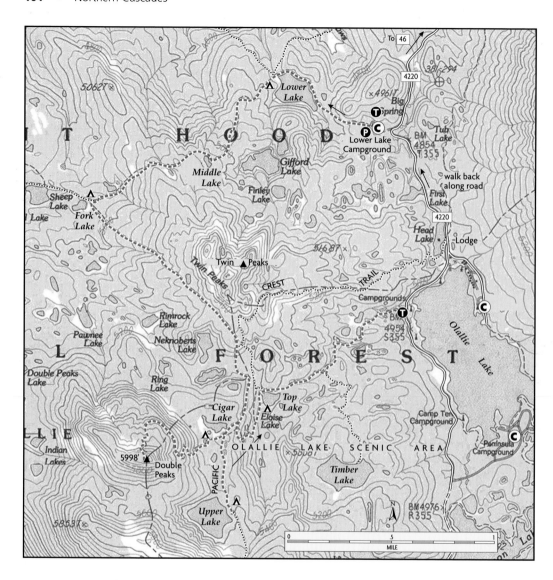

junction just below Cigar Lake and turn right (southeast). This trail switchbacks downhill 0.3 mile to a small meadow with an excellent campsite, then comes to a junction at the northwestern corner of Top Lake. Turn right and, 0.5 mile later,

at a junction with the side trail to Timber Lake (yet another good side trip), bear left. The trail ends in 0.7 mile at a gravel road beside Olallie Lake. It is an easy 1.2-mile stroll along this road back to Lower Lake Campground.

CENTRAL CASCADES

Mount Jefferson from near Scout Lake (Hike 40)

Volcanism and glaciers dominate the geologic history of Oregon, but it usually takes an expert to recognize the impact of these titanic forces on the land. In the central Oregon Cascades, however, even the untrained eye can pick out features that these grand creative and destructive forces have left behind. The legacy of volcanoes is apparent in the huge lava flows around McKenzie Pass, in the many cinder cones dotting the landscape, and in the tall volcanic peaks and eroded plugs that rise impressively above the horizon. The work of ice is seen in cirque lakes, moraines, and several active glaciers still present on the highest peaks. Surrounding all of these star attractions is a charming landscape that includes alpine wildflower gardens, waterfalls, and forested ridges with fine views of the distant higher peaks.

Although there have been periodic proposals to set aside the core of central Oregon's High Cascades as a national park, this idea has never gained the kind of support it deserves. For the time being, most of the high country is protected in wilderness areas, while the lower forested hills have fallen prey to the ravages of the chain saw.

40   JEFFERSON PARK

Distance: 7.5 miles round trip to Park Ridge; 11.5 miles round trip to Jefferson Park

Hiking time: 3.5 hours to Park Ridge; 6 hours to Jefferson Park (day hike or backpack)

Elevation gain: 1500 feet to Park Ridge; 2500 feet to Jefferson Park

Difficulty: Moderate

Season: Late July to October

Best: August

Maps: Green Trails No. 525 Breitenbush, No. 557 Mount Jefferson

Information: Willamette National Forest—Detroit Ranger District, (503) 854-3366

Permits and Reservations: To stay overnight in one of the 30 most desirable designated sites in Jefferson Park, you must have a reservation. Starting on May 1 you can make reservations by calling 1-877-444-6777 or go to www.recreation.gov. There is a $6 fee for processing.

Directions: From Salem, drive east on Oregon Highway 22 for 50 miles to Detroit. Turn left (northeast) onto paved Forest Road 46, following signs to Breitenbush, and drive 16.9 miles to a junction with FR 4220. (From Portland, you can reach this junction more quickly by driving 55 miles southeast of Estacada on Hwy 224 and FR 46.) Turn east and drive 1 mile to a gate, where the gravel road changes to dirt. From here, the road is bumpy and rough, but it remains passable if you drive slowly. The trailhead is 5.5 miles from the gate.

Mount Jefferson from Park Ridge

In the opinion of many veteran hikers, Jefferson Park is the most outstanding backcountry location in Oregon. When you are standing in this magnificent alpine wonderland, surrounded by wildflowers and relaxing beside a lake that perfectly reflects the sharp pinnacle of Mount Jefferson, it is hard to argue with this assessment. But word is definitely out, so you must share this paradise with other backpackers, day hikers, Pacific Crest Trail (PCT) through-hikers, photographers, and countless other awestruck dreamers. With such heavy use, it is crucially important that visitors adhere to Leave No Trace principles. The Forest Service requires that you camp in sites designated by wooden posts.

Three trails approach Jefferson Park. The shortest, easiest, and most popular is the Whitewater Trail, but this is also the least scenic alternative. A more attractive option is the South Breitenbush Trail, but this is also the longest and most difficult route with the most elevation gain. The most spectacular trail (a "10" on anybody's score card) follows the Pacific Crest Trail from the north. Even though the access road is rough and slow, this is clearly the "classic" approach.

From the trailhead, the Pacific Crest Trail goes south through delightful alpine meadows punctuated by patches of heather and huckleberries. The best views are of prominent Pyramid Butte to the west. After a little over 0.5 mile, bear left at an unsigned fork and go through an attractive forest that gradually opens to meadows filled with wildflowers. As you continue to gain elevation, the meadows give way in turn to rocks and snowfields. You eventually follow cairns that take you past a few small ponds, then climb a large, semipermanent snowfield on the north side of Park Ridge to the 6920-foot high point at about 3.7 miles.

Up to this point, Mount Jefferson has remained discreetly hidden from view, but at Park Ridge the towering, glaciated peak presents itself in all

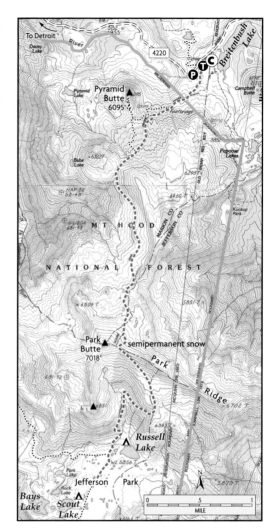

of its considerable glory. In the foreground, some 900 feet below, is Jefferson Park, with numerous small lakes and clumps of trees. Many agree that Park Ridge is the finest viewpoint in the state. Day hikers can turn around here, but backpackers will want to continue to the park itself.

Getting there involves a breathtakingly beautiful 2-mile walk that winds down to Russell Lake at the north end of Jefferson Park and a junction with the South Breitenbush Trail. More lakes and more wonders lie to the south and west around Scout and Bays lakes, but the quietest parts of the park are off-trail to the east. Many hours (or even days) of gawking are definitely in order.

41 TRIANGULATION PEAK

Distance: 4.2 miles round trip
Hiking time: 2 hours
Elevation gain: 700 feet
Difficulty: Easy
Season: Late June to October
Best: July
Map: Green Trails No. 557 Mount Jefferson
Information: Willamette National Forest—Detroit Ranger District, (503) 854-3366

Directions: From Salem, drive east on Oregon Highway 22 for 56 miles to a junction 6.2 miles east of Detroit. Turn left (north) on single-lane paved McCoy Creek Road (Forest Road 2233), go 4.2 miles, then turn left on a bumpy gravel road for 3.8 miles to a four-way junction. Turn right and proceed 1.3 miles to an unsigned junction. The trailhead is 20 yards down the road to the right.

Triangulation Peak is a rather nondescript summit that even those familiar with this region have a hard time recognizing from a distance. Once you reach the top, however, you soon realize that even a drab balcony provides the best seats in the house. Highlighting the view, about 6 miles to the southeast, is the snow-covered tower of Mount Jefferson. Mountains are like watercolor paintings—sometimes you have to step back to fully appreciate the view. Judging by Triangulation Peak, 6 miles is about the perfect distance. The trail to this viewpoint is easy enough for almost anyone, so this trip is an excellent choice when you want to introduce nonhikers to Oregon's great outdoors.

The gently graded trail sets off in a dense forest typical of the western Cascades, with the usual lush mix of Douglas firs, true firs, hem-

locks, and cedars. Huckleberries and beargrass compete for dominance on the forest floor. After a gradual downhill, the trail briefly skirts the edge of an old clearcut, from which you can see prominent Spire Rock jutting out of the side of Triangulation Peak to the east. You then return to forest and make a remarkably level 1.1-mile contour of a steep hillside to an obvious but unsigned fork at 1.7 miles. Bear right and ascend five moderately graded switchbacks to Triangulation Peak's rocky summit.

In July subalpine wildflowers abound, especially cliff penstemon, Washington lily, beargrass, buckwheat, woolly sunflower, and skyrocket gilia. Even more impressive than the blossoms, however, are the views. Mount Hood towers to the north, while the sharp spire of Three Fingered Jack and the snowy humps of North and Middle Sisters rise to the south. But it is the eastward view that really draws your attention, as Mount Jefferson fills the sky and demands at least an hour of awestruck gazing to fully appreciate.

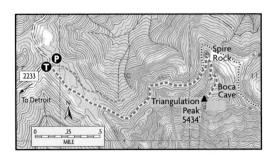

Mount Jefferson from Triangulation Peak

42 GRIZZLY PEAK

Distance: 10.4 miles round trip
Hiking time: 5.5 hours
Elevation gain: 2700 feet
Difficulty: Strenuous
Season: July to October
Best: July
Map: Green Trails No. 557 Mount Jefferson
Information: Willamette National Forest—Detroit Ranger District, (503) 854-3366
Permit and Reservation Information: The Forest Service has imposed a limited-entry permit system for this area. For hikes between Memorial Day and October 31, both dayhikers and backpackers must obtain a permit. Starting on May 1, you can reserve a spot by calling 1-877-444-6777 or going to www.recreation.gov. There is a $6 fee for processing.

Directions: From Salem drive Oregon Highway 22 east to a junction between mileposts 62 and 63. Turn left (east) on single-lane paved Pamelia Creek Road (Forest Road 2246) and drive 2.9 miles to a junction. Go straight and proceed 0.9 mile on gravel to the road-end trailhead.

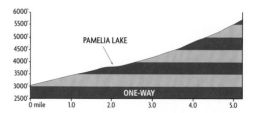

Grizzly Peak towers above a deep, forested valley southwest of Mount Jefferson and provides the best view of the mountain's rugged west face. But the trip to the summit is not all sweetness and light. A clue to the downside comes in the name. Since grizzly bears are only a distant memory in Oregon, some hikers have speculated that this peak was named because it is such a "bear" to reach the top. That is an overstatement, but you will get plenty of exercise.

The wide trail's first couple of miles are a pleasant walk through a shady old-growth forest of western red cedars, western hemlocks, and Douglas firs. Adding to the ambiance is cascading Pamelia Creek, always nearby with its soothing "river music." This crowded and easy part of the hike ends at a four-way junction at 2.2 miles, immediately before you reach the northwest tip of Pamelia Lake. The lake is worth a look, although the water level often drops 10

to 20 feet by mid- to late summer.

To reach Grizzly Peak, turn right at the junction, cross the usually dry outlet of Pamelia Lake, and begin climbing. The trail initially traverses rather gently uphill across the densely forested north slope of Grizzly Peak, then it makes three quick switchbacks followed by a winding ascent through an increasingly open forest of mountain hemlocks and lodgepole pines. In favored years, beargrass fills the forest here with its tall stalks and clusters of tiny white flowers. The views arrive with a bang at 4.4 miles when you hit the ridge top for the first time and come face to face with Mount Jefferson towering majestically above the Pamelia Lake valley. It is a stunning spectacle that calls for an extended rest stop to fully appreciate it.

But the climb is not yet complete, so keep going steadily uphill past more viewpoints, then at 5.1 miles make one switchback and soon attain

The view of Mount Jefferson from Grizzly Peak is ample reward for the climb.

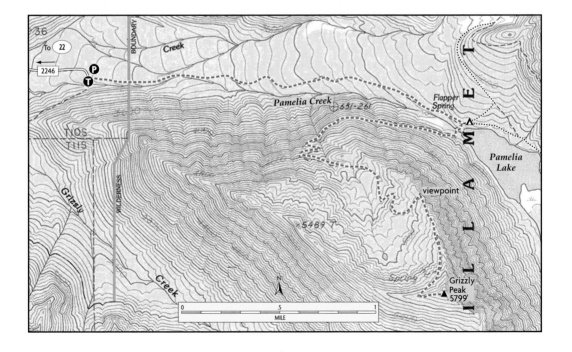

the summit. If the views were good below, then the scenery here, as George Orwell would say, is "double-plus-good." Mount Jefferson remains the star attraction and is, if possible, even more impressive from this higher grandstand than from below. In addition, you can see Mount Hood peeking over a ridge to the north, pointed Three Fingered Jack to the south, the rugged Cathedral Rocks to the southeast, and dozens of lesser peaks in the hills to the west. Lunch spots do not get much better than this.

If you want more exercise, continue cross-country along the view-packed ridge to the southeast. Most hikers, however, are satisfied with Grizzly Peak and choose to return the way they came.

43 SHALE LAKE LOOP

Distance: 16.3 miles round trip
Hiking time: 2 days (plus explorations)
Elevation gain: 2900 feet
Difficulty: Strenuous
Season: Mid-July to October
Best: Late July to mid-August
Maps: Green Trails No. 557 Mount Jefferson
Information: Willamette National Forest—Detroit Ranger District, (503) 854-3366
Permit and Reservation Information: The Forest Service has imposed a limited-entry permit system for this area. For hikes between Memorial Day and October 31, both dayhikers and backpackers must obtain a permit. Starting on May 1, you can reserve a spot by calling 1-877-444-6777 or going to www.recreation.gov. There is a $6 fee for processing.

Directions: From Salem, drive 60 miles east on Oregon Highway 22 to a junction between mileposts 62 and 63. Turn left (east) on Pamelia Creek Road (Forest Road 2246) and drive 2.9 miles on this single-lane paved route to a junction. Go straight and proceed 0.9 mile on gravel to the trailhead at road's end.

The impressive views of the sharp pyramid of Mount Jefferson's south face over tiny Shale Lake are second only to the much more famous ones from Jefferson Park on the mountain's north flank (Hike 40). That fact alone makes this trip worthwhile, but that is only one of the many benefits this hike has to offer. You are also treated to deservedly popular Pamelia Lake, a large, lower-elevation gem surrounded by stately forest; two small but scenic higher-elevation lakes in Hunts Cove that are surrounded by wildflower-covered meadows; a

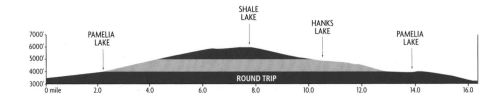

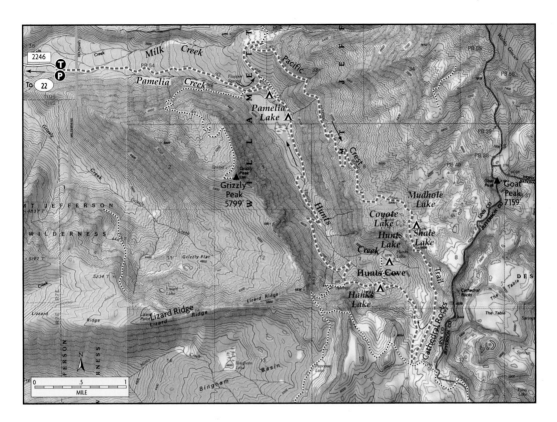

stupendous viewpoint of Mount Jefferson over a red cinder–covered ridge; the jagged crags of Goat Peak and the Cathedral Rocks; and access to enough superb off-trail destinations to keep a hiker busy for several days. All in all this is one of the more diverse and enjoyable hikes in the central Oregon Cascades.

For its first 2.2 miles the trail follows the same route as Hike 42 through a beautiful old-growth forest to the shores of Pamelia Lake. For a very easy first day you could spend the night at any of several fine campsites along the north shore of this 45-acre lake. Unfortunately, the lake's water level drops considerably by late summer, so it loses much of its appeal.

To continue the recommended clockwise loop, turn left at a four-way junction near the northwest tip of Pamelia Lake and climb for 0.1 mile to a second junction. Go left again and ascend through forest for 0.6 mile to a junction

with the Pacific Crest Trail (PCT).

Turn right (southbound) on the PCT and make a long, gradual, switchbacking ascent, mostly through forest but also passing a couple of viewpoints where you can look down to Pamelia Lake. Eventually, the trail enters more varied and interesting terrain where the forests are more open and interspersed with small meadows that host a wealth of midsummer wildflowers. At 7.5 miles you reach very shallow Mudhole Lake and, just beyond, smaller but deeper Shale Lake. Both of these lakes offer outstanding views across their waters to pointed Mount Jefferson. To the east you can see ruggedly scenic Goat Peak. Camps are plentiful here, although they are very popular, especially with through-hikers on the PCT. The best sites are along the west side of Mudhole Lake and on a low rise between the two lakes.

From a base camp at Shale Lake there are

Mudhole Lake offers a scenic rest stop.

many excellent off-trail possibilities to entice adventurous hikers. With a good map and GPS device you can explore other nearby pools, including Coyote Lake and several others lacking names. Almost all of these tiny lakes offer excellent mountain views and campsites that are less crowded than those at Shale Lake. You could also climb Goat Peak or scramble up the generally untechnical south ridge of Mount Jefferson all the way to within a few hundred yards of the summit. (Past that, only serious climbers need apply.) Finally, you can wander southeast from Shale Lake through open forests and over timberline meadows and cinder fields to The Table, where you can either explore or simply bask in the views from this amazingly flat-topped grandstand.

Back at Shale Lake, the southbound PCT soon passes a couple of smaller ponds, then visits a fine cliff-top viewpoint overlooking Hunts Cove. From there the trail cuts across the west side of the extremely rugged Cathedral Rocks and comes to a junction in a wide saddle at 9.3 miles (excluding side trips). Looking south from here rewards you with a terrific view of Mount Jefferson rising over a sloping field of red cinders. For a side trip to an even better viewpoint of Mount Jefferson, continue hiking south on the PCT up a series of switchbacks for 1.2 miles to a dramatic ridge-top vista that overlooks the varied volcanic landscape of cinder cones, lava flows, and basalt cliffs around The Table.

Back at the saddle junction, you have a choice of return trails. The shorter and more interesting option is to go north down a gully on an old and unmaintained but still easy-to-follow trail. In 1.1 miles this rather steep path takes you down to a junction on the north shore of clear Hanks Lake. There are good campsites at this pretty subalpine lake as well as at nearby Hunts Lake, 0.4 mile up the trail to the right.

To complete the recommended loop, turn left at the junction beside Hanks Lake and gradually descend for 0.6 mile to another junction. Keep right (north) and drop steadily in long traverses and switchbacks to a crossing of Hunts Creek, then very gradually descend back to Pamelia Lake and the junction at its northwest corner. Go straight and return 2.2 miles to your car.

44 TABLE LAKE LOOP

Distance: 18-mile loop; 5.2-mile side trip to Bear Butte viewpoint; 23 miles
 total
Hiking time: 2–3 days
Elevation gain: 3000 feet; 900 feet to Bear Butte viewpoint; 3900 feet total
Difficulty: Strenuous
Season: July to October
Best: Mid-July to mid-August
Maps: Green Trails No. 557 Mount Jefferson, No. 558 Whitewater River
Information: Deschutes National Forest—Sisters Ranger District, (541) 549-7700

Directions: Drive US 20 to 7.6 miles east of Santiam Pass or 12.4 miles west of Sisters, then turn north on paved Forest Road 12. After FR 12 turns to gravel at 4.6 miles, continue on another 11.9 miles, then fork left on FR 1292, following signs to Jefferson Lake Trail. Turn left again after 0.4 mile and proceed 2.4 miles to the trailhead.

This loop trip is well suited to backpackers looking to escape the crowds in other parts of the Mount Jefferson Wilderness. Two factors ensure a lower trail population. The first is that the trailhead is on the east side of the range, which forces hikers coming from the Willamette Valley to drive an additional hour to start their hike. Second, the approach route has no realistic destination for day hikers, so usually only backpackers and equestrians take this trail. Fortunately, you do not have to sacrifice scenery for solitude, because the beauty here exceeds all expectations. **Note:** In late 2003 the B&B Complex Fire burned much of this area; expect a blackened landscape with limited shade for several years.

The trail immediately takes a bridge over rush-

ing Candle Creek, goes between a pair of 800-year-old Douglas firs, and wanders through forest for 0.4 mile to a junction at the start of the loop. For a gentler ascent, go straight on the Jefferson Lake Trail. The forest at this relatively low elevation is a unique mix that includes both ponderosa pines and western hemlocks, two species that normally do not grow together. As you gain elevation, the mix of species changes to mostly lodgepole pines, mountain hemlocks, and subalpine firs.

The most notable physical feature as you slowly gain elevation is a jumbled lava flow on your right. This massive display of volcanism will be your companion for much of the climb and is so old that full-sized trees now grow on its surface. You cross a small part of the uneven flow, then travel through an eerie section of fire-scarred snags standing above a brushy landscape dominated by ceanothus and fireweed. The continuous fire zone ends at 1.9 miles at trickling Cougar Spring, after which you go in and out of burn areas for the next 1.5 miles.

After reentering the forest, the trail winds through the top of the ancient lava flow, then at 6.3 miles comes to a junction with the 0.5-mile

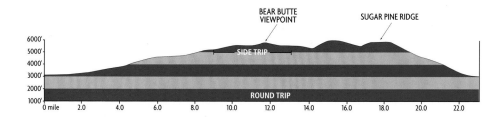

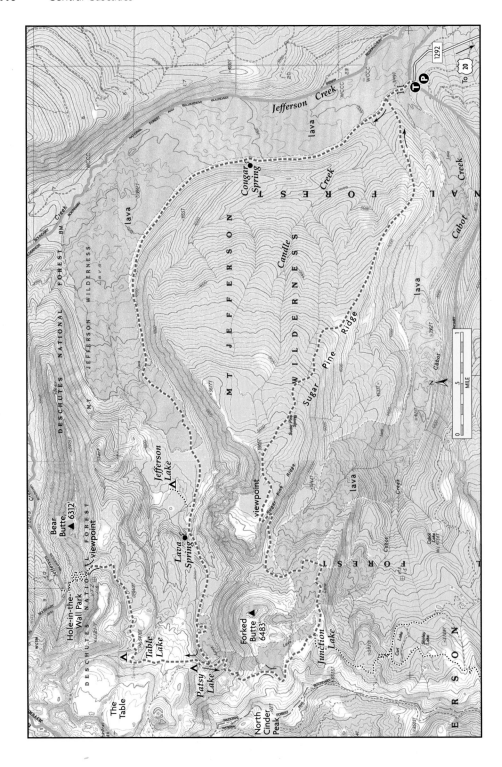

spur trail to Jefferson Lake. This small lake sits in a pretty meadow and has a nice campsite but no view of its namesake peak. The main trail goes straight at the junction, does a bit of moderate climbing to Lava Spring, then goes up and down through forests, meadows, and around lava to a junction at 8.3 miles beside the outlet to small Patsy Lake.

There are adequate campsites at Patsy Lake, but for better ones turn right (north), make a short switchbacking climb, then cross a rolling meadowy plain to Table Lake 9.4 miles from the start. This narrow and very scenic lake features a large spring, flower-covered meadows, and several excellent campsites above its northwest end. Fires are prohibited within 0.25 mile of the lake.

A mandatory 1.5-mile side trip from Table Lake follows a sometimes sketchy trail through gorgeous subalpine terrain to a stupendous ridge-top viewpoint beside the pinnacle of Bear Butte. The scene of Mount Jefferson towering above a deep, meadow-filled depression called Hole-in-the-Wall Park is one of the best views in Oregon.

To do the loop, return to Patsy Lake at 13.5 miles, go south, and climb over a windy pass between Forked Butte's cinder cone and the crags of North Cinder Peak. You then drop to a junction at 15.3 miles beside a minuscule pond with the rather generous title of Junction Lake. Turn left on a circuitous trail that winds mostly downhill through meadows and lava to a wide

The volcanic landscape of Sugar Pine Ridge

saddle. From there, two uphill switchbacks go through an old burn area filled with silvery snags and unusual wildflowers, such as Washington lily and boykinia, to the top of Sugar Pine Ridge at 17 miles. For a great view of Mount Jefferson, drop your pack and make the short scramble northwest to the top of a craggy knoll.

From Sugar Pine Ridge, it is 5 miles of downhill, often through shadeless burn areas, to a log over Candle Creek and a reunion with the Jefferson Lake Trail at 22.4 miles. Turn right to return to your car.

45 DUFFY LAKE AND SANTIAM LAKE

Distance: 9.6 miles round trip
Hiking time: 5 hours (day hike or backpack)
Elevation gain: 1200 feet total
Difficulty: Moderate
Season: Late June to October
Best: July (but be ready for mosquitoes)
Map: Geo-Graphics Mount Jefferson Wilderness
Information: Willamette National Forest—Detroit Ranger District, (503) 854-3366

Directions: Take Oregon Highway 22 to milepost 76, 5.8 miles north of the intersection with US 20, then turn east on one-lane paved Big Meadows Road (Forest Road 2267). Stay on the main road for 3.1 miles to the trailhead.

Three Fingered Jack stands sentry over Santiam Lake.

The sparkling lakes, dense forests, and lovely meadows in the high country northwest of Three Fingered Jack have been a popular destination for generations of Oregon hikers. Many people now in their eighties retain fond memories of family outings to Marion Lake or overnight scout trips into Eight Lakes Basin. As often happens with such memories, the clouds of mosquitoes that chased many of those hikers out of the high country are forgotten, leaving only the pleasant thoughts of good fellowship and grand scenery.

The mosquitoes are still there, waiting for a new generation of hikers to attack, but massive fires in 2003 scorched so much of this area that for the time being it is better to focus on the still-unscathed and lovely lakes farther south near the base of Three Fingered Jack.

The gently graded trail meets a horse trail from a separate equestrian trailhead, then ascends through forest. After 1.6 sometimes dusty miles, you pass the Turpentine Trail coming in from the left, then level off and go through meadows beside the sluggish headwaters of the North Santiam River. Shortly after an unbridged but easy crossing of the river is a junction at 3.3 miles. Go straight on the more heavily used trail and walk 0.4 mile to a junction at the southwest

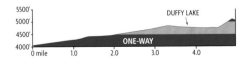

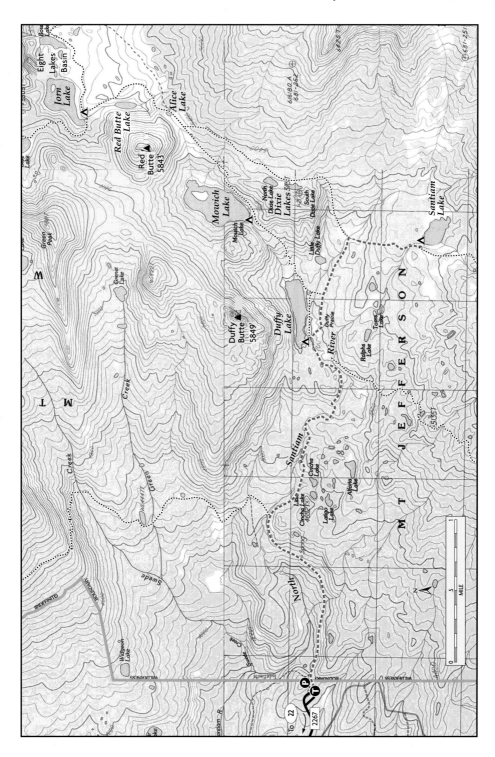

corner of popular Duffy Lake. The pyramid-shaped summit of Duffy Butte dominates the north side of this lake and several good campsites are located around the lakeshore.

Going straight at the junction would lead to Eight Lakes Basin, with its thousands of acres of blackened snags and, for the next couple of decades, virtually no shade. For a much more scenic destination, turn right and in about 0.3 mile come to a second junction. Go straight and gradually ascend to a junction at 4.2 miles in a pretty meadow, which in July is covered with a beautiful pink mat of shooting stars. To visit Santiam Lake, go right and climb an eroded trail 0.6 mile to this meadow-rimmed lake with many good campsites. The view across the lake's waters to the jagged summit of Three Fingered Jack is classic.

46 CANYON CREEK–FIRST CREEK MEADOWS LOOP

Distance: 8-mile loop
Hiking time: 5 hours (day hike or backpack)
Elevation gain: 1400 feet
Difficulty: Strenuous
Season: Mid-July to October
Best: Late July and early August
Map: Geo-Graphics Mount Jefferson Wilderness
Information: Deschutes National Forest—Sisters Ranger District, (541) 549-7700

Directions: Drive US 20 to 7.6 miles east of Santiam Pass or 12.4 miles west of Sisters, then turn north on paved Forest Road 12. Drive 3.8 miles to a junction, go left on FR 1230, drive 1.5 miles, then turn left on FR 1234. Climb 5 miles on this bumpy, gravel road to the Jack Lake trailhead.

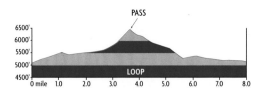

This is a magnificent, cross-country variation on the popular trail into Canyon Creek Meadows below Three Fingered Jack's precipitous east face. After taking you through that meadow's famous wildflower bonanza, this loop goes off trail to a spectacular meadow on the rarely visited southeast side of the mountain. On weekends during the peak flower show in late July, entire divisions of booted infantry depart from the trailhead. Try to visit on a weekday. **Note:** In late 2003 the B&B Complex Fire burned all of this area except around Canyon Creek Meadows; expect a blackened landscape for several years.

Follow the wide and often dusty trail around the north side of tiny Jack Lake, then slowly ascend 0.3 mile through a mountain hemlock and lodgepole pine forest to a prominent fork. Bear left and go gradually uphill through attractive woods before descending slightly to a junction at 2 miles at the lower end of Canyon Creek Meadows. The trail to the right loops back to Jack Lake. Your trail goes straight and travels through increasingly scenic wildflower meadows bisected by the clear flow of Canyon Creek. The impressive striated crags of Three Fingered Jack rise to the southwest. Although the scenery is outstanding, mosquitoes can be a problem during the flower season, so bring repellent.

From the upper end of the last meadow, the trail steeply ascends through barren, rocky terrain to a pass at 3.5 miles, directly beneath the sheer cliffs of Three Fingered Jack. This desolate

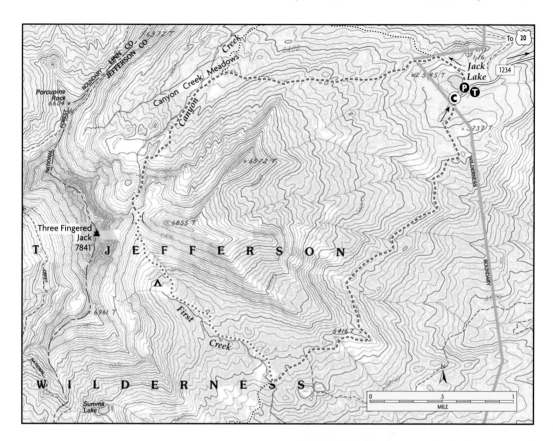

spot is often cold and windy, but it provides first-rate views north to Mount Jefferson and south to the Three Sisters.

The trail ends here, but to do the recommended loop, carefully pick your way 0.5 mile down the steep, rocky slope on the south side of the pass to a rather barren, pumice-covered meadow at the head of trickling First Creek. Backpackers will find some nice campsites around this meadow. To finish the cross-country section, go southeast through meadows and open forests, generally staying fairly close to small First Creek. About 0.5 mile below the first meadow, look for a shallow pond a little northeast of the creek. On a calm morning this pond presents breathtaking reflections of Three Fingered Jack. About 0.6 mile below this pond you intersect a maintained trail at about 5 miles. Turn left, climb over a low ridge, then make a 2-mile downhill traverse back to Jack Lake.

Canyon Creek Meadows offers excellent views of Three Fingered Jack.

47 IRON MOUNTAIN LOOP

Distance: 5-mile loop; 1.4-mile side trip to lookout; 6.4 miles total
Hiking time: 3.5 hours
Elevation gain: Loop, 1000 feet; lookout, 800 feet; 1800 feet total
Difficulty: Moderate
Season: Mid-June to early November
Best: Mid- to late July
Map: USGS Harter Mountain
Information: Willamette National Forest—Sweet Home Ranger District, (541) 367-5168

Directions: From Sweet Home, drive US 20 east 35 miles to Tombstone Pass. There is a large parking area on the south side of the highway.

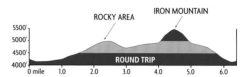

Iron Mountain is a justifiably popular western Cascades destination that packs a lot of high-

lights into a single hike. There are great views, a picturesque fire lookout, old-growth forests,

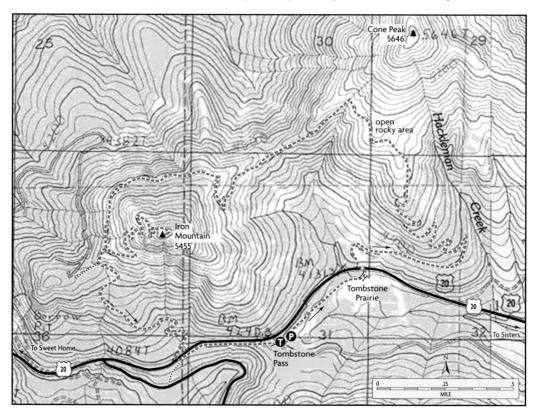

Iron Mountain from the rocky meadow below Cone Peak

craggy rock formations, and some of the most outstanding wildflower meadows in the Oregon Cascades. Botanists especially love this outing, because the region supports more tree species—seventeen—than any other place in Oregon and more than 300 types of wildflowers. Most hikers reach the top via a crowded and dusty trail from the south, but a longer and more attractive option is this loop from Tombstone Pass.

The trail starts just south of the restroom and goes east, gradually descending along the wooded hillside below US 20. After 0.4 mile you pass Tombstone Prairie, take a bridge over a usually dry creek, and cross the highway. The trail resumes about 25 yards to the left (west) and rapidly climbs away from the sounds of traffic through an old-growth forest of mixed conifers. The well-graded route then takes you through a wet meadow choked with bushes and tall wildflowers such as thimbleberries, tiger lilies, coneflowers, bracken ferns, columbines, cow parsnips, and knotweeds.

Above this meadow, ten uphill switchbacks lead to an open, rocky area at 2.2 miles that hosts an assortment of colorful wildflowers that prefer a drier environment. Especially common are cat's ear, stonecrop, phlox, skyrocket gilia, larkspur, owl's clover, wallflower, buckwheat, and sulphur flower, although that is a very shortened list. If you can tear your eyes away from the blossoms, there are great views west to Iron Mountain and its distinctive thumblike rock pinnacle.

The trail returns to forest, winds downhill to a small saddle, then traverses the woodsy north side of Iron Mountain to a fork at 3.7 miles. To reach the lookout, bear left on a dusty trail that switchbacks steeply uphill 0.7 mile. The wildflower gardens here support, in addition to the varieties mentioned above, such colorful favorites as flax, penstemon, yarrow, and several kinds of saxifrage. Drawn to all of these flowers, hummingbirds seem to be everywhere. From the ground-level, wooden lookout building at the summit, there are views of all the snowy Cascade peaks from Mount Hood to Diamond Peak.

To finish the trip, return to the trail fork at 5.1 miles, turn left, pass a junction with the Iron Mountain Cutoff Trail after 100 yards, then descend through old-growth forest to US 20 at 6.1 miles. The popular Iron Mountain trailhead is a short distance down the other side of the highway, but to close the loop, turn left and follow the road shoulder for 0.3 mile back to Tombstone Pass.

48 BROWDER RIDGE

Distance: 8.4 miles round trip to Browder Ridge;
   10.4 miles round trip to Heart Lake
Hiking time: 4 hours
Elevation gain: 2100 feet
Difficulty: Moderate
Season: June to October
Best: Mid- to late July
Map: USGS Tamolitch Falls, Echo Mountain
Information: Willamette National Forest—Sweet Home Ranger District, (541) 367-5168

Directions: Drive US 20 to 41 miles east of Sweet Home or 2.4 miles west of the intersection with Highway 126, then turn south on initially paved then gravel Forest Road 2672 (Hackleman Creek Road). Drive 1.7 miles to a fork, bear right on FR 1598, and drive 2.9 miles to the Gate Creek trailhead.

Browder Ridge is a little-known alternative to nearby and much more popular Iron Mountain (Hike 47). Although the trail is less crowded, the scenery is equally spectacular, with similarly impressive old-growth forests at lower elevations, the same grand meadows filled with acres of wildflowers along the ridge top, and equally breathtaking views from the summit.

Despite the trailhead's name, the trail does not follow Gate Creek. Instead it leaves the stream immediately and switchbacks up a hillside covered with an impressive old-growth forest

of Douglas firs. But these are only the first and most notable of the conifer species you encounter on this hike. There are also Pacific silver and noble firs, western red and Alaska yellow cedars, western white pines, and western and mountain hemlocks. In fact, this is one of the most diverse forests in Oregon. After about 1 mile, you leave the forest and enter a large meadow with your first nice views. The trail then makes one switchback and begins a generally level traverse along a ridge to the west. This attractive route goes in and out of forests for a little over 1.5 miles to a junction at 3.1 miles, where you turn right, following signs for Heart Lake.

The trail curves northeast and soon enters a

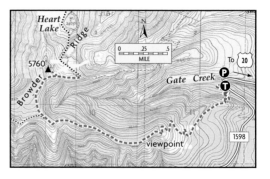

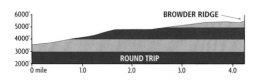

spectacular sloping meadow that features outstanding wildflower displays. There are many species—buckwheat, lupine, yarrow, tiger lily, paintbrush, orange mountain dandelion, Washington lily, groundsel, and woolly sunflower—but the most abundant flower is wild carrot, millions of which carpet these slopes in July. Views are very good from this meadow, especially southeast to the Three Sisters.

For even better views, keep hiking to a forested saddle at 4 miles, about 150 yards before the trail begins its steep, switchbacking descent to Heart Lake. Leave the trail here and scramble west up the spine of a narrow ridge 0.2 mile to a small open area rimmed with ground-hugging juniper at the summit of Browder Ridge. The expansive views extend north to Mount Hood and south to Diamond Peak, but lesser summits also provide interesting viewing. Especially worth noting are Carpenter Mountain to the south and Coffin Mountain to the north, both of which host fire lookouts.

Three Sisters from Browder Ridge

49 MCKENZIE LAVA FLOW AND GEORGE LAKE

Distance: 5.2 miles round trip to Little Belknap Crater;
    12 miles round trip to George Lake
Hiking time: 3 hours to Little Belknap Crater; 2 days to George Lake
Elevation gain: 1100 feet to Little Belknap Crater; 2400 feet to George Lake
Difficulty: Moderate
Season: Late June to October
Best: July
Map: Geo-Graphics Mount Washington Wilderness
Information: Deschutes National Forest—Sisters Ranger District, (541) 549-7700

Directions: Drive Oregon Highway 242 to exactly 0.5 mile west of McKenzie Pass or 15.5 miles west of Sisters to a parking area on the north side of the highway. The small trailhead parking area is marked with a brown hiker sign.

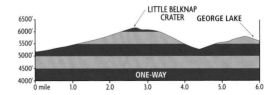

Nowhere is the volcanic history of the Cascade Range on better display than here. The massive lava flows around McKenzie Pass are so desolate they look as if they spewed out of the ground only yesterday. This hike takes you across these jagged flows all the way to their source at Little

Mount Washington towers over George Lake.

Belknap Crater. From there the stark panorama is punctuated by views of the Three Sisters, a trio of tall, relatively young volcanoes. If you prefer an overnight outing, continue to George Lake, a tranquil, forest-rimmed pool directly beneath the pinnacle of Mount Washington, an ancient volcanic plug that is now extinct. The sharp lava quickly destroys tennis shoes, so wear good boots. Also remember that a dog's unprotected paws will be cut to shreds.

The Pacific Crest Trail (PCT) immediately enters the Mount Washington Wilderness in a sparse forest of lodgepole pines, mountain hemlocks, and subalpine firs. After 0.4 mile you cross a narrow tongue of lava, then round the west and north sides of a *kipuka,* a forested "island" that the lava missed. Once you leave the *kipuka,* the color green becomes a distant memory as the trail climbs through a uniformly black landscape of jumbled rocks. On a sunny day it can be very hot and you will discover that sitting down to rest is

uncomfortable without a pad to protect you from the solar-heated rocks and sharp edges. On the other hand, the views are wonderful, especially south to glacier-clad North and Middle Sisters, north to the bulky hump of Belknap Crater, and east to distinctive Black Crater (Hike 50). The trail is obvious—and very easy to maintain, since deadfall should not be a problem for at least a few thousand years.

The exposed and often windy route steadily ascends through the stark lava, which initially appears lifeless but actually supports many lichens, scattered bushes, and a few tufts of grass. Near the top of the lava flow, at the 2.4-mile point, is a junction marked by a large cairn. The 0.2-mile, dead-end trail to the right visits Little Belknap, taking you near three lava tube caves, which once enclosed flowing rivers of molten rock. This makes a good turnaround point for day hikers.

Backpackers should stick with the PCT, which

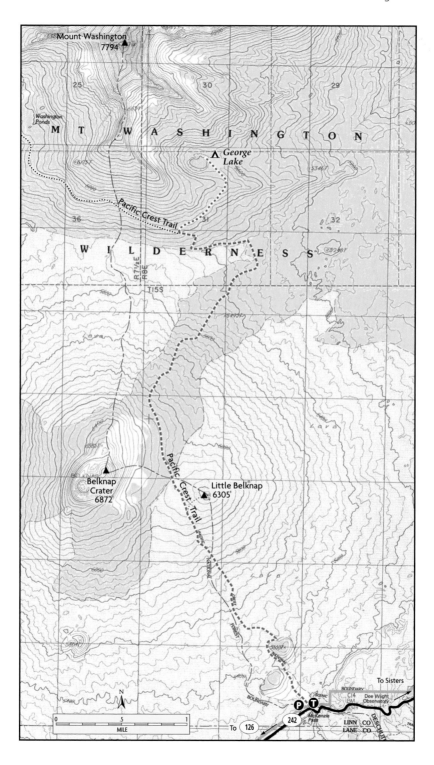

goes straight at the junction and heads north toward the sharp pinnacles of Mount Washington and distant Mount Jefferson. The route soon leaves the lava for the friendlier environment of a mountain hemlock forest more typical of the Oregon Cascades. You steadily descend through this forest for about 2 miles, loop around the end of another, much older, lava flow, then begin to go uphill.

To find George Lake, which has no official trail, leave the PCT about 0.5 mile after you begin climbing and travel northeast over a woodsy ridge generally contouring or slightly gaining elevation. Occasional orange ribbons and paint splotches on trees help with navigation. After about 0.6 mile you reach a ridge top, then descend 0.2 mile to the lake with its welcome water and good campsites.

Before your return the next day, take the time to scramble up the ridge north of George Lake to a stunning viewpoint of Mount Washington's precipitous east face.

50 BLACK CRATER

Distance: 7.2 miles round trip
Hiking time: 3.5 hours
Elevation gain: 2500 feet
Difficulty: Strenuous
Season: July to October
Best: Mid- to late July
Map: Geo-Graphics Three Sisters Wilderness
Information: Deschutes National Forest—Sisters Ranger District, (541) 549-7700

Directions: Drive Oregon Highway 242 to 12 miles west of Sisters or 3 miles east of McKenzie Pass, and park at the Black Crater trailhead.

The best place to study the volcanic landscape around McKenzie Pass is from the top of Black Crater, an old cinder cone that towers above the lava flows and forests east of the Cascade Divide. Even novices will be impressed by the views, but the ideal hiking companion for this trip is a geology professor, preferably one who specializes in volcanology. An expert can spend hours pointing out features such as cinder cones, eroded plugs, lava vents, *kipukas* (isolated tree "islands" the lava missed), and much more. It is all fascinating and extremely scenic.

With plenty of climbing to do, the dusty trail wastes no time with preliminaries and sets off at a moderately steep grade through a forest com-

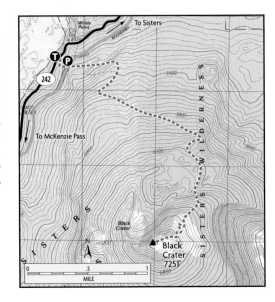

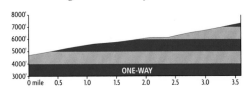

Mount Washington acts as a backdrop to the cinder-strewn landscape of Black Crater.

posed primarily of mountain hemlocks and true firs. The undergrowth is sparse, with wildflowers limited to a few lupines and cat's ears. A series of four mostly long, rounded switchbacks leads to a gentler section of trail through a rolling landscape of forests and waterless depressions. After this, the trail curves to the right and climbs an increasingly exposed ridge in moderately steep traverses and switchbacks. The path ends at the summit, which is topped with scenic red-orange cinders.

The views from Black Crater's high point are superb, stretching north to Mount Hood, south to Broken Top, and east to the vast deserts of southeastern Oregon. The stars of the show, however, are the Three Sisters, or "Faith, Hope, and Charity," as the early settlers called them. In addition to those virtues, the trio possesses beauty in abundance. Middle Sister is just barely visible from this angle, shyly peeking over her northern sibling's shoulder.

After absorbing the scenic beauty, spend an hour or so studying the diverse landscape. In addition to the volcanic features mentioned above, your geologist companion will note how ice age glaciers carved an impressively deep gash in Black Crater's northeastern flank just below the summit. The trail dead-ends here, so return the way you came.

51 SOAP CREEK

Distance: 8.5 miles round trip
Hiking time: 4 hours (day hike or backpack)
Elevation gain: 1750 feet
Difficulty: Strenuous
Season: Mid-July to mid-October
Best: Late July and August
Map: Geo-Graphics Three Sisters Wilderness
Information: Deschutes National Forest—Sisters Ranger District, (541) 549-7700

Directions: Drive Oregon Highway 242 to 1.4 miles west of Sisters, then turn left (southwest) on Forest Road 15. Stay on paved then gravel FR 15 at all intersections for 10.6 miles to the road-end Pole Creek trailhead.

North Sister over Soap Creek

The alpine terrain encircling the Three Sisters may be the most beautiful landscape in Oregon. No matter what trail you take here, the scenery is spectacular. The problem is that no matter what trail you take here, you have to fight off hordes of other admirers. To escape the crowds, leave the official trails and explore on your own. One excellent option follows a boot path along splashing Soap Creek to a spectacular plain high on the east side of North Sister. Here you can enjoy both outstanding scenery and relative solitude.

The often dusty trail climbs gradually through a viewless forest of mostly lodgepole pines, where many of the trees have been killed by a beetle infestation, leaving numerous dead and dying snags. After 1.4 miles you bear left at a junction, then descend a bit to Soap Creek at 2 miles.

The main trail crosses Soap Creek, but for this hike you turn right about 40 yards before the creek onto an unsigned path. Follow this unmaintained climbers route as it winds uphill, generally staying a little back from Soap Creek but always within earshot of this cheerful, flower-banked stream. At about 3.5 miles the trail gets a bit sketchy, but the creek remains an unerring guide. Although the open forest provides frequent tantalizing glimpses of the surrounding mountains, the best views do not occur until you hop over Soap Creek and reach a rolling plain almost directly beneath the towering and colorfully striated east face of North Sister. Broken Top and the upper third of South Sister are also visible from this area, which makes the already amazing scenery even better. Stunted whitebark pines and tiny alpine wildflowers such as pussy toes, pink heather, paintbrush, partridge foot, and aster add life and color to the plain. Without question, this is one of the most dramatic locations in Oregon.

You can camp almost anywhere on the plain, with Soap Creek providing water and the towering mountains giving you a first-rate view from your tent's front porch. Return the way you came or explore a bit to nearby ridges and meadows for even more great scenery.

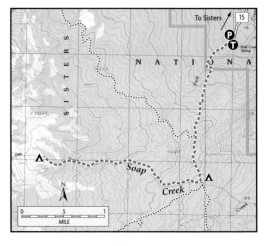

Camp Lake at the base of South Sister

52 NORTHERN THREE SISTERS LOOP

Distance: 36-mile loop, including 0.3-mile side trip to Collier Glacier View
Hiking time: 4–6 days
Elevation gain: 5300 feet
Difficulty: Strenuous
Season: Mid-July to October
Best: Late July and August
Map: Geo-Graphics Three Sisters Wilderness
Information: Deschutes National Forest—Sisters Ranger District, (541) 549-7700, and Willamette National Forest—McKenzie River Ranger District, (541) 822-3381
Permit and Reservation Information: The Forest Service has imposed a limited-entry permit system for entry into the Obsidian area northwest of North Sister. For hikes between Memorial Day and October 31, both dayhikers and backpackers must obtain a permit. Starting on May 1, you can reserve a spot by calling 1-877-444-6777 or going to www.recreation.gov. There is a $6 fee for processing.

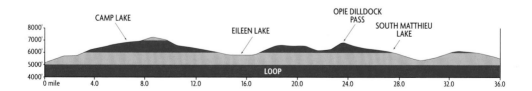

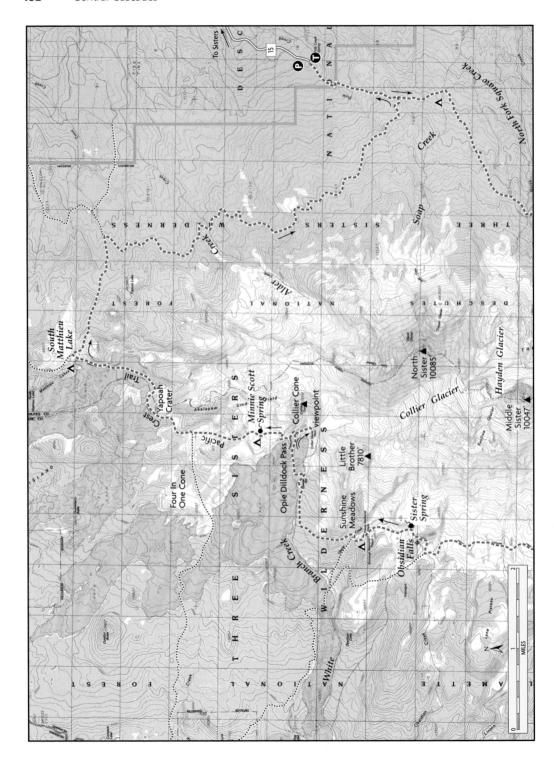

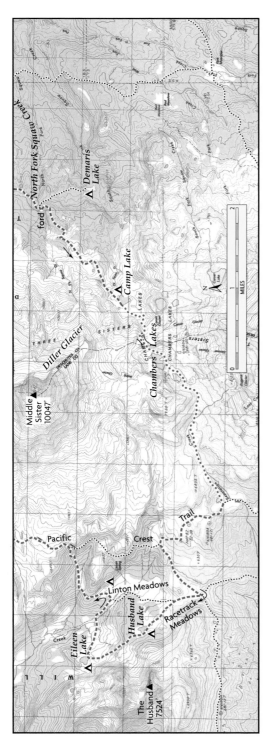

Directions: Drive Oregon Highway 242 to 1.4 miles west of Sisters, then turn left (southwest) on Forest Road 15. Stay on paved then gravel FR 15 at all intersections for 10.6 miles to the road-end Pole Creek trailhead.

As the centerpiece of Oregon's most-visited wilderness, the Three Sisters draw a lot of attention. And they deserve it. This comely trio dressed in white hats and blouses with flower-patterned skirts beckon with a decidedly alluring appeal that is difficult to resist. Fortunately for the legions of hiking suitors, plenty of trails lead to intimate locations where you can get up close and personal with the lovely ladies. The best option is the 55-mile loop all the way around the group, a seductive adventure that will leave you thoroughly satisfied. If your courting time is limited, however, try this shorter version, which focuses on the two charismatic sisters to the north and offers more than enough beauty to bring you under the spell of these enchanting siblings.

The often dusty trail climbs gradually through viewless forest for 1.4 miles to a junction and the start of the loop. A clockwise tour is easier to navigate, so turn left and descend to a junction at 2 miles immediately after the trail crosses Soap Creek. Make sure your water bottles are full, because this clear stream is the last good water source for 5 uphill miles.

Turn right and climb through a dry and rather monotonous lodgepole pine forest that has very limited ground cover and equally limited views. The ascent is steady but not overly steep as it goes in and out of dry gullies and through increasingly open forests to a potentially difficult crossing of North Fork Squaw Creek at 4.6 miles. This glacial stream can be a raging torrent of meltwater on hot afternoons, so try to cross in the morning. In addition, the silt tends to clog your water filter, so do not use this creek for drinking water.

On the other side of the crossing is a junction. An 0.8-mile side trail goes left to Demaris Lake, which has decent campsites and partial views of South Sister. For the truly exceptional scenery, however, take the trail to the right.

This path ascends into an alpine wonderland of scattered trees, rolling meadows, and excellent views of the glaciers on the east face of Middle Sister. The breathtaking scenery keeps pulling you along. The trail eventually levels and arrives at the heather-rimmed shores of Camp Lake at 7 miles. The views of South Sister across this often ice-covered pool are world class. As the name implies, there are glorious campsites here, although they are exposed to the wind and overused. Fires are banned within 0.5 mile of the lake.

The trail ends at Camp Lake. Continuing the loop requires a cross-country transit through the high divide between South and Middle Sister. The most difficult part is at the start, where you must scramble about 1 mile over rocks and semi-permanent snowfields to the top of a small ridge west of Camp Lake. Once that is accomplished, the going becomes relatively easy as you drop to a pair of shallow, milk-colored lakes in the Chambers Lakes chain at about 9 miles. The route passes the south shores of these two lakes, then goes southwest down a gully that eventually hosts the intermittent flow of Separation Creek. About 2 miles below the Chambers Lakes, you intersect the Pacific Crest Trail (PCT) at 11 miles. Turn right (north) on the PCT and travel through rolling meadows and open forests to a junction at about 12.5 miles. The most direct course is straight on the PCT, but if you have the time, take the more scenic route past beautiful Linton Meadows and Eileen Lake. To visit these spots, turn left and proceed to a four-way junction at 13.5 miles in pumice-covered Racetrack Meadows.

Turn right (north), passing great viewpoints of red-topped South Sister, pyramid-shaped Middle Sister, and craggy The Husband, and walk 0.3 mile to a fork. Take the left path past Husband Lake in 0.5 mile to small but gorgeous Eileen Lake at 15.5 miles. The trail then turns right and drops 1.1 miles to a junction in bright-green Linton Meadows, where a group of large springs feed a cascading creek. From here, a fairly steep 1.4-mile trail takes you back uphill to the PCT.

The gently graded PCT heads north and soon enters the Obsidian Limited Entry Area, where a permit is required. At about 19.5 miles, at a junction near Obsidian Creek, turn right and pass joyfully cascading Obsidian Falls. Just above this falls, you walk through a delightful wildflower meadow to Sister Spring, the source of Obsidian Creek, then turn north past small ponds and rolling meadows. Nice campsites abound, but fires are banned and Leave No Trace principles are strictly enforced.

At the north end of these meadows is a junction at 21 miles. Turn right, still on the PCT, round a ridge on the west side of Little Brother, then climb beside the intermittent flow of White Branch Creek. The trail soon leaves the creek and climbs over stark lava flows to Opie Dilldock Pass at 23 miles, where an unsigned side trail goes 0.3 mile to Collier Glacier View. From this grandstand you can see Collier Glacier, reputed to be the largest in Oregon, flowing out of the col between North and Middle Sisters.

The PCT continues north to the pumice-covered meadow around tiny Minnie Scott Spring (possible camps) at 24.5 miles, then descends to a junction at the north end of a flower-choked meadow at 25.5 miles. Turn right, staying on the PCT, round the cinder cone of Yapoah Crater, then go through more lava to a junction beside tiny South Matthieu Lake at 27.5 miles. This small, circular pool has a great view of North Sister and popular but exposed campsites. Fires are prohibited, and the Forest Service requires that you camp only in designated sites.

The PCT continues north from South Matthieu Lake, but your loop goes right (east) and gradually descends for 1.8 miles through forested terrain to another junction at 29.3 miles. Turn right, following signs to Green Lakes, and go south on an irregular uphill grade through viewless lodgepole pine forests. The trail is sometimes dusty but is rarely steep. After 2 miles, hop over Alder Creek, then do more up-and-down hiking for 3.5 miles back to the junction with the Pole Creek Trail at 34.5 miles and the close of the loop; turn left and hike out.

Lake below Bend Glacier on Broken Top

53 BROKEN TOP LOOP

Distance: 23-mile loop
Hiking time: 2–3 days
Elevation gain: 2800 feet
Difficulty: Strenuous
Season: Mid-July to early October
Best: Late July and August
Map: Geo-Graphics Three Sisters Wilderness
Information: Deschutes National Forest—Sisters Ranger District, (541) 549-7700, and Bend/Fort Rock Ranger District, (541) 383-4000

Directions: From downtown Sisters, turn south on Elm Street (Forest Road 16), following signs to Three Creek Lake. Drive 15.8 miles to a junction at the northeast side of Three Creek Lake. Turn right on the spur road to Driftwood Campground and almost immediately pull into the trailhead parking lot on the right.

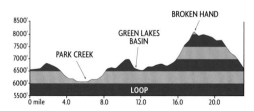

Judging by the names, the central Oregon Cascades is where mountains go to hold family reunions. Gathered at the party are not only the Three Sisters, but also The Husband, The Wife, Little Brother, Mount Bachelor, and even a few relatives whose family ties are less obvious, such as Kwolh Butte and Tot Mountain—Chinook jargon for "aunt"

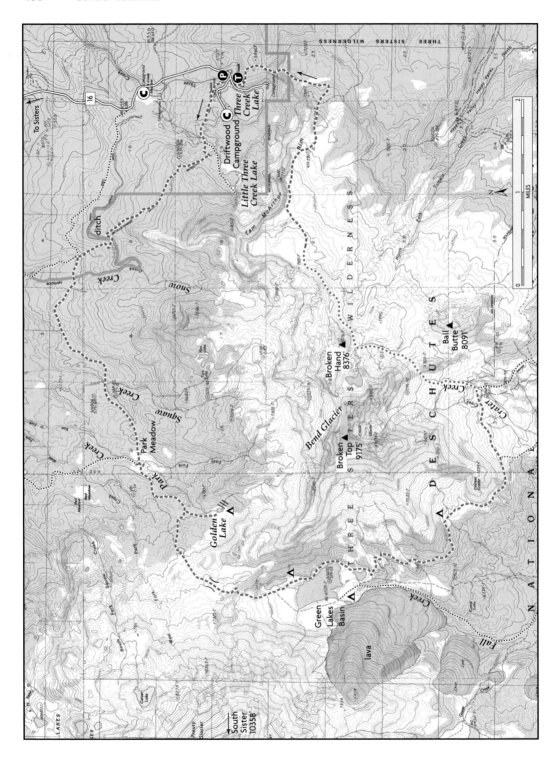

and "uncle." The most notable party-crasher is Broken Top, a handsome, 9175-foot interloper whose status as a family outcast is unfortunate. Not only does this stranger possess a ruggedly handsome profile, he has a real sense of style, clothing himself in picturesque wildflower meadows and glaciers. To judge the merits of this outsider for yourself, try this rugged loop around the mountain's base, which connects parts of several scenic trails with a fairly long but relatively easy cross-country traverse.

A counterclockwise loop is easier to navigate, so head northwest from the parking lot and follow an up-and-down trail through open forest for about 1 mile to a junction. The trail to the left goes a few hundred yards to Little Three Creek Lake, which features very photogenic views of the cliffs of Tam McArthur Rim. However, the loop trail goes straight and gradually makes its way up to a ridge at 1.6 miles, where you obtain your first good views of the Three Sisters filling the skyline to the west.

From here, descend to the Snow Creek irrigation ditch at 2.9 miles and a four-way junction 0.5 mile later. Turn left and follow a remarkably gentle but dusty trail that loops southwest, crosses the silty flow of Squaw Creek at about 5.3 miles, then comes to Park Meadow at 6.4 miles. This subalpine wonderland features scattered wildflower glades, a small pond, a clear creek, and your first view of Broken Top's jagged summit to the south.

At a junction on the west side of Park Creek, turn left and make a short, fairly steep climb of a hillside clothed in a dense mountain hemlock forest. About 0.8 mile from Park Creek, the trail curves to the right in a pumice-covered meadow. An unsigned, 0.6-mile use path goes south from here to Golden Lake. This sparkling little jewel sits in a small wildflower-covered basin, has a couple of good campsites, and features superb views of Broken Top in one direction and Middle and North Sister in the other. Adding to the scene is a cascading waterfall on the inlet creek. Adventurers can follow a boot path beside the inlet creek to a pair of gorgeous ponds on the north side of Broken Top.

After you've had your fill of wandering, return to the Golden Lake turnoff. The main trail goes straight (left), gradually ascends through increasingly open terrain to a 7000-foot pass at about 9.5 miles, then descends 1 mile into Green Lakes Basin. This stunningly beautiful location, where three spring-fed lakes nestle beneath South Sister on one side and Broken Top on the other, is justifiably one of the most popular backcountry destinations in the state. On an August weekend, as many as 350 people camp here. To reduce your impact, visit on a weekday and plan to camp elsewhere. If you must stay in the basin, the Forest Service requires that you use designated sites; fires are prohibited.

At a junction at the south end of the last lake at about 11.5 miles, bear left and begin a long, very scenic, up-and-down traverse through meadows and open forests on the west and south sides of Broken Top. About 1.5 miles from the last Green Lake, the trail crosses a creek (campsite here), then reaches a sketchy junction at 14.3 miles where you stay left on the main trail. Cross Crater Creek at about 15.2 miles in a gently sloping wildflower meadow where the trail turns south. Leave the trail and go north through an obvious gap to a sloping plain southeast of Broken Top.

At the north end of this plain, at about 16.8 miles, do not miss a fantastic 0.4-mile detour to the source of the small creek that flows across this area. The scramble route leads up a rocky gulch to a spectacular meltwater lake filled with icebergs that break off an adjacent glacier. It is a remarkable location but a potentially dangerous one, because sudden large waves occasionally surge across the lake when a particularly large chunk of ice calves off into the water.

To complete the loop, head east-northeast around the south side of Broken Hand to the sketchy boot path at the top of Tam McArthur Rim at about 19.5 miles. This route grows more obvious the farther east you go and eventually becomes a maintained trail. After passing a couple of outstanding cliff-top viewpoints, the trail drops fairly steeply at about 22 miles to the trailhead at Three Creek Lake.

54 SWAMPY LAKES

Distance: 7.7 miles round trip
Hiking time: 4 hours (day hike or backpack)
Elevation gain: 1300 feet
Difficulty: Moderate
Season: June to early November
Best: June
Map: USGS Tumalo Falls
Information: Deschutes National Forest—Bend/Fort Rock Ranger District, (541) 383-4000

Directions: From downtown Bend, take Galveston Avenue over the Deschutes River at Drake Park and go west through several intersections on what becomes Skyliners Road, then Forest Road 4603. About 10 miles from the city the road changes to good gravel, then proceeds 2.5 miles to the road-end Tumalo Falls trailhead.

The well-named Swampy Lakes are nestled in a scenic meadow east of Mount Bachelor, where visitors can enjoy excellent views of both that snowy landmark and nearby Tumalo Mountain. The lakes are a popular destination with cross-country skiers in the winter but are virtually deserted once the snow melts. That is a shame, because the trail has a lot to offer, including impressive waterfalls, pleasant forests, and colorful wildflowers. Unfortunately, Swampy Lakes also offer a lot of something else: mosquitoes (hardly surprising, given the name). As a result, this hike is best done as a day trip, at least until mid-August when the insect hordes have died down.

Two trails lead from the parking lot to Swampy Lakes, and this trip combines them into a loop.

The more scenic alternative starts counterclockwise and in 0.2 mile adds a 0.1-mile side trip to the right to Tumalo Falls, a dramatic, 85-foot falls that plummets in a nearly perfect drop over a basalt cliff. Return from the Tumalo Falls spur trail and turn right (west) up the canyon of Bridge Creek. This pleasant route goes through open, fire-scarred terrain, gradually gaining elevation for 1 mile to a nice waterfall on Bridge Creek. A short distance above this falls, turn left at a junction at 1.4 miles and cross Bridge Creek,

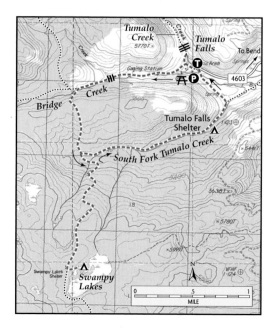

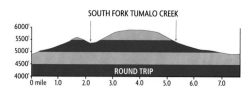

then go over a low ridge to a junction beside the crossing of South Fork Tumalo Creek at 2.1 miles. The trail to the left (east) is the return route of the loop.

To reach Swampy Lakes, go straight, switchback up a forested hillside for 1.5 miles, then level off and arrive at a junction on the edge of the meadow holding Swampy Lakes. The best views are in a marshy area about 350 yards to the south, but the best campsites are near a wooden shelter 0.1 mile down the trail to the left at 3.8 miles. For the loop, return to the junction beside South Fork Tumalo Creek (5.6 miles from the start), turn right, and follow the creek through dense forest for 1.2 miles to a campsite beside a wooden shake shelter. Below this, the trail goes back into the old burn area and descends 0.9 mile to the east end of the Tumalo Falls trailhead.

Mount Bachelor and Tumalo Mountain rise over Swampy Lakes meadow.

55 TODD LAKE LOOP

Distance: 1.8-mile loop
Hiking time: 1 hour
Elevation gain: 100 feet
Difficulty: Easy
Season: Late June to October
Best: July
Map: Geo-Graphics Three Sisters Wilderness
Information: Deschutes National Forest—Bend/Fort Rock Ranger District, (541) 383-4000

Directions: From Bend take the Cascade Lakes Highway southwest 23 miles to a junction about 2 miles west of the Mount Bachelor Ski Area. Turn right (north) on gravel Forest Road 370 and drive 0.6 mile to the Todd Lake trailhead.

Tranquil Todd Lake is a popular destination near Bend that stands out as a particularly beautiful lake in an area with intense competition in that category. From the meadows at the north end of this shimmering lake are stunning views of Mount Bachelor, while in the open forest at the south end of the lake are idyllic picnic spots. The loop is very easy, so hikers who want a little more exercise can ascend a trail that goes northeast to a spectacular ridge-top viewpoint of the Todd Lake Basin and Mount Bachelor.

The wide trail begins on an old road for a few hundred yards to a junction. For a counterclockwise circuit, stay on the east side of the lake and proceed through a lovely forest on the slopes beside the lake to a junction at 0.2 mile with the

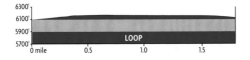

Mount Bachelor is reflected in Todd Lake.

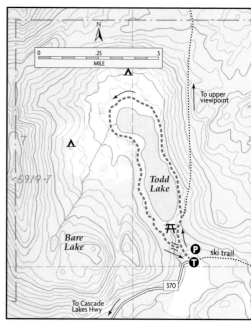

ridge trail. (More energetic hikers can follow this trail about 0.8 mile to a nice viewpoint.)

The loop trail around the lake stays near the shore and goes gently up and down to the north end of the lake at about 1 mile, where an extensive meadow provides an ideal foreground for views across the water to Mount Bachelor. On a calm morning, the reflection of the mountain in the still water is breathtaking. The meadow is rather marshy, especially early in the season, so tread carefully. Expect a lot of elephant heads and other water-loving wildflowers in July.

The trail continues around the north and west sides of the lake, past possible campsites and great lunch spots to the picnic area at the south end of the lake. Just below this spot, cross the bridge over the outlet creek at the south end of Todd Lake to complete the circuit.

56 REBEL ROCK LOOP

Distance: 12.4-mile loop
Hiking time: 7 hours
Elevation gain: 3300 feet
Difficulty: Very strenuous
Season: Late June to October
Best: July
Map: Geo-Graphics Three Sisters Wilderness
Information: Willamette National Forest—McKenzie River Ranger District, (541) 822-3381

Directions: From Eugene, drive Oregon Highway 126 east 45 miles, then turn south on paved Forest Road 19, following signs to Cougar Reservoir. After 0.5 mile, turn right and go 10 miles around the west side of Cougar Reservoir. After the road takes a bridge over the head of the reservoir, proceed 4 miles to the Rebel Creek trailhead.

The high, forested ridges and deep, green canyons in the western Three Sisters Wilderness are laced with numerous scenic trails rarely hiked by the booted masses headed for the higher trails around the famous mountain trio. Before you make the same mistake, take a day to enjoy this trip, the best of several hikes in this attractive area. The loop samples all that this region has to offer: old-growth forests, a beautiful clear creek, a great ridge-top viewpoint, and lovely wildflower meadows. When you throw in an interesting old fire lookout building, you have a real winner.

The trail starts with a brief uphill away from splashing Rebel Creek to a fork and the start of your loop. A clockwise tour allows for a more gentle ascent, so turn left on the Rebel Creek Trail.

The pleasant creekside route wanders gradually uphill through a splendid old-growth forest of huge Douglas firs, western hemlocks, and western red cedars. Beneath this towering canopy of living skyscrapers rises a green understory of smaller trees such as red alder and vine

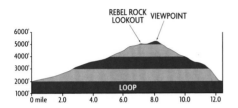

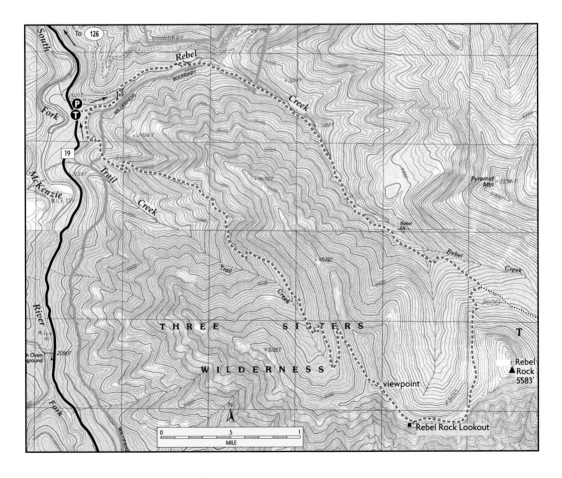

Rebel Rock Lookout

maple, both eking out an existence on limited sunlight. Even lower on the light-starved food chain is a mass of ferns and mosses on the forest floor. In the next 1.1 miles you cross the creek twice on log bridges, where you can look for dippers, perky little gray birds that use their wings to "swim" under mountain streams gathering small bits of food. After the second crossing, the trail ascends several moderately steep and irregularly spaced switchbacks on the wooded hillside south of the creek.

At a junction at 5.7 miles in a small meadow of waist-high thimbleberry, turn right on the Rebel Rock Trail and traverse a steep, brushy meadow with good views west to a ridge on the other side of the canyon. The ascent ends at a ridgeline, where the trail curves right and loses elevation. About 0.5 mile later, pass through a small rocky area where you can see Rebel Rock Lookout hanging precariously onto the lip of a steep drop-off to the west. To visit this abandoned facility, go another 300 yards, then look for a low rock cairn on the left at 7.5 miles. Turn left and follow an 80-yard spur trail downhill through brush and

forest to the abandoned lookout. The southward panorama over the deep canyon of South Fork McKenzie River is inspiring.

The main trail goes northwest from the lookout junction and climbs in 0.5 mile to an opening on the ridge. The vista here is even better than from the lookout, with outstanding views of the Three Sisters as well as other Cascade peaks from Mount Hood to Diamond Peak. Nearer at hand is Rebel Rock, with a distinctive, thumblike rock pillar on its south side.

From this viewpoint, the trail makes a lengthy, toe-jamming descent. It begins with two long switchbacks in a sloping meadow, then a series of shorter switchbacks through an increasingly dense forest bring you near Trail Creek. As you gradually descend, the vegetation changes from a subalpine mountain hemlock and noble fir forest with an understory of beargrass and huckleberry, to a lower-elevation zone featuring western hemlocks and Douglas firs towering over a mass of salal and sword fern. The last mile descends steeply to the junction above Rebel Creek just a few yards from the trailhead.

57 IRISH MOUNTAIN–MINK LAKE LOOP

Distance: 37-mile loop
Hiking time: 3–5 days
Elevation gain: 1500 feet
Difficulty: Moderate
Season: July to October
Best: Late August and September
Map: Geo-Graphics Three Sisters Wilderness
Information: Deschutes National Forest—Bend/Fort Rock Ranger District, (541) 383-4000

Directions: From Bend, take the Cascade Lakes Highway 47 miles, then turn right on paved Forest Road 4635, following signs to Cultus Lakes. After 1.8 miles go straight at two successive junctions and follow a gravel then dirt road 0.7 mile to the trailhead.

When the "10,000 Lakes" of Minnesota get tired of the cold weather and flat terrain back home, they go on vacation to the southern Three Sisters Wilderness. Judging by the number of lakes here, many decided to stay (Minnesota will have to change its license plates). Hundreds of lakes and ponds dot the forested landscape here, a paradise for lake lovers—including mosquitoes, whose uncountable billions make travel here miserable until mid-August. Long but relatively easy trails reach many of the lakes, and good-to-excellent campsites seem to pop up around every corner. So for great late-summer backpacking, grab the fishing pole, bring the kids, pack your swimsuit, and give this loop a try.

In a forest of lodgepole pines, true firs, and Engelmann spruces, the dusty trail goes west around the north side of large Cultus Lake. This lake is popular with boaters, so expect to hear the sounds of revving motors, especially on summer weekends. After 0.8 mile you pass a boat-in campground, then go very gently up and down, mostly through an open forest where many of the larger pines were killed by a beetle infestation. At the 2.5-mile point, at the junction with the trail to the Corral Lakes, go straight and soon reach a second junction and the start of the loop.

Either clockwise or counterclockwise is fine, but to save the prettier lakes for last, stay left. Drop to a log bridge over a small creek, then come to the busy boaters campground at the west end of Cultus Lake. Go south through the camping area and follow a trail to a fork near Deer Lake at 4.3 miles. Bear right and spend the next 4.5 miles winding gradually uphill past countless small- to medium-sized lakes on the well-named Many Lakes Trail. Plenty of places to camp and wonderful lunch spots can be found around every turn.

The route ends at a remote trailhead on rough Forest Road 600 at 9 miles. (It is possible to start your hike here, which would take 5.8 miles off the round-trip distance. Doing so, however, requires driving this miserably rough and dusty road. This is theoretically possible for passenger cars, but it

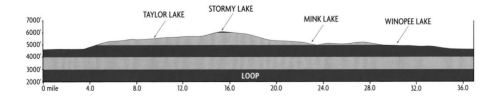

might cost you an axle or worse.) Turn right (west) and follow the road for 2 miles to the primitive car campground between Irish and Taylor lakes. The trail resumes at the unsigned crossing of the Pacific Crest Trail (PCT) at the west end of the lakes.

Go right (north) on the PCT as it skirts the west side of large Irish Lake, then gradually wanders uphill in open forest past Riffle Lake and several small ponds to a nice campsite at about 13.5 miles

beside Brahma Lake, which features a picturesque island. After looping around the east side of this gem, the trail climbs more noticeably up a miniature gully to inviting Jezebel Lake and over a little ridge to small Stormy Lake at 15.5 miles. The towering pinnacle of Irish Mountain makes an idyllic backdrop to this lake and will make you sorry to leave the excellent campsites here.

You now negotiate a long downhill mostly in forest but also past several small ponds and

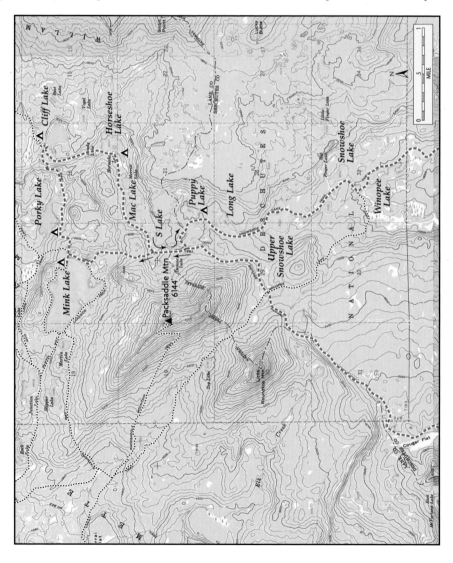

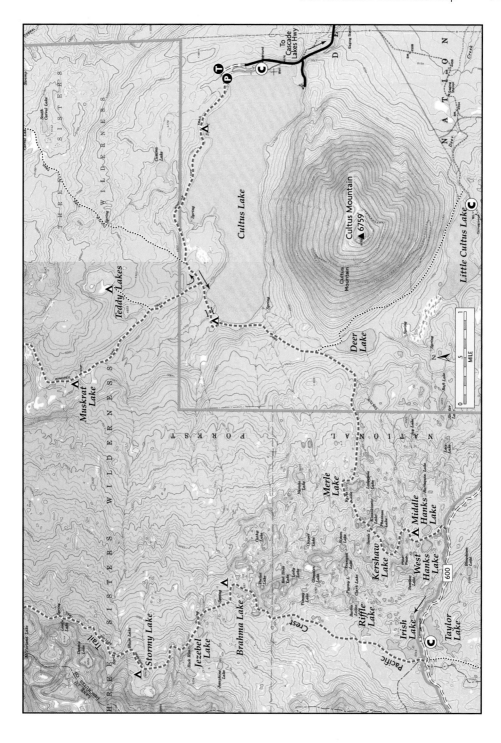

Porky Lake is just one of the many lovely lakes found on this loop.

viewpoints. About 5 miles from Stormy Lake is a four-way junction at 20.5 miles beside a grassy pond in a wide saddle. For a shorter loop, you could turn right here and return to the Cultus Lake trailhead in about 10 miles. Since this option misses many of the best lakes, however, it is better to stay on the PCT another 1.2 miles to a junction with the Snowshoe Lake Trail, the recommended return route.

Unless you are really pressed for time, take at least a day to enjoy a side loop to large Mink Lake. To reach it, go 0.4 mile north on the PCT, then turn left at a junction at 22 miles. This trail goes over a little ridge and drops to the east side of Mink Lake in about a mile. Camps abound around this mile-long and very scenic lake, with the best views near a shelter on the northeast side. From a base camp here you can explore more trails to dozens of nearby lakes or the viewpoint atop Packsaddle Mountain. To resume the loop, take the trail that goes east from the northeast tip of Mink Lake, passes attractive Porky Lake, and comes to a junction with the PCT at 25 miles near Cliff Lake. Turn right and return past a string of lovely, clear lakes (all with good campsites) to close the Mink Lake loop; go left to return to the Snowshoe Lake junction at 27.5 miles.

To close the Cultus Lake loop, go left on the Snowshoe Lake Trail past four large scenic lakes, most notably Puppy, Upper Snowshoe, and Snowshoe. Ospreys and bald eagles are often seen fishing at these lakes. At about 30 miles you come to a junction at the north end of large, irregularly shaped Winopee Lake, surrounded by beautiful meadows well worth exploring but with a lot of standing water. The woodsy 2.1-mile trail to the right is the other end of the shorter loop option.

Stay left to take the trail through forest on the east side of Winopee Lake, then follow its sluggish outlet creek (barely a trickle by late summer) through a series of lovely meadows for 2 miles to Muskrat Lake. This beautiful pool surrounded by lush meadows features an old cabin, now used as a shelter. The log structure was built around 1920 by a man who tried to earn money by raising muskrats here. The cabin is now falling into disrepair but is still worth visiting. The best campsites are in the woods near the inlet creek.

The remarkably level trail now heads south-southeast 1.4 miles to a junction at 33.5 miles with the spur trail to Teddy Lakes. Go straight and soon hear the drone of motorboats on Cultus Lake informing you that the hike is almost over. In 0.7 mile reach the junction near the northwest end of Cultus Lake, which closes the loop at a little over 34 miles; turn left back to the trailhead.

58   PAULINA LAKE LOOP

Distance: 8.4-mile loop
Hiking time: 4 hours
Elevation gain: 500 feet
Difficulty: Moderate
Season: June to October
Best: Late June and July
Maps: USGS East Lake, Paulina Peak
Information: Deschutes National Forest—Bend/Fort Rock Ranger District, (541) 383-4000

Directions: Drive US 97 to a junction 23 miles south of Bend or 6 miles north of La Pine. Turn east, following signs to Newberry Crater, and climb 13.2 miles on paved Forest Road 21 to a junction just before an entrance booth. Turn left, cross a bridge over Paulina Creek, and drive 0.2 mile to the trailhead parking area near rustic Paulina Lake Lodge.

Long before Mount Mazama committed suicide by blowing a hole in its head and filling the top with water, another prehistoric Oregon volcano met a similar fate. Newberry Volcano was (and still is) a massive shield volcano that scientists believe once looked similar to the Crater Lake model. Over the millennia, however, the mountain's 17-square-mile caldera has filled with lava and obsidian flows, pyroclastic material, and sedimentary rock, so today the caldera walls range from as high as 1600 feet at Paulina Peak to as low as 10 feet near the outflow of Paulina Creek. And although nothing can compare to the scenic beauty of Crater Lake (see Hikes 67 and 68), Newberry National Volcanic Monument boasts plenty of attractions of its own, including two stunning lakes, open forests, and high viewpoints of the Cascade Range to the west. Newberry Crater also has a more varied

and interesting volcanic history: massive flows of obsidian, about 400 nearby cinder cones, and numerous lava caves.

Probably the most scenic trail in the crater is the loop around Paulina Lake, the more westerly of two large lakes in the caldera. This trail not only has great views of jagged Paulina Peak but samples the area's volcanic highlights with a trip to the top of a cinder cone and past a massive obsidian flow, where you can reach out and touch huge boulders of natural black glass.

The loop is equally good in either direction, but going counterclockwise gets you past the lake's developed areas more quickly. So from the parking lot walk back along the road to the bridge over Paulina Creek, then turn left to pick up the south shore trail, which goes past Paulina Lake Campground, picnic sites, and summer homes. At 2.4 miles from the trailhead, you intersect the paved access road to Little Crater Campground.

You could turn left and follow the road through the busy campground, but for a quieter option pick up a trail on the other side of the road and climb through open forest to the summit of Little Crater, a cinder cone topped with tan-colored pumice and cinders, at 3.2 miles. At the top are outstanding views south to the jumbled Big Obsidian Flow and southwest to jagged Paulina Peak. A rough loop trail goes around the uneven edge of this cinder cone's summit crater, but stay left for this hike.

The well-graded trail slowly descends to the north end of Little Crater Campground, then closely follows Paulina Lake's scenic east shore.

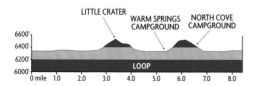

At 4.8 miles the trail takes you over the uneven edge of the Inter Lake Obsidian Flow. Here you can marvel at the assortment of rocks and boulders of streaked black glass. Just past this flow is a nice beach and the primitive boater's campground at Warm Springs at 5.4 miles. Beneath the lake water here are some large hot springs, which attest to the fact that this volcano is still active. The views southwest to Paulina Peak are superb.

From here, the trail climbs over a small headland with more excellent views, passes a secluded swimming beach and primitive boaters camp at North Cove at 6.7 miles, then completes the loop with a gentle traverse through open forest on the west side of Paulina Lake.

Paulina Peak over Paulina Lake

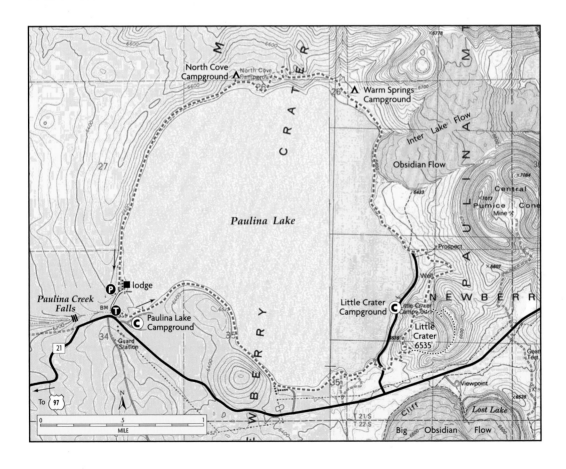

SOUTHERN CASCADES

Phantom Ship, Crater Lake National Park (Hike 67)

The southern Oregon Cascades are world famous as the home of Crater Lake, a nearly circular body of water filling a volcanic caldera that is the star attraction of the state's only national park. The remarkably blue waters of this lake have impressed visitors at least since June 12, 1853, when John Hillman and a party of prospectors reached the rim near a peak that now bears Hillman's name. Showing almost no imagination, the group christened this marvel "Deep Blue Lake" (a name that was, fortunately, changed to Crater Lake in 1869). But, of course, long before Hillman and his party "discovered" the lake, Native Americans had known of its presence and considered it sacred. Millions of visitors since might understand this belief, because viewing this masterpiece of creation is very much a spiritual experience.

Less well-known than this singular highlight of the southern Cascades are their many other beauty spots. The region includes lake-dotted mountain basins, wildflower-covered ridges, some of the most beautiful waterfalls in Oregon, and several towering remnants of extinct volcanoes, such as Diamond Peak, Mount Thielsen, and Mount McLoughlin. In other words, more than enough to draw visitors even if Crater Lake did not exist.

59 DIVIDE LAKE

Distance: 8 miles round trip
Hiking time: 4 hours (day hike or backpack)
Elevation gain: 1300 feet
Difficulty: Moderate
Season: July to October
Best: Mid-July to late August
Map: USFS Diamond Peak Wilderness
Information: Willamette National Forest—Middle Fork Ranger District, (541) 782-2283

Directions: From Eugene, drive Oregon Highway 58 southeast 38 miles to a junction 1.5 miles past Oakridge. Turn right, following signs to Hills Creek Dam, drive 0.5 mile, then go straight on Forest Road 23. Drive 19.1 miles on this paved then gravel road to the Vivian Lake trailhead.

Despite impressive scenery, numerous lakes, and relatively easy access, Diamond Peak is the most overlooked major mountain in Oregon. This may be due to the mountain's lack

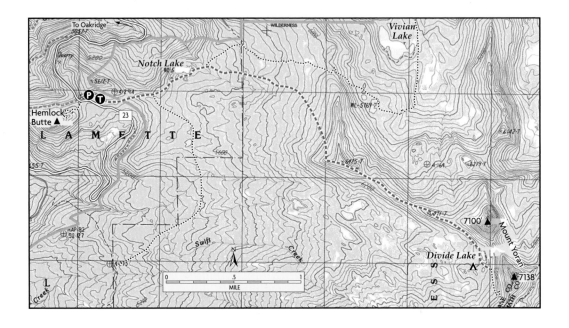

of a single summit, which makes the peak less distinctive than its neighbors, or it could be the clouds of mosquitoes that plague early-summer visitors. Regardless, the Diamond Peak Wilderness remains relatively undiscovered by the booted masses. The scenic trail to Divide Lake, tucked neatly into a small basin on the northwestern shoulder of Diamond Peak, provides a good sampling of this area's charms, allowing you to judge the merits of this wilderness for yourself.

The trail begins in a recovering clearcut but soon enters a cool forest of mountain hemlocks and Pacific silver firs. Huckleberries crowd the forest floor, providing delicious diversions in late August. After 0.5 mile of very gentle climbing, reach a junction with the Diamond Peak Tie Trail; go straight and in about 0.3 mile reach sparkling Notch Lake, ringed with scenic rocks and patches of pink heather.

About 200 yards past Notch Lake is a junction. Turn right on the Mount Yoran Trail and begin a steady but generally well-graded ascent. After 1.4 uphill miles you reach the top of a ridge, then descend 150 feet and come to a boulder field with the hike's first good views, at 2.3 miles. The jagged, snowy ridge of Diamond Peak fills the skyline to the southeast, effectively drawing your attention away from the distant clearcuts on the ridges to the southwest.

From here, follow the undulating ridge top southeast past more viewpoints, then angle slightly downhill to a good campsite beside small Divide Lake at 4 miles. The location of this deep, turquoise-colored pool, beneath the twin rock pinnacles of Mount Yoran, make it a dramatic spot to eat your lunch or spend the night.

To explore further, you can either scramble cross-country west to any of several nearby lakelets or stick with the trail as it switchbacks south up to a junction with the Pacific Crest Trail. From there, you can turn south to explore the view-packed alpine slopes on the east side of Diamond Peak before returning the way you came.

Mount Yoran over Divide Lake

60 MOUNTAIN VIEW LAKE

Distance: 12.2 miles round trip
Hiking time: 6 hours (day hike or backpack)
Elevation gain: 1100 feet
Difficulty: Moderate
Season: July to October
Best: July (if you can stand the bugs; otherwise mid-August to October)
Map: USFS Diamond Peak Wilderness
Information: Deschutes National Forest—Crescent Ranger District, (541) 433-3200

Directions: Drive Oregon Highway 58 to 7.5 miles southeast of Willamette Pass, then turn west, following signs to Crescent Lake. After 2.3 miles, turn right on paved Forest Road 60, drive 4.7 miles (exactly 0.2 mile past the Tandy Bay turnoff), then turn right at a poorly signed junction with FR 6010. Slowly drive 3.9 miles on this rough and bumpy dirt road to the Snell Lake trailhead. This road may be impassable when wet.

The name "Mountain View Lake" tells you everything you need to know about the merits of this destination. Although this pool provides the best view anywhere of Diamond Peak's long snowy ridge, very few people go here, because the water is too shallow for fish and the small lake is not identified on any map. As a result, the trail provides solitude and avoids the choking dust that plagues the more popular paths to nearby Diamond View and Fawn lakes. July is the most spectacular time to visit, because snow still covers the mountain and the views are at their best. Another advantage of a visit at this time is that the dense clouds of mosquitoes that

follow you around will provide shade by effectively blocking out the sun (just kidding—but only a little).

Follow the Snell Lake Trail, which goes north, almost immediately enters the Diamond Peak Wilderness, and begins a gradual uphill through an open forest of mountain hemlocks and lodgepole pines. As is typical for forests east of the Cascade Divide, the ground cover is limited to a few grouse whortleberries. In 0.5 mile the winding path reaches 9-acre Snell Lake, which features a lovely view of Diamond Peak to the northwest over its tranquil waters. The trail goes around the west side of this irregularly shaped lake, then continues its gentle climb.

The trail passes numerous small ponds (a.k.a. mosquito nurseries), then, at the 2.8-mile point, reaches a possible campsite beside narrow Effie Lake. After this, you climb six short switchbacks to the top of a small ridge, contour past more ponds, and reach cascading Mountain Creek at 4.3 miles. Ford or jump over this pretty creek; then it is another easy mile to a prominent junction at 5.3 miles. Turn left and climb for 0.8 mile to Mountain View Lake. On a calm morning, Diamond Peak is perfectly reflected in the shallow water, although stopping for more than a few seconds to enjoy the view will invite an all-out attack by millions of our invertebrate enemies. If your hike is in mid-August or later, however, you can spend a blissful bug-free night at a good campsite above the lake's southwest shore.

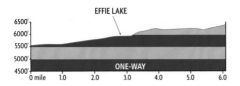

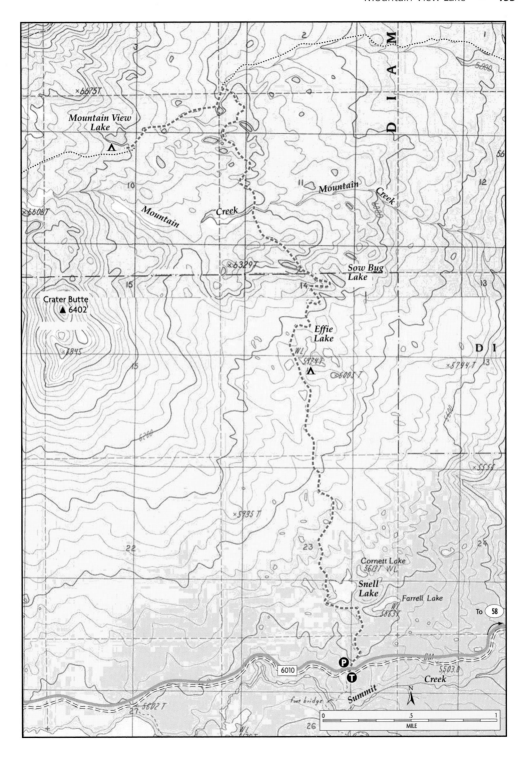

Mountain View Lake nestles at the foot of Diamond Peak.

61   INDIGO LAKE

Distance: 3.8 miles round trip to lake, plus 0.8-mile loop around lake; 4.6 miles total

Hiking time: 2 hours to lake; 0.5-hour loop; 2.5 hours total (day hike or backpack)

Elevation gain: 600 feet

Difficulty: Easy

Season: Late June to October

Best: July and August

Map: USGS Cowhorn Mountain

Information: Willamette National Forest—Middle Fork Ranger District, (541) 782-2283

Directions: From Eugene, drive Oregon Highway 58 southeast 38 miles to a junction 1.5 miles past Oakridge. Turn right, following signs to Hills Creek Dam, and go 0.5 mile to a junction. Turn right on Diamond Drive (Forest Road 21) and go 32 miles to a junction where you turn left on FR 2154. This route soon changes from pavement to badly washboarded gravel and goes 6.4 miles to a T-junction. Turn right and proceed 2.8 miles to the signed trailhead at Timpanogas Lake Campground.

If you started at the mouth of the Willamette River near Portland and traveled upstream, sticking with the larger branch every time a tributary entered the flow, your 309-mile-long journey would end at Timpanogas Lake, the source of Oregon's largest river. For that reason alone it is worth visiting, but if you require more encouragement, consider that this mountain lake also serves as the jumping-off point for several excellent and relatively easy hikes. The best destination is Indigo Lake, a stunning pool at the base of Sawtooth Mountain that makes a great first backpacking trip for youngsters or an easy day hike for the older set. Before starting your hike, walk to the road bridge over the outlet from Timpanogas Lake and stop for a moment to contemplate that this small creek grows to become the mighty Willamette.

From the trailhead, go left on the Indigo Lake Trail. This wide path makes two long, gently graded uphill switchbacks through an attractive forest of mountain hemlocks and Pacific silver firs. After 0.7 mile you come to a junction. Go straight on the leftmost of the three trails that meet here, immediately hop over a small creek, and continue gradually uphill through an attractive forest with an understory of heather and huckleberries. At about 1.5 miles the trail passes a pair of small meadows filled with shooting stars, then comes to a campsite at the north end of Indigo Lake at 1.9 miles. Picnic tables and an outhouse give this campsite amenities that backpackers usually must forgo.

The star attraction at Indigo Lake is the view across the sparkling waters to the cliffs and talus slopes of Sawtooth Mountain, towering majestically above the south shore. An 0.8-mile path circles the lake, taking you past numerous fishing spots and a great swimming hole at the south end of the lake.

Sawtooth Mountain over Indigo Lake

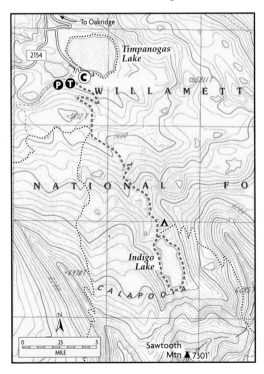

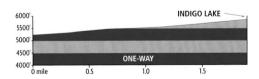

If this short hike has not given you enough exercise, follow a relatively new trail that leaves from just before the camping area at the north end of Indigo Lake and switchbacks up the ridge to the southeast. This scenic path leads to some excellent viewpoints and provides access to a scramble route to the top of Sawtooth Mountain.

62   WOLF CREEK FALLS

Distance: 2.4 miles round trip
Hiking time: 1.5 hours
Elevation gain: 240 feet
Difficulty: Easy
Season: All Year
Best: April to June
Maps: USGS Red Butte
Information: Bureau of Land Management—Roseburg District, (541) 440-4930

Directions: From Roseburg, drive Oregon Highway 138 east 17 miles to Glide, then turn right (south) on Little River Road (a.k.a. County Road 17). Follow this good paved road for 10.6 miles to the Wolf Creek Falls picnic area and trailhead, a little before you reach the Wolf Creek Job Training Center.

The drainages of both the North Umpqua River and its largest tributary, Little River, are blessed with an unusual wealth of beautiful waterfalls, every one of which is worth visiting. For the hiker, arguably the best of this spectacular lot is Wolf Creek Falls, a lovely sliding fall at the end of a woodsy path that is easy enough for families with young children.

The trail starts by crossing a large, curving wooden bridge over Little River before reaching a possibly unmarked junction with an old trail that goes left toward Wolf Creek Campground.

Go straight, take a bridge over Wolf Creek, then begin an easy ramble up the forested banks of that pretty stream. The trail is shaded by a dense canopy of bigleaf maples and Douglas firs, while the forest floor is covered with a green mat of shrubs and wildflowers. One plant that is sometimes found amid this dense greenery is poison oak, so watch your dog and children closely to keep them from getting nasty rashes. Wildflowers are abundant in April and May, with plenty of the usual forest varieties such as oxalis, trillium, inside-out flower, wood violet, and starflower.

The trail's first 0.5 mile is gentle, smooth, and wheelchair-accessible, all the way to a picnic table beside Wolf Creek. Beyond this point the tread is a little rougher and steeper but still relatively easy hiking. At 1.1 miles you pass a 20-foot falls, which some hikers mistake for the main Wolf Creek Falls and are disappointed. Those who persevere, however, and continue another

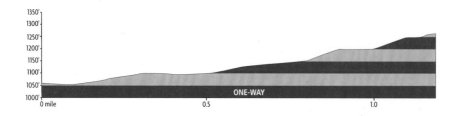

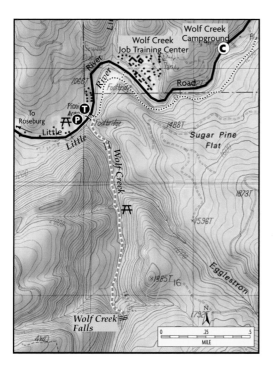

0.1 mile to the real Wolf Creek Falls are rarely disappointed. This near-perfect 75-foot fall, which slides down a steep rock face, is both beautiful to look at and exceptionally photogenic. It's hard not to linger here, so give in to the urge and enjoy a leisurely lunch before returning to your car.

Wolf Creek Falls

63 TOKETEE FALLS

Distance: 0.8 mile round trip
Hiking time: 1 hour
Elevation gain: 200 feet
Difficulty: Easy
Season: All year (except during severe winters)
Best: May and June
Map: USGS Toketee Falls
Information: Umpqua National Forest—Diamond Lake Ranger District, (541) 498-2531

Directions: From Roseburg, take Oregon Highway 138 east to a junction with the paved Toketee–Rigdon Road between mileposts 58 and 59. Turn north and proceed 0.2 mile to a fork, bear left, cross a bridge, then immediately turn left onto the spur road to the Toketee Falls trailhead.

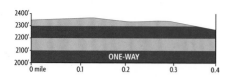

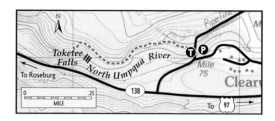

Toketee means "graceful" in the Chinook jargon used by early settlers, trappers, and Native Americans, and there could be no better word to describe the waterfall that carries this name. Here the North Umpqua River plunges in a delicately beautiful falls over the side of an impressive columnar basalt amphitheater framed by towering old-growth forests. All of this combined makes Toketee one of Oregon's most dramatic cascades. Photographers apparently agree with this assessment, because the falls is often depicted in calendars and travel brochures of the state. So why not pack your camera and see what all the fuss is about?

The hiker-only trail starts beside a huge, leaky pipe, through which most of the North Umpqua River's flow is diverted to feed a power station farther down the canyon. The trail takes a gentle, wandering course through a lush forest of giant Douglas firs, western red cedars, and western hemlocks. In the spring this forest is brightened by the blossoms of thimbleberry, Oregon grape, and Pacific rhododendron, while in the fall the yellow leaves of bigleaf maple and the orange leaves of vine maple keep the color show going. Throughout the year the clear waters of the North Umpqua River cascade past moss-covered cliffs, providing scenes of stunning beauty.

Toketee Falls

At the end of its short course, the trail descends a series of wooden steps to an overlook platform immediately downstream from the falls. This short and easy hike is ideal for families with children or those who are just passing through and looking for a quick leg-stretcher.

If you want a little more exercise, take time to visit some of the other outstanding waterfalls that grace this area. Towering Watson Falls is a good option, reachable by a short trail off a well-signed side road just 2 miles east of the Toketee–Rigdon Road turnoff. Another excellent choice is Clearwater Falls, a mossy cascade near a small campground another 10 miles east of Watson Falls.

64 TIPSOO PEAK

Distance: 6.2 miles round trip
Hiking time: 3.5 hours
Elevation gain: 1500 feet
Difficulty: Moderate
Season: Mid-July to October
Best: Late July and August
Map: USFS Mount Thielsen Wilderness
Information: Umpqua National Forest—Diamond Lake Ranger District, (541) 498-2531

Directions: From Roseburg, take Oregon Highway 138 east to a junction at milepost 75 about 4 miles north of Diamond Lake. Turn east onto gravel Forest Road 4793, following signs to Cinnamon Butte Lookout, and drive this washboard-riddled road for 1.7 miles to a fork. Bear right on FR 100 and proceed 3.3 miles to the trailhead. Drive slowly over the last 0.6 mile, because the road is crossed by a series of deep, diagonal waterbars that have a nasty habit of ambushing your car's suspension system.

While the longer trails up nearby Mounts Thielsen and Bailey draw thousands of hikers, surprisingly few people take the well-graded trail to the top of Tipsoo Peak. The oversight is hard to understand, because at 8034 feet, this unassuming summit provides a first-rate panorama that includes almost half the state of Oregon—not that you will notice much of it, because almost all of your attention is likely to be drawn to the outstanding perspectives of Mount Thielsen and Howlock Mountain just a short distance to the south.

The trail starts in a mountain hemlock forest with very limited undergrowth. Shade, on the other hand, is plentiful—a blessing, because this keeps you cool during the steady climb on two long switchbacks to the boundary of the Mount Thielsen Wilderness at 1.1 miles. From here, ascend gentle switchbacks to a series of grassy meadows, where the plant life becomes more varied and attractive. Tiny, showy alpine wildflowers

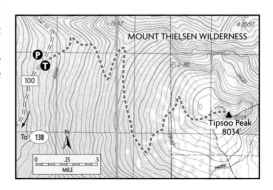

include large numbers of partridge foot, dwarf lupine, and pink heather.

As you continue uphill, the views become more impressive, but the meadows are less lush due to the harsher environment and poor volcanic soils. In fact, by the time you make the steep, 0.2-mile climb to the top, almost nothing is left but rough lava and red cinders. Even the trees have a difficult time surviving. The only remaining specimens are a few windblown snags of whitebark pines and mountain hemlocks.

Of course, by this time the outstanding views are probably all you will notice anyway. In the distance to the north are the Three Sisters and Diamond Peak. Somewhat closer are Diamond Lake and Mount Bailey to the southwest and shimmering Miller Lake to the east. The most dramatic scene is to the south: the sharp spire of Mount Thielsen and the contorted crags of Howlock Mountain. Directly below your viewpoint is the pumice-covered flat of Tipsoo Meadow, a sparsely forested plain created 7700 years ago when the cataclysmic eruption of Mount Mazama buried this area under enormous quantities of pumice. The vegetation has yet to recover from this event, finding it hard to get a foothold without topsoil or surface water. Early morning provides the most dramatic lighting for photographs.

Howlock Mountain and Mount Thielsen from Tipsoo Peak

65 THIELSEN CREEK MEADOWS LOOP

Distance: 15.7 miles round trip
Hiking time: 8 hours (day hike or backpack)
Elevation gain: 2000 feet
Difficulty: Strenuous
Season: Mid-July to October
Best: Mid-July to mid-August
Map: USFS Mount Thielsen Wilderness
Information: Umpqua National Forest—Diamond Lake Ranger District, (541) 498-2531

Directions: From Roseburg, take Oregon Highway 138 east to the Diamond Lake Resort turnoff between mileposts 78 and 79. Turn west and almost immediately pull into the Howlock Mountain/Thielsen Creek trailhead.

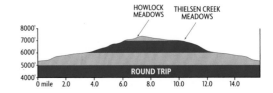

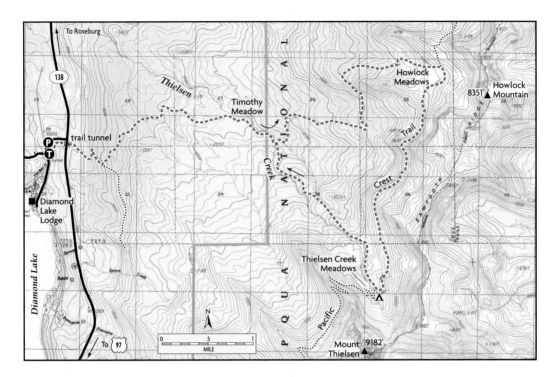

The distinctive spire of Mount Thielsen, the "Lightning Rod of the Cascades," rises impressively above the open forests east of Diamond Lake, drawing rave reviews from thousands of campers, anglers, and car-bound tourists. Although the world-class views across the lake are enough for the average sightseer, hikers will naturally get itchy feet and look for ways to get closer to the mountain. The best way to satisfy this desire is an attractive loop that visits a wildflower glen beneath the towering cliffs on the north side of Mount Thielsen and a less well-known meadow near the jagged spine of Howlock Mountain. **Warning:** A trail-riding service uses this area, so the trails are pounded to dust by countless hooves.

From the trailhead signboard, take the left fork and walk 0.2 mile to a tunnel beneath Highway 138. Immediately after, stay right at two successive junctions with unofficial horse trails, then climb gradually but steadily in an open forest of lodgepole pines, mountain hemlocks, and Pacific silver firs. About 1.1 miles from the trailhead is a junction with the Spruce Ridge Trail to the

right. Go straight and continue uphill to Timothy Meadow, a bright green swath of grasses and flowers studded with trees and bisected by the clear waters of Thielsen Creek. At the far end of this oasis, hop across the creek and reach a junction at 3.5 miles at the start of the loop.

To save the best scenery for last, veer left and make a long ascent through a rather monotonous mountain hemlock forest that takes you to the edge of the rolling pumice plain of Howlock Meadows at 6.7 miles. This spot was buried in the enormous eruption of Mount Mazama some 7700 years ago and has yet to develop an adequate layer of topsoil. Only a few stunted flowers and grasses survive. Camping here yields an evening enjoying fine views of jagged Howlock Mountain, but the only water is from lingering snow patches through July.

The trail skirts the north side of Howlock Meadows to a junction with the Pacific Crest Trail (PCT) at 7 miles. Turn right (south), loop around the meadows, then begin an up-and-down (mostly down) traverse of a viewless hillside covered with large mountain hemlocks. The

traverse ends at Thielsen Creek Meadows at 10 miles, which has a spring-fed creek, good campsites, and great views of Mount Thielsen looming like an enormous black wall above the meadows. There is a junction here with the Thielsen Creek Trail. The best views are about 100 yards to the right (downstream) from this crossing.

If you spend the night at Thielsen Creek, you can enjoy an outstanding side trip. It leads to the summit of Mount Thielsen, which athletic hikers can reach by a very steep climbers route that intersects the PCT 2.2 miles south of Thielsen Creek.

To complete the loop, from the PCT in Thielsen Creek Meadows turn right (west) on the Thielsen Creek Trail and descend through open forest with views back to towering Mount Thielsen. The route generally stays fairly close to the creek all the way to the junction at 12.2 miles with the Howlock Mountain Trail at the upper end of Timothy Meadow. Turn left, cross the creek, and return 3.5 miles the way you came.

Mount Thielsen over Thielsen Creek

66 ROCKY RIDGE

Distance: 7 miles round trip
Hiking time: 3 hours
Elevation gain: 1300 feet
Difficulty: Moderate
Season: Late June to early November
Best: Early to mid-July
Map: USFS Rogue–Umpqua Divide Wilderness
Information: Umpqua National Forest—Tiller Ranger District, (541) 825-3100

Directions: From Medford, drive Oregon Highway 62 northeast 58 miles to a junction, where you veer left on Hwy 230. Go 0.9 mile, then turn left on gravel Forest Road 6510. After 1.7 miles bear right at a junction, go 0.5 mile, then turn left on FR 6515. Drive 6.8 miles on this narrow gravel road, passing the impressive rock spires of Rabbit Ears, then turn right on rough dirt FR 530. Slowly drive 1.8 miles to the trailhead, where the road makes a sharp right turn.

The Rogue–Umpqua Divide Wilderness, a narrow preserve in the forested hills west of Crater Lake, protects a little-known landscape of subalpine lakes, unusual rock formations, view-packed ridges, and some of the best wildflower meadows

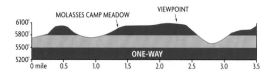

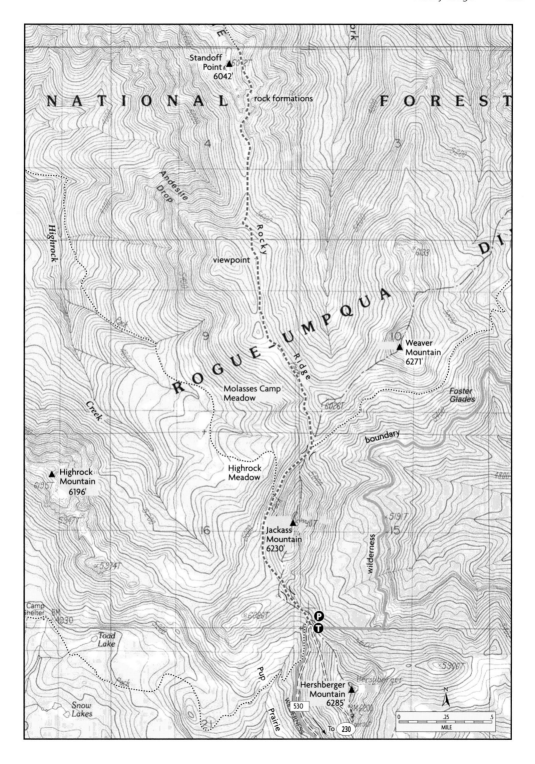

Standoff
Point
6042'

rock formations

N A T I O N A L

F O R E S T

Andesite
Drop

Highrock

Rocky

viewpoint

R O G U E – U M P Q U A

D I

Weaver
Mountain
6271'

Ridge

Foster
Glades

Molasses Camp
Meadow

Creek

boundary

Highrock
Mountain
6196'

Highrock
Meadow

wilderness

Jackass
Mountain
6230'

Camp
shelter

Toad
Lake

Pup

Hershberger
Mountain
6285'

Snow
Lakes

Prairie

530

To 230

N

0   .25   .5
MILE

Highrock Mountain over Molasses Camp Meadow

in Oregon. With no major peaks or eye-popping alpine scenery to draw the crowds, this area's more subtle charms see relatively few hikers. The most popular destination is Fish Lake, but the best scenery is along Rocky Ridge, a rugged divide loaded with picturesque rock formations and wonderful viewpoints with unusual perspectives of the upper Rogue River drainage.

Two trails start from the trailhead. Go north on the Rogue–Umpqua Divide Trail, which climbs 0.3 mile through dense forest to a saddle, then makes a mostly downhill traverse around the west side of Jackass Mountain. At 0.8 mile, bear right at a fork, then complete the half-circle around Jackass Mountain to a junction at 1.2 miles. Here you go left and ascend 0.2 mile to

sloping Molasses Camp Meadow, where you often see deer and elk and are always treated to a wonderful view of craggy Highrock Mountain to the southwest. In early July this meadow is filled with a white-blooming variety of lupine.

The well-graded trail now switches to the east side of Rocky Ridge, contours to a viewpoint at 2.3 miles, then gradually descends 0.4 mile to a narrow saddle. Soon after, you reach an area of towering rock walls and pinnacles at 3 miles guarding the south side of Standoff Point. These ruggedly scenic ancient volcanic rocks create a natural rock garden with stonecrop, paintbrush, woolly daisy, yarrow, penstemon, and several other colorful species blooming from late June to mid-July.

The trail cuts around and through these rock formations, then climbs rather steeply to the hike's highest and best viewpoint: the east shoulder of Standoff Point. From here, a grand vista east takes in the two-pronged tower of Castle Rock; the distant, rounded form of Mount Bailey; and pointed Mount Thielsen. You can even see Hillman Peak and several other high points on the rim of Crater Lake. The trail beyond this viewpoint follows a narrow ridge with good views, but most hikers turn around here.

If you still have energy when you return to the trailhead, hike 0.5 mile down the Acker Divide Trail to the lush wildflower gardens of Pup Prairie.

67 WIZARD ISLAND

Distance: 2.2-mile round-trip approach; 2.5 miles round trip on Wizard Island; 4.7 miles total
Hiking time: 1 hour, approach trail; 1–2 hours on Wizard Island; 2–3 hours total (plus 1.5-hour round-trip boat ride and possible waiting time)
Elevation gain: 650 feet, approach trail; 800 feet on Wizard Island; 1450 feet total
Difficulty: Moderate
Season: July to October
Best: July to October
Map: Trails Illustrated—Crater Lake National Park
Information: Crater Lake National Park, (541) 594-3000

Directions: From Medford, drive Oregon Highway 62 northeast 58 miles to its junction with Hwy 230, where you veer left. Take Hwy 230 north and east 24 miles to Hwy 138, then turn right and continue 4 miles to Crater Lake National Park's North Entrance Road.

Head south to its junction with Rim Drive in the northwest section of the park, go left (east) 4.5 miles on Rim Drive, then turn into the large parking lot for the Cleetwood Cove Trail.

The world-famous, awe-inspiring views from the rim of Crater Lake are impossible to improve upon. Millions of tourists have seen these vistas, and countless postcards and calendar photographs ensure that all Oregonians (and much of the rest of the world) are intimately familiar with these breathtaking scenes. But relatively few of those admiring masses have achieved a water-level perspective from inside the caldera. This unusual hike provides that opportunity by taking you to the top of Wizard Island, the distinctive cinder cone featured in so many of those famous photographs. **Note:** Dogs are prohibited on this trail, as they are on all trails in the park. Also, Wizard Island has no piped water and almost no shade; bring a hat and extra water.

Your first stop is at the booth beside the parking lot to purchase a ticket for the boat tour. A schedule posted at this booth informs you that tours leave about once an hour, sometimes more frequently on busy summer weekends. The tours are popular, so arrive as early in the day as possible. Due to time constraints, the boat operators do not allow anyone to off-load on Wizard Island after 3:00 PM. Be sure to schedule enough time to hike on Wizard Island and catch a return boat afterward.

The wide approach trail departs from the south side of Rim Drive opposite the parking lot and descends in long, moderately graded switchbacks 1.1 miles to the dock facility at the lakeshore. It takes about thirty minutes to reach the bottom, depending on how many slow-footed tourists are traveling in front of you.

The 45-minute boat ride includes, in addition to awesome scenery, fascinating narration

from a park ranger who explains the geologic history of the lake, answers questions, and identifies landmarks along the way. At Wizard Island, those off-loading for the hike are assigned numbers that give them priority to catch later boats.

The trail departs from the dock area and climbs 0.1 mile over jumbled lava flows to a junction. (Those not up for the climb to the top

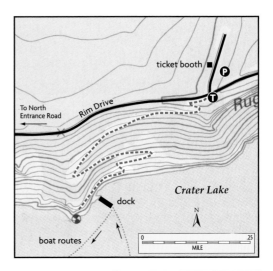

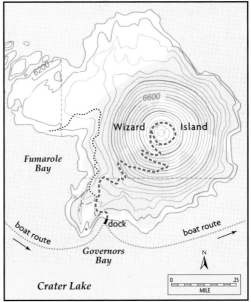

Hillman Peak from the top of Wizard Island

of the island can turn left on a shorter trail that goes 0.4 mile over sharp lava to Fumarole Bay.) Stay right on the summit trail and steadily ascend (gently at first, then steeply) through lava, cinder fields, and open forests of Shasta red firs and mountain hemlocks 1.1 miles to the view-packed summit. A 0.3-mile loop trail goes around the edge of the small summit crater.

Those who hike very quickly can zip to the top and back in an hour, just in time to catch the next departing boat. A more reasonable itinerary allows for two hours, but be prepared to wait—there may be no room on the boat if not enough passengers disembark at the island. The return boat ride takes a different course, so you can enjoy more great views of the caldera walls. Be sure to save enough energy for the 650-foot climb back to the trailhead on Rim Drive.

68 GARFIELD PEAK

Distance: 3 miles round trip
Hiking time: 2 hours
Elevation gain: 1000 feet
Difficulty: Moderate
Season: Mid-July to October
Best: Mid-July to August
Map: Trails Illustrated—Crater Lake National Park
Information: Crater Lake National Park, (541) 594-3000

Directions: From Medford, drive Oregon Highway 62 northeast 75 miles to the South Entrance Road of Crater Lake National Park and proceed to the main parking lot for the Rim Village Visitor Center.

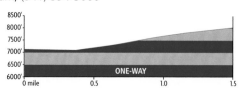

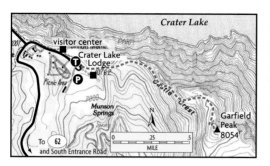

View of Crater Lake from Garfield Peak

Several short trails lead to viewpoints along the rim of Crater Lake, and for terrific scenery you really cannot go wrong taking any (or all) of them. One of the best starts from Crater Lake Lodge, with its classic view of Wizard Island, and climbs near the precipitous edge of the crater to the top of windswept Garfield Peak. Visitors are sometimes surprised to learn that Garfield Peak was named not for the U.S. president but for his son, also named James Garfield, who served as the Secretary of the Interior under President Theodore Roosevelt. Mr. Garfield was the first cabinet secretary to visit Crater Lake after it became a national park in 1902. From the summit of his namesake peak, you can revel in a magnificent panorama of the deepest and perhaps the most beautiful lake in the United States. **Note:** Dogs are prohibited on this trail, as they are on all trails in the park.

Walk a short distance east to historic Crater Lake Lodge and follow the paved trail that starts beside the back porch. This scenic route soon changes to a dirt surface, goes through a saddle at 0.2 mile, and slowly ascends past ever more impressive viewpoints and sloping meadows filled with July and August wildflowers. Several moderately graded switchbacks lead into a higher and harsher environment of stunted trees, small alpine wildflowers, and rocks. Snowfields often remain on the trail well into August. At the summit, you can spend hours enjoying the views. If you forgot to bring a windbreaker, however, your time may be limited, because cold winds often blow over the summit, sending chills down the spines of unprepared hikers.

69 SEVEN LAKES BASIN AND SKY LAKES

Distance: 30 miles round trip
Hiking time: 3–4 days
Elevation gain: 3900 feet
Difficulty: Moderate
Season: July to October
Best: Mid-August to October
Map: USFS Sky Lakes Wilderness
Information: Fremont–Winema National Forest—Klamath Falls Ranger District, (541) 883-6714

Directions: From Fort Klamath on Oregon Highway 62 south of Crater Lake National Park, drive 4 miles west on Nicholson Road to a fork. Bear left onto a gravel road, following signs to Sevenmile Trailhead. Drive 0.4 mile, then bear right on gravel Forest Road 3334 and drive 5.6 miles to the road-end trailhead.

Tread carefully in the delicate environment around Cliff Lake.

The Sky Lakes Wilderness protects a narrow strip of forested mountains along the Cascade Divide south of Crater Lake. The wilderness is popular with lake lovers, who delight in the region's countless lakes and ponds. Unfortunately, all that water feeds an enormous population of invertebrate vampires. So in July, you will cover the miles very quickly, because the mosquitoes instill a strong desire to keep moving. It is better to go from late August to mid-September, when the bugs are mostly gone and the huckleberries are ripe.

The trail immediately crosses the meager flow of Sevenmile Creek, then climbs gradually through a pleasant forest of Shasta red firs, lodgepole pines, and mountain hemlocks. The ground

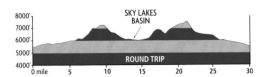

cover is dominated by grouse whortleberry and huckleberry. After 1.8 miles of gentle climbing, you come to a junction with the Pacific Crest Trail (PCT).

For a worthwhile side trip, visit Ranger Spring, the source of the Middle Fork Rogue River: turn right, walk 250 yards, then turn left on a dead-end trail that goes 0.8 mile to the ice-cold springs. Return to the PCT (now having hiked 3.6 miles), where the main route goes left (south).

Follow a woodsy, undulating course to a junction at 6.2 miles at the edge of Seven Lakes Basin. To start your loop through this popular basin, turn right and go 0.3 mile to meadow-rimmed Grass Lake, a scenic introduction to this area, with campsites and a particularly good view from the north shore. The next lake you come to is Middle Lake, which features campsites and a nice view of Violet Hill to the west. At a junction at 7.1 miles with the Lake Ivern Trail, go straight and you'll soon come to Cliff Lake. Although all the lakes in Seven Lakes Basin are scenic, Cliff Lake is the most dramatic (and popular) with outstanding views

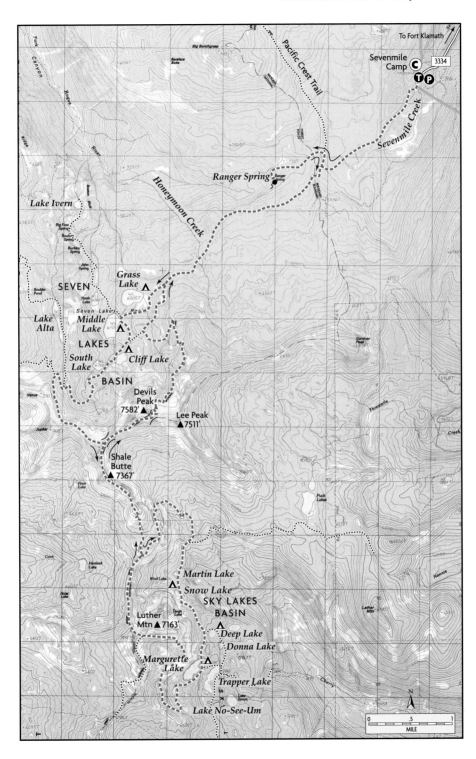

Seven Lakes Basin and Sky Lakes map showing trails, peaks, and lakes.

- To Fort Klamath
- Sevenmile Camp
- 3334
- Pacific Crest Trail
- Sevenmile Creek
- Big Bunchgrass
- Boneface Butte
- Rogue River
- Fork Canyon
- Ranger Spring
- Honeymoon Creek
- Lake Ivern
- Big Foot Spring
- Boulay Spring
- Buckley Spring
- John Spring
- Boulder Pond
- SEVEN
- Grass Lake
- North Lake
- Seven Lakes Basin
- Lake Alta
- Middle Lake
- LAKES
- South Lake
- Cliff Lake
- BASIN
- Devils Peak 7582'
- Lee Peak 7511'
- Venus
- Jupiter
- Shale Butte 7367'
- Finch Lake
- Gardner Peak
- Threemile Creek
- Puck Lakes
- Hemlock Lake
- Creek
- Hole Lake
- Wind Lake
- Martin Lake
- Snow Lake
- SKY LAKES BASIN
- Luther Mtn 7163'
- Trap Lake
- Deep Lake
- Donna Lake
- Luther Mtn
- Nannie
- Margurette Lake
- Trapper Lake
- Lake Sonya
- Cherry
- Lake No-See-Um
- N
- 0   .5   1
- MILE

of craggy Devils Peak looming above the south shore. The Forest Service has roped off trampled lakeshore campsites for restoration; please camp only at designated sites away from the shore or, even better, make your visit to this lake a day trip.

Continue west past South Lake, then gently ascend to a junction with the trail to Lake Alta at 9.2 miles. Bear left, then left again at a second junction in 0.2 mile and climb a view-packed route to a reunion with the PCT at 10.5 miles in a saddle southwest of Devils Peak; this ends the western half of the Seven Lakes Basin loop.

To reach the Sky Lakes Basin loop, turn right (south) and round the talus slopes on the west side of Shale Butte, where you obtain the first good views of Mount McLoughlin to the southwest. Descend a scenic ridgeline and come to a sign at the junction with the Snow Lakes Trail at 12.2 miles. Turn left to start the loop, and pass viewpoints and several small lakes in a circuitous, switchbacking descent to a junction with the Nannie Creek Trail at 14.5 miles. Go straight and soon pass several small lakes with views of the rocky crags and talus slopes of nearby Luther Mountain; there are campsites at both Martin and Snow lakes. At a junction with the Donna Lake Trail at 15.9 miles, go straight again; then in 0.4 mile reach Margurette Lake, the largest and prettiest in the Sky Lakes Basin. Some areas near the lakeshore are closed for restoration, but there are plenty of legal campsites in the nearby forest.

Above the northeast shore of Margurette Lake is a junction. Trapper Lake, a short walk to the left, is worth a visit, but the recommended Divide Trail goes right and winds uphill past numerous small lakes to a stunning viewpoint of the Sky Lakes Basin, snowy Mount McLoughlin, huge Upper Klamath Lake, and even California's Mount Shasta. From here, the trail makes several short uphill switchbacks to a ridge-top junction with the PCT at 19 miles. Turn right and walk 1.1 miles on this view-packed trail back north to close this loop at the Snow Lakes junction. Go straight and retrace your steps to the junction southwest of Devils Peak at 21.8 miles.

To close the Seven Lakes Basin loop, stay on the PCT as it takes you past Devils Peak (well worth a scramble to the top), then switchbacks down to the junction near Grass Lake at 25.5 miles. From there, return 4.5 miles the way you came.

70 MOUNTAIN LAKES LOOP

Distance: 17.1 miles round trip
Hiking time: 2 days
Elevation gain: 2700 feet
Difficulty: Strenuous
Season: July to October
Best: July
Map: USFS Mountain Lakes Wilderness
Information: Fremont-Winema National Forest—Klamath Falls Ranger District, (541) 883-6714

Directions: From Klamath Falls, drive Oregon Highway 140 northwest 22 miles, then turn left on gravel Forest Road 3637, following signs to the Varney Creek trailhead. Drive 1.8 miles to a prominent junction, turn left onto FR 3664, then go 2 miles to a road-end parking area 100 yards past the signed trailhead.

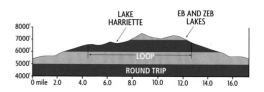

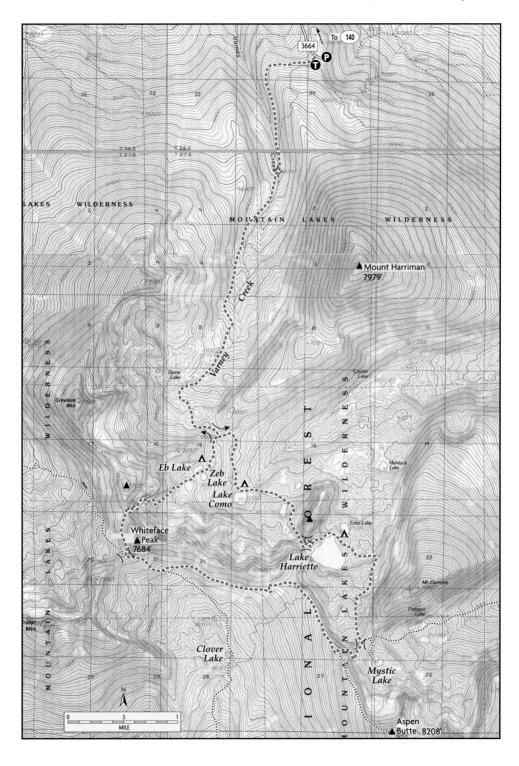

Lake Harriette

Although the Mountain Lakes area was one of the first in the country to receive official wilderness designation, this small preserve is still generally overlooked by the hiking public. Set to the east of the Cascade Divide, this compact area of rugged peaks and sparkling lakes lies in the rain shadow of the mountains to the west. As a result, the weather is better for hiking and the forests are drier, which allows species such as white fir to thrive here even though the tree does not grow in the main part of the Cascade Range.

The trail climbs gradually across a hillside covered with ponderosa pines, Douglas firs, and white firs to a crossing of small Varney Creek on a plank bridge. You then make a long, gentle climb through open areas choked with head-high manzanita bushes and forested areas with lodgepole pines, Engelmann spruces, Shasta red firs, and mountain hemlocks. The ground cover is generally sparse with only scattered grasses, wildflowers, and low bushes.

At the 4.5-mile point is a junction and the start of the loop. A clockwise circuit is recommended, so bear left and go up and down for 0.6 mile to Lake Como, which has good campsites and a scenic setting beneath the talus slopes of Whiteface Peak. The trail then climbs to a 6900-foot pass, descends three switchbacks, and comes to Lake Harriette at 6.3 miles. It is the largest, deepest, and arguably the most scenic lake in this wilderness. The shoreline is rimmed by heather and mountain hemlocks, and several scenic peaks and ridges surround the basin. Not surprisingly, Lake Harriette is the most popular location in the Mountain Lakes Wilderness. Don't expect to be alone.

Beyond this lake, the trail makes a fairly steep climb to a junction in a 7350-foot pass at 8.2 miles. The main trail turns right, then gains another 250 feet to a view-packed ridge. The loop trail, which is often sketchy in this area, descends a gentle ridge past a pair of excellent viewpoints above Lake Harriette.

The rocky trail then turns left off the ridgeline and makes a rolling traverse across talus slopes and through mountain hemlock forests to a junction with the Clover Creek Trail at 10.2 miles. Bear right and steadily climb 0.6 mile through open forest to a junction in a high pass. Turn right, cut across the west face of Whiteface Peak, then go down five steep switchbacks to Eb and Zeb lakes. The trail goes through the strip of forested land between these shallow twins, passes a good campsite above their north shores at 12.3 miles, then goes downhill to a junction with the Varney Creek Trail in 0.3 mile to close the loop. Turn left and return the way you came.

NORTHEASTERN OREGON

Near the trailhead in Smith Rock State Park (Hike 71)

Not to disparage the beauties of better-known hiking regions such as the Oregon coast, the Cascade Range, and the Columbia River Gorge, but many veteran hikers agree that the Beaver State's best scenery lies in its northeastern corner. The dominant geographic features of this diverse region are the forested hills of the Blue Mountains and the gently rolling wheatfields of the Columbia Plateau. The latter is something of a wasteland for hikers, because most of the land is privately owned.

The Blue Mountains, on the other hand, have a wealth of trails to explore. The most spectacular paths wind through two subranges of "the Blues": the Strawberry Mountains and the Elkhorn Range, where peaks reach skyward in impressive displays of rugged granite. The other subranges of the Blue Mountains present no such jagged skylines, but they feature outstanding highlights of their own, such as the incredible wildflower displays of the Ochoco Mountains and the impressive canyons of the Wenaha, Umatilla, and John Day rivers. If you are willing to make the somewhat longer drive to this little-known region, you will find more than enough great trails to keep you happily hoofing it for decades.

71 SMITH ROCK STATE PARK LOOP

Distance: 3.8 miles round trip
Hiking time: 2.5 hours
Elevation gain: 800 feet
Difficulty: Moderate
Season: All year
Best: April and May; September and October (avoid midsummer heat)
Map: USGS Redmond
Information: Smith Rock State Park, (541) 923-7551

Directions: From Redmond, take US 97 north 4.5 miles to Terrebone. Turn right (east), following signs to Smith Rock State Park, and keep following signs for 3.4 miles to one of the park's several parking lots. Finding a place to park can be difficult, especially on weekends, because climbers arrive by the hundreds and they tend to be *very* early risers.

Smith Rock State Park is famous among rock climbers as a great place to go vertical. Less well known is that the park is an equally good destination for those who prefer to travel horizontally. The orange, yellow, and red walls of rhyolite rock hold climbing pitons well but are also spectacularly scenic attractions for those who prefer to just look on and marvel. The meandering Crooked River, which has carved deeply into the rock, adds greatly to the scenery and provides a natural hiking corridor around the dramatic rock formations. Good trails follow the wildlife-rich river, travel through stands of ponderosa pines and western junipers, and climb to impressive viewpoints where you can sit for hours watching climbers inch their way up the rock walls. To protect the park's sensitive soils, land managers ask that all hikers stay on the trail.

The trail starts on a dirt maintenance road that

drops off the edge of a rimrock mesa near the restroom and switchbacks down to a bridge over the Crooked River. Immediately on the other side of this span is a junction at 0.4 mile. For a counterclockwise loop, angle right and climb rather steeply to the wide top of Misery Ridge. The going becomes much easier on this rolling, sagebrush-dotted ridge top, where the trail goes west to an amazing viewpoint at 1 mile of the most distinctive feature in the park, Monkey Face. This almost 400-foot-tall, free-standing tower is a major challenge for rock climbers and an impressive sight for hikers. A side trail goes to an overlook directly across from the tower,

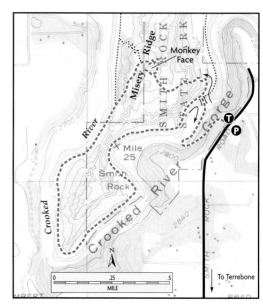

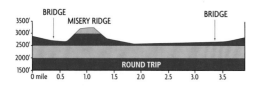

where you can sit and talk to climbers as they rest in the small cave that forms the "mouth" of Monkey Face.

To complete the recommended loop, switch-back steeply downhill around the north side of Monkey Face to a junction near the pillar's base. The trail straight ahead drops directly to the Crooked River, but the recommended route goes left and makes a more gradual downhill traverse to the riverbank at 1.6 miles. If you turn around here and look back at Monkey Face, you will immediately recognize how this landmark got its descriptive name.

The gentle trail follows the river upstream around a sharp bend at 2.2 miles and past a stunning series of cliffs and spires that are often crawling with rock climbers. If you can take your eyes off the scenery, the river corridor is a good place to watch for wildlife, most notably Canada geese, prairie falcons, golden eagles and other raptors, and porcupines. There are also a few rattlesnakes, so watch your step. Numerous short side paths lead to marked climbing routes. At 3.4 miles, the trail returns to the bridge and the close of the loop.

Monkey Face

72 STEINS PILLAR

Distance: 4 miles round trip
Hiking time: 2 hours
Elevation gain: 700 feet
Difficulty: Easy
Season: April to November
Best: May and June
Map: USGS Steins Pillar, Salt Butte
Information: Ochoco National Forest, (541) 416-6500

Directions: From Prineville, drive US 26 east 8.5 miles to a junction at the east end of Ochoco Reservoir. Turn left (north) on Mill Creek Road, following signs to Wildcat Camp, and drive 6.8 miles on this initially paved then gravel road to a junction with Forest Road 500. To see the pillar from below, go straight and drive 1.4 miles to a signed viewpoint pullout. To reach the trailhead, turn right (east) on FR 500 and go 2.1 miles to the unsigned trailhead parking area and turnaround loop on the left.

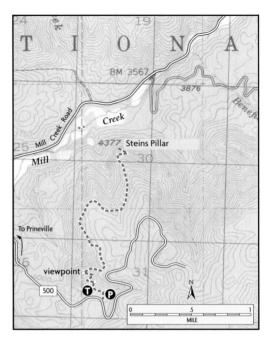

Steins Pillar

The first time Steins Pillar comes into view, it is almost hard to believe what you are seeing. You just do not expect a 350-foot-tall tower to rise directly out of the otherwise undistinguished hills in the western Ochoco Mountains. You look on in awe and contemplate how this narrow, mis-

placed pinnacle of pinkish yellow volcanic tuff ended up in this unlikely spot and feel an uncontrollable urge to reach out and touch the pillar to ensure that your eyes aren't deceiving you. Since private land blocks access from the road, to convince yourself that it is not an optical illusion, you have to go around to a scenic trail that takes you to the base of the remarkable pillar.

The trail departs from the northeast side of the turnaround loop and soon crosses a woodsy gully below a small spring. Follow the trickling creek downstream for 200 yards, then curve right and climb four rounded switchbacks through a forest of ponderosa pines and Douglas firs. Reversing the usual pattern in Oregon, the environment becomes drier as you gain elevation, so by the time you reach a rocky viewpoint at 0.4 mile, you are surrounded by a scrubland of aromatic sagebrush and western junipers. From this viewpoint, you take in excellent views west to the snowcapped Three Sisters and Mount Bachelor. In May, tiny wildflowers such as desert parsley, prairie star, and phlox add patches of color to the dry surroundings.

From the viewpoint, the trail turns east, ascends a bit more, then begins a rolling traverse north through partial forest and across open slopes. Even though you know it is coming, little in the terrain suggests the presence of a towering pinnacle just ahead. At the 1.3-mile point, the trail tops a spur ridge, curves right, then goes mostly downhill through forest to a rocky overlook beside massive Steins Pillar. To actually touch the rock, follow a steep climbers path that goes down to the base of the pillar, where daring souls begin their route to the top.

73 JOHN DAY FOSSIL BEDS TRAILS

Distance: Carroll Rim Trail, 1.6 miles round trip; Painted Hills Viewpoint Trail, 0.6 mile round trip; Painted Cove Trail, 0.2-mile loop; Blue Basin Loop, 4-mile loop; 6.4 miles total

Hiking time: Carroll Rim, Painted Hills Viewpoint, and Painted Cove trails, 1.5 hours; Blue Basin Loop, 2 hours; 3.5 hours total

Elevation gain: Carroll Rim Trail, 400 feet; Painted Hills Viewpoint Trail, 100 feet; Painted Cove Trail, 50 feet; Blue Basin Loop, 1050 feet; 1600 feet total

Difficulty: Easy to moderate

Season: All year (avoid midsummer heat)

Best: Spring and fall

Maps: USGS Painted Hills, Picture Gorge West, Picture Gorge East

Information: John Day Fossil Beds National Monument, (541) 987-2333

Directions: To reach the Painted Hills unit of John Day Fossil Beds National Monument, take US 26 to a junction 3.5 miles west of Mitchell. Turn north on paved Burnt Ranch Road and follow it 5.7 miles to a signed junction. Turn left and drive 1.1 miles on this initially paved then gravel road to a ridge-top junction and parking for the Carroll Rim Trail. The Painted Hills Viewpoint trailhead is 0.2 mile south. Continue west on the gravel road 1.1 miles to reach the Painted Cove trailhead.

To reach the monument's Sheep Rock unit (Blue Basin Loop), return to US 26 and drive 37 miles east to a junction with Oregon Highway 19. Turn left (north) and drive 5.4 miles to the trailhead parking lot.

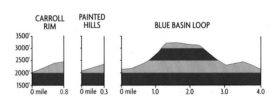

In the rolling, juniper-dotted hills of north-central Oregon are several isolated pockets of colorful volcanic ash and clay. These places have gained fame in the scientific community, because they preserve a remarkably complete fossil record of North America's plant and animal life over the last 55 million years. But you do not have to be a paleontologist to appreciate this region; admiring the colorful scenery takes no expertise. Although most of the trails are short, by combining several hikes you can enjoy two full days of very scenic hiking. **Note:** Collecting fossils is prohibited on national monument land.

For the best overview of the Painted Hills, take the well-graded Carroll Rim Trail from the small pullout beside the ridge-top road junction. It begins from the north side of the road, then makes one long switchback up an open, sun-exposed hillside to a ridge-top viewpoint at 0.8 mile. From here you have a thrilling view of the colorfully striated hills.

For a closer look at those spectacular hills, follow the popular Painted Hills Viewpoint Trail as it climbs 0.3 mile to a classic postcard viewpoint of the hills. The colors change depending on lighting and moisture content but always feature

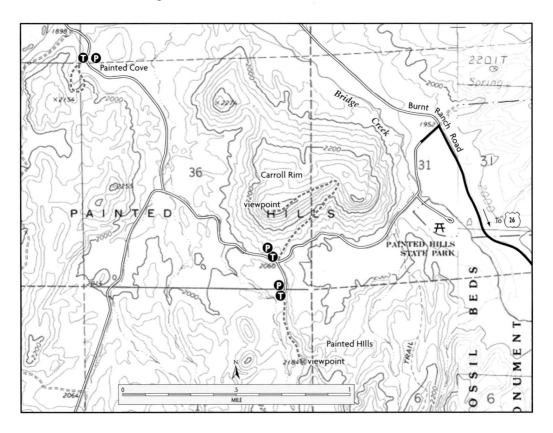

reds, tans, pinks, yellows, and blacks.

The short but excellent Painted Cove Trail loops 0.2 mile through an incredibly colorful area with several interpretive signs that explain the geologic history of these hills. In May, you might also see the showy, pinkish white blossoms of bitterroot.

The longest and most difficult trail is the Blue Basin Loop in the monument's Sheep Rock unit. The trail forks beside the parking lot. For a clockwise circuit, bear left, skirt an irrigated field, then go gradually up a usually waterless drainage. On your right are scenic light tan or greenish white outcroppings of fluted badlands. In May, look for larkspurs, prairie stars, lomatiums, dandelions, brodiaeas, and other wildflowers brightening the grassy areas below the badlands.

A few uphill switchbacks take you to the trail's high point at 1.5 miles and a 0.1-mile spur trail to a grand vista of the John Day Valley and the bad-

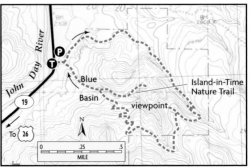

lands of Blue Basin (actually more a light green color). The trail then loops around the head of the basin, goes over a pair of fence stiles at the borders of a private inholding, then descends numerous short switchbacks to a junction at 3 miles with the 0.4-mile Island-in-Time Nature Trail.

The trailhead is 0.2 mile to the left, but it is worthwhile to first turn right on the wide, gravel,

The Painted Hills in John Day Fossil Beds National Monument

dead-end nature trail into Blue Basin. The route is very scenic with eroded cliffs and spires. Interpretive signs stress the importance of the thousands of fossils that have been discovered here.

74 ARCH ROCK

Distance: 0.7 mile round trip
Hiking time: 0.5 hour
Elevation gain: 300 feet
Difficulty: Easy
Season: May to October
Best: Late May to mid-July
Map: USGS Susanville
Information: Malheur National Forest—Blue Mountain Ranger District, (541) 575-3000

Directions: From Pendleton, take US 395 south 77 miles to a junction immediately before a bridge over the Middle Fork John Day River. Turn left (southeast) on paved Middle Fork Road (County Road 20) and go 22.4 miles to a junction. Turn right on gravel Forest Road 36, drive 5.3 miles, then bear left on FR 3650. The signed trailhead is on the left 0.3 mile along this narrow, gravel road.

From John Day, take US 26 east 8.5 miles, then turn left (north) onto paved Keeney Fork Road (County Road 18). Drive 9.7 miles to a junction at Fourcorners, turn right on gravel FR 36, then proceed 8.9 miles to the FR 3650 turnoff. The trailhead is on the left 0.3 mile along this road.

Arch Rock is a beautiful result of ancient vocanic activity.

Although the name exhibits a remarkable lack of imagination, Arch Rock is an accurate description of this photogenic stone arch on a flower-covered hillside in Malheur National Forest. The short trail to the arch is easy enough for anyone, but it remains virtually unknown to all but a few locals. This is due entirely to the arch being so far off the beaten track, not because of a lack of scenery.

The trail, officially designated a national recreation trail, steadily ascends a grassy hillside dotted with ponderosa pines, western larches, Douglas firs, and grand firs. In late spring and early summer, wildflowers such as prairie star, lomatium, clarkia, wood violet, and glacier lily add color to the grasslands. You soon pass several lichen-covered rock outcroppings, which, like Arch Rock, are composed of solidified volcanic ash and mudflows that cooled millions of years ago. These exposed outcroppings are still standing because they have withstood the effects of erosion better than the surrounding rock.

The trail takes you over a grassy hump at 0.3 mile just above Arch Rock, then goes down one

switchback to a close-up view of the trail's star attraction. The hole in the arch, easy to reach, is large enough to walk through.

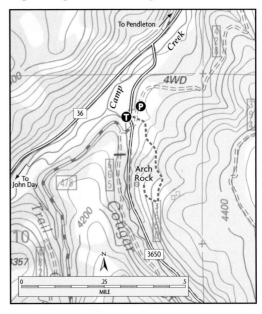

75   BALDY MOUNTAIN

Distance: 6 miles round trip
Hiking time: 3 hours
Elevation gain: 1300 feet
Difficulty: Moderate
Season: Late June to October
Best: July
Map: USFS Strawberry Mountain Wilderness
Information: Malheur National Forest—Blue Mountain Ranger District, (541) 575-3000

Directions: From John Day, drive US 26 east 5.5 miles to a junction halfway between mileposts 168 and 169. Turn right (south) onto Pine Creek Road (County Road 54) and stick with this road as it changes from pavement to good gravel then rough dirt and climbs past several mining shacks and old homesteads. At 7.1 miles from US 26, the road, now Forest Road 5401, comes to a fork. Bear right, following signs to Pine Creek Trail, and proceed 1.5 miles to the road-end parking lot just past a junction with a gated jeep road.

When the Oregon Wilderness Act of 1984 expanded the boundaries of the Strawberry Mountain Wilderness, Baldy Mountain finally received the protection it deserved. But the upgrade in status has not led to fame; surprisingly few people take this viewpoint hike to the rolling meadowlands at the mountain's summit. Perhaps one reason is that the trail is relatively new, having only recently been rerouted to climb at a gentler grade and include superb views that extend over the upper John Day Valley to Dixie Butte and the distant Elkhorn Range. Closer at hand are towering Strawberry Mountain and the jagged spine of the Strawberry Range. More

treasures come in the form of wildflowers, which abound in the open terrain and invite visitors to lie back and soak in the scenery for as long as the daylight holds out.

The trail follows the gated jeep road for 150 yards to a junction, where you veer left (uphill) on a jeep track toward Chambers Mine. This route makes a moderately steep ascent through open forests of lodgepole pines and Douglas firs with some ponderosa pines and grand firs mixed in. The grassy slopes beneath these trees host flowers such as bistort, yarrow, groundsel,

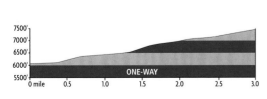

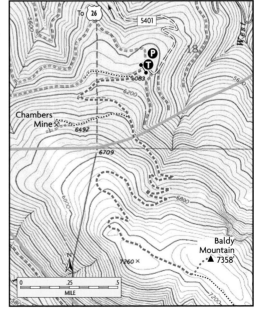

Strawberry Mountain from Baldy Mountain

lupine, and paintbrush. At the jeep track's second switchback, turn left on the Pine Creek Trail at 0.7 mile.

The well-graded trail climbs steadily but not steeply through open forest and across grassy slopes on five gentle switchbacks that crisscross the trickling headwaters of a seasonal creek. Eventually the trail leaves the forest and at 2 miles climbs a view-packed ridge on the northwest side of aptly named Baldy Mountain. The stunted alpine vegetation here is interesting and attractive, but it is the excellent views that really blow you away.

Near the top of the wide and often windy summit, the trail cuts across the west side of the peak, so you must leave the path and wander 0.1 mile up the gentle, open slopes to reach the grassy top. Views are superb in all directions, but the best ones are of the snowy pinnacle of Strawberry Mountain to the east.

76 STRAWBERRY LAKES LOOP

Distance: 13.7-mile loop; 2.2-mile side trip to Strawberry Mountain; 1-mile side trip to Little Strawberry Lake; 0.6-mile side trip to Slide Lake; 17.5 miles total
Hiking time: 2–3 days
Elevation gain: 4200 feet total
Difficulty: Strenuous
Season: July to October
Best: Late July; mid-October
Map: USFS Strawberry Mountain Wilderness
Information: Malheur National Forest—Prairie City Ranger District, (541) 820-3800

Directions: From John Day, drive US 395 south 10.1 miles, then turn left (east) onto paved County Road 65. Drive 13.8 miles to a junction, turn left on Forest Road 16 for 2.6 miles, then turn left onto gravel FR 1640 and climb 9.7 miles to the trailhead, where the road makes a sharp right turn.

The eastern third of the Strawberry Mountain Wilderness contains several small, scenic lakes that lie hidden beneath the range's rugged cliffs and peaks. You can visit almost all of these lakes in a magnificent loop that also takes you past a towering waterfall, through high meadows, and over lofty ridges with outstanding views. Most people start at Strawberry Campground on the north side of the wilderness and only get as far as popular Strawberry Lake. But if you are doing the loop, it is better to begin at the less-crowded trailhead described here, which takes 2 miles and 500 feet of elevation gain off the difficulty of the trip.

The trail's first 1.3 miles follow a rocky roadbed on the side of an exposed ridge with terrific views west along the rugged spine of the Strawberry Range. The abandoned road ends at a junction on a windswept ridge. Turn right and cross the west side of a high ridge with good views northwest of the fire-scarred valley of Indian Creek and north to the sharp pinnacle of Strawberry Mountain. The trail heads directly for that lofty goal, climbing through burned areas to a ridge-crest junction at 2.5 miles.

The loop trail goes right, but unless there are thunderstorms in the area (a common occurrence), go the extra 1.1 miles to visit the summit of Strawberry Mountain. To reach it, take the gradual uphill trail across the mountain's rocky east face, then turn left and steeply ascend for 0.3 mile over loose talus, shale, and alpine wildflowers to the summit. At 9038 feet, this is one of the highest mountains in Oregon, so it is not surprising that the views are superb. In the haze to the south is the looming form of Steens Mountain, while to the northeast rise the jagged peaks of the Elkhorn Range and Wallowa Mountains. Closer at hand are the John Day Valley and the contorted ridges and lake basins of the

Strawberry Lake

Strawberry Range, over which this mountain reigns supreme.

After returning to the loop trail at 4.7 miles, turn left (east) and descend a steep slope, where snow often lingers into early August. The trail then switchbacks down to the lovely meadows of Twin Springs Basin at 5.5 miles. Here are the roofless remains of a small log cabin and several very good campsites with fine views of Strawberry

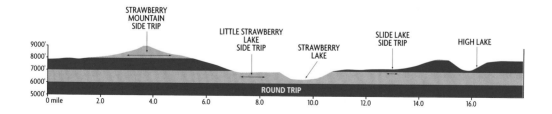

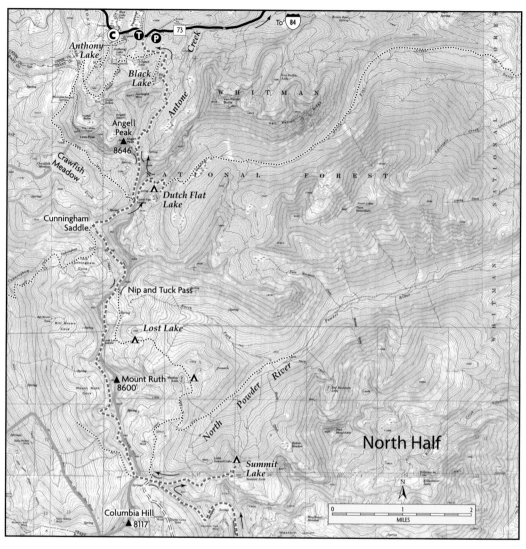

North Half

species puts on an impressive show of golden yellow in mid-October.

In 0.5 mile you cross Lake Creek. Unfortunately, you must get your feet wet, because for the benefit of the two-wheeled terrors, hiker-friendly stepping stones have been removed. An unrelenting uphill then leads to a large meadow in a basin choked with Douglas' knotweed and other wildflowers. From here, a series of short switchbacks climbs a scree slope with fine views of the towering, reddish-brown cliffs enclosing this canyon.

A final climb takes you to a knoll just above gorgeous Lower Twin Lake, where there are excellent campsites at 3.1 miles amid the scattered whitebark pines and subalpine firs. No trail goes to Upper Twin Lake, but it is easy to find in a small basin to the north. Keep an eye on the nearby cliffs for mountain goats, which initially look like small, moving snow patches. Fill your water bottles at Twin Lakes, because this is the last reliable source for more than 10 miles.

The trail switchbacks 0.9 mile up a rocky hillside to a junction with the Elkhorn Crest Trail. Turn left and walk 1 mile to a high saddle.

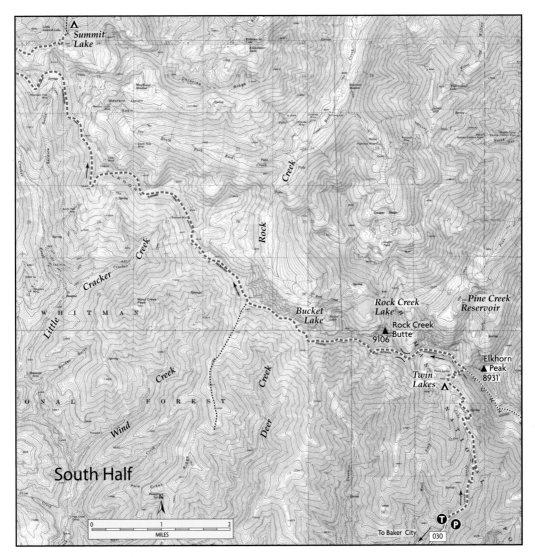

Shortly beyond this point you can leave the trail and make a moderately steep scramble to the top of 9106-foot Rock Creek Butte, the highest summit in the Elkhorn Range. The views from here are about as good as views get, extending northeast over the Powder River Valley to the Wallowa Mountains, southwest to the Strawberry Mountains, and almost straight down to the shimmering waters of Rock Creek Lake (Trip 79).

For the next 10 miles the Elkhorn Crest Trail makes a gentle traverse, generally staying on the west side of the divide. Along the way you pass

occasional examples of old mining activity and numerous good viewpoints of the Sumpter Valley. The trail has remarkably little up and down, so the miles go by quickly. The only junction is at 8.3 miles, where you continue straight.

Unfortunately, there are no reliable water sources, so by the time you reach a junction at 14.9 miles in a saddle east of Columbia Hill you will be thirsty and looking for a place to camp. To satisfy both needs, turn sharply right and walk 1.5 miles past great viewpoints of Mount Ruth, then through a burn area to large, deep, and very

Craggy ridges rise above Upper Twin Lake

scenic Summit Lake. A granite peak looms above the southern shore, making for memorable views from the excellent campsites near the outlet. Ospreys can often be seen diving for fish, and do not be surprised if mountain goats stomp around your camp during the night.

Back on the Elkhorn Crest Trail at 17.9 miles, go north 0.1 mile and come to a remote trailhead at the end of a rough jeep road. Cross the road and briefly climb to a junction in a saddle where you enter the wilderness and finally leave the motorcycles behind. Turn sharply right and gradually ascend sloping meadows, burn areas, and sagebrush-covered hillsides on the south and west sides of Mount Ruth. Views are excellent from the trail, but for even better ones, scramble to the summit of Mount Ruth, a steep but nontechnical endeavor best done via the north ridge. Once around Mount Ruth, the trail follows an undulating ridge, then descends to a junction at about 21.4 miles with the trail to Lost Lake.

The Elkhorn Crest Trail goes straight at the junction, immediately goes through tiny Nip and

Tuck Pass, then contours for 1.1 miles around a large basin to a junction at Cunningham Saddle. Veer right and traverse a hillside with great views of Crawfish Meadow and a jagged ridge to the south to a four-way junction at 23.3 miles in Dutch Flat Saddle. The trail to the right (east) drops 600 feet to meadow-rimmed Dutch Flat Lake, a 0.9-mile side trip well worth the effort because the lake features a small island, scenic campsites, and fine views of an unnamed granite peak to the west.

To complete the hike, return to the junction in Dutch Flat Saddle (now at 25.1 miles), go right (north), and climb to an 8200-foot pass beside jagged Angell Peak. The well-engineered trail then winds downhill, eventually crossing into the next drainage to the north and descending to an intersection at 27.5 miles with the spur trail to Black Lake. Go straight, then veer right just 30 yards later at a junction with a connector trail to Anthony Lake. The final 0.6 mile is an easy stroll through meadows and open forest to the Elkhorn Crest trailhead.

79 ROCK CREEK LAKE

Distance: 8.4 to 17 miles round trip (depending on how far you can drive)
Hiking time: 4 to 10 hours or overnight
Elevation gain: 2500 to 2800 feet
Difficulty: Strenuous
Season: July to mid-October
Best: Late July to mid-August
Maps: USGS Bourne, Elkhorn Peak (trail not shown)
Information: Wallowa-Whitman National Forest—Whitman Ranger District,
(541) 523-6391

Directions: From Baker City, drive 10 miles north on Old US Highway 30 to Haines. Turn left (west) on Anthony Lakes Highway and drive 1.6 miles to a junction where the main road makes a sharp right turn. Go left for 0.25 mile, then turn right (west) on South Rock Creek Road. Stick with the main road for 3.7 miles to the end of pavement just past the old town of Rock Creek. From here you proceed 2.1 miles on the public gravel road, ignoring several turnoffs labeled "No Trespassing," to a point where the gravel abruptly changes to rough and rocky dirt. From here it becomes a guessing game as to when the benefits of less hiking distance outweigh the costs of potential damage to your car. Most people can drive another 2.2 miles, now on Forest Road 5520, to a wide spot on the left at the unsigned Killamacue Lake trailhead just before the road crosses Killamacue Creek. From here the road deteriorates even further so only very daring drivers in tough cars can continue another 2.1 miles, through Eilertson Meadow and over two bridged crossings of Rock Creek, to Camp Lee, an obvious campsite on the left complete with an old picnic table. Beyond this point the road gets even worse (if that's possible) and is effectively impassible for anything short of a tank. From Camp Lee it is 0.7 mile to the official trailhead.

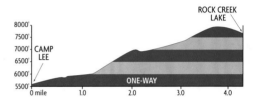

Rock Creek Lake, which sits directly beneath the imposing 1400-foot cliffs of Rock Creek Butte, is as dramatically scenic a spot as you are likely to find. It is also so isolated that solitude is the norm. Typically your only company will be mountain goats, several of which roam the surrounding cliffs. The lake even has a good population of brook trout (as well as a few lake trout) to entice the angler. The problem is getting there. The trail itself, although steep and challenging, is nothing out of the ordinary. The real difficulty comes with the road access to the trailhead. The last few miles of Forest Road 5520 are so rough that only those in rugged, high-clearance, four-wheel-drive vehicles can reach the official trailhead. But for the dedicated hiker who is willing to park and walk that extra road mileage, the rewards are tremendous. The best plan is to accept the extra exercise and make this either a very long day hike or a moderately rugged overnight outing.

From Camp Lee, hike the jeep road that goes uphill and follow it for 0.7 mile, past three spur routes leading to private mining claims, to a prominent fork. Veer left and walk 150 yards to the official trailhead.

Now on a foot trail, you immediately cross North Fork Rock Creek either on very rickety logs or, more safely, by wading. Meander

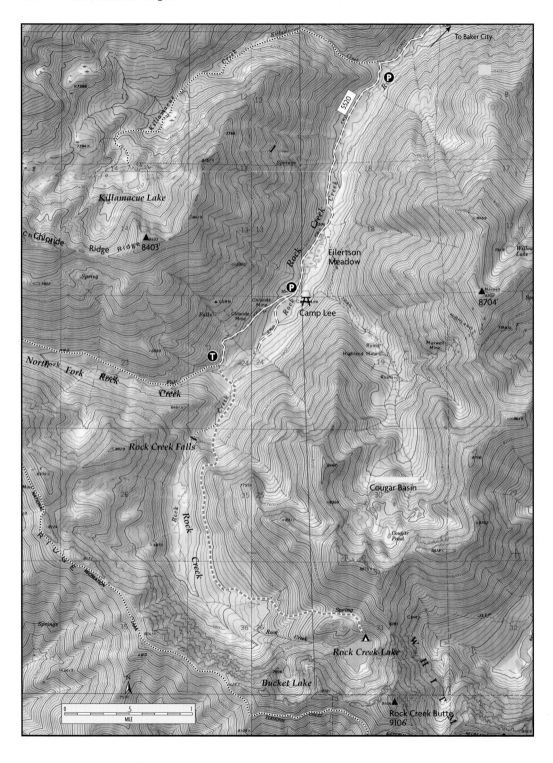

Rock Creek Lake

through a mixed conifer forest of spruces, firs, and larches. After crossing the main branch of Rock Creek on a sturdy log, you then climb lazily in dense forest to a junction. The trail to the right reaches Rock Creek Falls in 0.5 mile. These falls are worth a visit if you have some extra time.

The main trail goes left at the junction, takes you to an easy hop-over crossing of a small creek, then begins climbing in earnest as it charges up a steep avalanche chute covered with thick brush. After 0.3 mile you gratefully leave the brush for a woodsy hillside but continue with the steep uphill. Your legs and lungs get a workout as you rapidly ascend in short switchbacks to a fine overlook of Rock Creek Canyon. From here you lose about 100 feet, then curve to the left and begin a long traverse of a wooded slope hundreds of feet above distantly murmuring Rock Creek. After staying almost level on this hillside for about 1 mile, the trail goes steeply uphill through open forest.

Near the top of the climb you cross a series of sloping meadows with good views of the extremely steep Elkhorn Ridge to the west. A prominent rock pinnacle jutting out from the cliffs on the other side of Rock Creek provides an impressive landmark as you complete the final part of your hike. The way goes through two wet meadows before dropping about 200 feet to the shores of very deep Rock Creek Lake, 4.2 miles from Camp Lee.

This awesome 35-acre lake is set in a stupendous cliff-walled cirque, surrounded on three sides by 1400-foot headwalls. Snow often lingers on the far shore into early August, so the swimming is too cold to be recommended. A couple of small and wildly scenic campsites are on the north shore.

80

NINEMILE RIDGE

Distance: 7.2 miles round trip
Hiking time: 4.5 hours
Elevation gain: 2200 feet
Difficulty: Strenuous
Season: Late April to November
Best: Late May
Map: USFS North Fork Umatilla Wilderness
Information: Umatilla National Forest—Walla Walla Ranger District, (509) 522-6290

Directions: From Interstate 84 about 7 miles east of Pendleton, take exit 216 and drive 2 miles north to a flashing stoplight. Turn right on Mission Road, drive 1.7 miles, then turn left onto Cayuse Road. Stay on this road for 10.5 miles, then turn right on Bingham Road, which immediately crosses a set of railroad tracks. After 16 miles this road, which becomes Forest Road 32, turns to gravel and comes to Umatilla Forks Campground. About 0.2 mile past the campground, bear left at a junction, following signs to Buck Creek Trail, and drive 0.2 mile to the small trailhead parking lot.

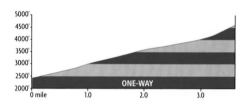

The Blue Mountains rise like a green wall above the rolling wheatfields east of Pendleton, forming a dramatic transition zone between the semi-desert steppe of the Columbia Plateau and the coniferous forests of the Blue Mountains. Over the millennia, the Umatilla and Walla Walla rivers have carved deep gashes into that barrier,

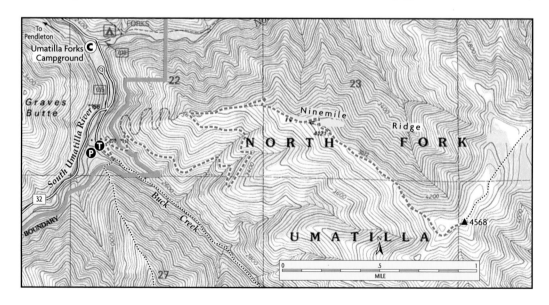

Along lower Ninemile Ridge Trail

resulting in scenic canyons that provide habitat for a diverse community of plants and animals. The best time to visit this area is late May, when the open slopes put on one of the most outstanding wildflower displays in the state. Several trails explore this realm, but for the best combination of views and flowers, take the uncrowded route up Ninemile Ridge.

Walk 150 feet along the gentle Buck Creek Trail, then turn left onto a trail marked only with a small brown post informing you that the route is open to hikers and horses. The trail makes a short traverse to an unsigned junction, where you bear right and begin to switchback steeply uphill through a dense Douglas fir forest. The understory is surprisingly lush for this relatively dry area, with a rich assortment of ferns, shrubs,

and forest wildflowers. At about 0.4 mile, you enter the first meadows.

These steep meadows provide outstanding views of the surrounding canyonlands, but flower lovers will probably miss these views, because their attention will be drawn to all the colorful blossoms. In late May the grassy hillside resembles a huge painter's palette with the blues of brodiaea and larkspur; the yellows of lomatium, balsamroot, and a type of yellow lupine; the pinks of shooting star, onion, and clarkia; and the white of prairie star.

The trail makes a gradual uphill traverse in and out of little gullies and through meadows divided by strips of trees to a switchback, where you leave the last of the trees and cross an enormous flower-covered meadow. At the

2-mile point you hit the top of the ridge, a good turnaround point for hikers seeking a shorter trip. Those who want an even better view can continue 1.6 miles to the ridge's 4568-foot high point. In addition to the terrific views, it is inter- esting to see how the flowers gradually change to stunted, subalpine varieties, with phlox and blue (instead of yellow) lupine. The trail beyond this high point is less scenic and gets rather sketchy, so turn around here.

81 WENAHA RIVER TRAIL

Distance: 13 miles round trip
Hiking time: 6 hours (day hike or backpack)
Elevation gain: 600 feet
Difficulty: Moderate
Season: All year (except during winter storms)
Best: Late April and early May
Map: USFS Wenaha-Tucannon Wilderness
Information: Umatilla National Forest—Pomeroy Ranger District, (509) 843-1891

Directions: From Enterprise, drive 34 miles north on Oregon Highway 3, then turn left (west) on the road to Flora. Drive 3 miles to Flora, a virtual ghost town, and continue 4 miles to the end of pavement. The road's next 7 miles snake down to the bottom of the Grande Ronde River Canyon. Take a bridge over the river, turn left on a paved road, and drive 1.6 miles to Troy. At the north end of town, turn right on Bartlett Road, following signs toward Pomeroy, and drive 0.3 mile to the trailhead at the road's first switchback.

The rushing waters of the Wenaha River have carved an impressive, 2000-foot-deep canyon into the uplifted tablelands of the northern Blue Mountains. The canyon is a scenic mas- terpiece, with rocky ledges and grassy slopes perfectly mixed with groves of pines and firs that add touches of green to the dry surround- ings. At the bottom of the canyon, the clear river flows in glassy eddies and rushing rapids that serenade the visitor with the constant sound of "river music." But excellent scenery is only one reason to hike the Wenaha River Trail. Anglers can try their luck at snagging some of the river's large trout, while wildlife lovers will delight in the better-than-average chance of seeing elk and bighorn sheep. In April and May, botanists will have fun examining the wide variety of flow- ering plants, including species that prefer dry, semidesert slopes and moisture-loving varieties along the river. Keep an eye out for the twin haz- ards of rattlesnakes and poison ivy.

From the trailhead you drop to a grassy, river-level flat. Then you go upstream, alter- nating between gentle flats and rocky slopes a little above the river. Stately ponderosa pines are scattered on the dry hillsides, while the wetter lowland areas host Douglas firs, grand firs, and black cottonwoods. The mostly treeless benches above the river are covered with bunchgrass and wildflowers such as phlox, balsamroot, and sul- fur flower. Keep an eye on the ledges above the trail for bighorn sheep. Views of the canyon and access to outstanding fishing spots are frequent.

At about the 4.5-mile point, you pass through a gate with a confusing sign saying this is the Wenaha-Tucannon Wilderness boundary (although the maps all say you won't reach it for

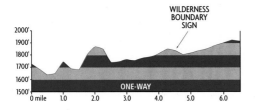

WILDERNESS
BOUNDARY
SIGN

2000'
1900'
1800'
1700'
1600'
1500'
ONE-WAY
0 mile   1.0   2.0   3.0   4.0   5.0   6.0

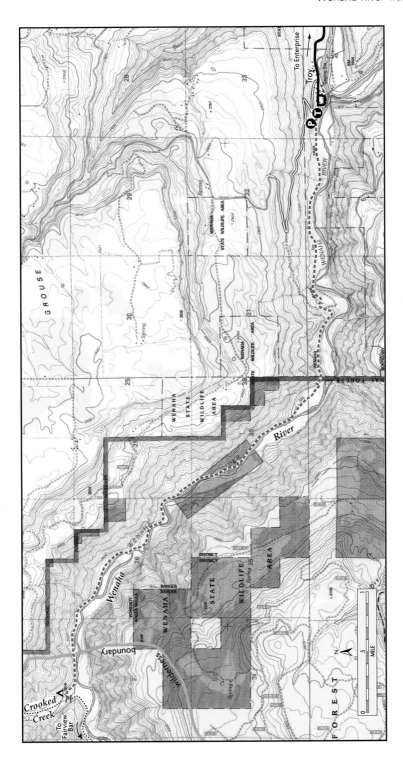

Wenaha River Canyon near Dry Gulch

another 2 miles). Then do more ups and downs for 2 miles to a junction just before the bridge over Crooked Creek. There are some mediocre campsites to the right. Backpackers can also continue another 2.2 miles to Fairview Bar, a particularly attractive river-level flat with fine campsites under the shade of large ponderosa pines.

WALLOWA MOUNTAINS AND HELLS CANYON

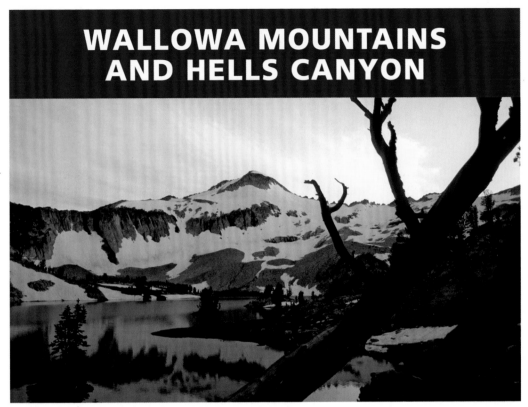

Sunset at Glacier Lake, Wallowa Mountains (Hike 87)

Tucked neatly into the northeastern corner of Oregon are the two most outstanding hiking areas in the state. The jagged, white-granite peaks, sparkling lakes, and wildflower-covered meadows of the Wallowa Mountains make this range one of the most beautiful in the nation. In fact, there is so much outstanding scenery here that a lifetime would be inadequate to see all of its glories.

Just a short distance east of the Wallowa Mountains, which include most of the state's highest peaks, is the state's biggest ditch—and a radically different hiking experience. Hells Canyon is not only the deepest gorge in Oregon, it lays claim to being the deepest one in North America. Trails through this gaping chasm boast not only breathtaking views but an unusual abundance of wildlife, including elk, bighorn sheep, and black bears. But time your visit between early spring and early summer—depending on elevation—because at the wrong time of year the canyon is blisteringly hot and literally crawling with ticks, black widow spiders, and rattlesnakes. (After all, it's not called "Hells" Canyon for nothing.)

Although most of the Wallowa Mountains and part of Hells Canyon are preserved as wilderness, the surrounding terrain receives inadequate protection in the Hells Canyon National Recreation Area. A dedicated coalition of environmentalists, anglers, Native Americans, and local businesses is working hard to expand wilderness protection and generally improve the management of these precious lands for wildlife and recreation. For more information about these worthy efforts, contact the Hells Canyon Preservation Council (see Appendix B, Selected Conservation and Hiking Groups, at the back of this book).

82 WEST LOSTINE RIVER LOOP

Distance: 36-mile loop (includes 3.3-mile road section and 6.2-mile side trip to Chimney and Hobo lakes)
Hiking time: 3–5 days
Elevation gain: 6900 feet
Difficulty: Strenuous
Season: July to October
Best: Mid-July to August
Map: Imus Geographics—Wallowa Mountains
Information: Wallowa Mountains Office, (541) 426-5546

Directions: From La Grande, drive Oregon Highway 82 east 55 miles to Lostine. Turn south, following signs to the Lostine River campgrounds, and proceed 14.9 miles on paved then gravel Forest Road 8210 to the Bowman/Frances Lake trailhead. If you have two cars, leave one here for the return. Drive the road's final 3.3 miles to busy Two Pan trailhead, the recommended starting point.

Alpine lakes, high passes, idyllic meadows, wildlife—words such as "sublime" and "enchanting" come to mind but somehow seem woefully inadequate. To say that this hike is the Wallowa Mountains at their best is meaningless, because every part of this magnificent range is superlative, but at least you can say that nowhere is the mountain scenery any better. And while the country is far from lonesome, it is not as crowded as the famous Lakes Basin. So strap on your boots and enjoy!

The wide and heavily used trail climbs 0.2 mile to a junction immediately after a sign for the wilderness boundary. Bear right and soon cross East Fork Lostine River on a concrete bridge. The trail then follows West Fork Lostine River, climb-

ing in fits and starts beside this joyfully cascading stream to an upper glacier-carved valley. At 2.8 miles, just as you leave the forest for the meadows of the upper valley, the trail splits. Veer right on the Copper Creek Trail, immediately pass a spacious horse camp, then make a calf- to knee-deep ford of West Fork Lostine River.

Refreshed by this chilly ford, hike steadily uphill for a little under 1 mile to an easy ford of rollicking Copper Creek, then ascend through meadows and forest to a second, somewhat simpler crossing near the base of a scenic meadow. There is a good campsite immediately before this crossing and two more in the meadow just beyond. The trail soon pulls away from this meadow and switchbacks up a rocky slope to a smaller but equally beautiful meadow that is more alpine in character with heather, owl's clover, Cusick's speedwell, and other high-elevation wildflowers. The views improve as you ascend to an exposed 8500-foot plateau, where there is a junction at 8 miles. Go right and descend ten switchbacks to a meadow just above irregularly shaped Swamp Lake. This gorgeous alpine lake features a small island, exposed but scenic campsites, and excellent views of the snow-streaked

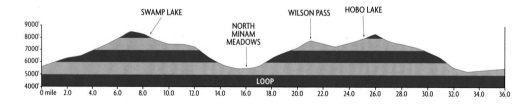

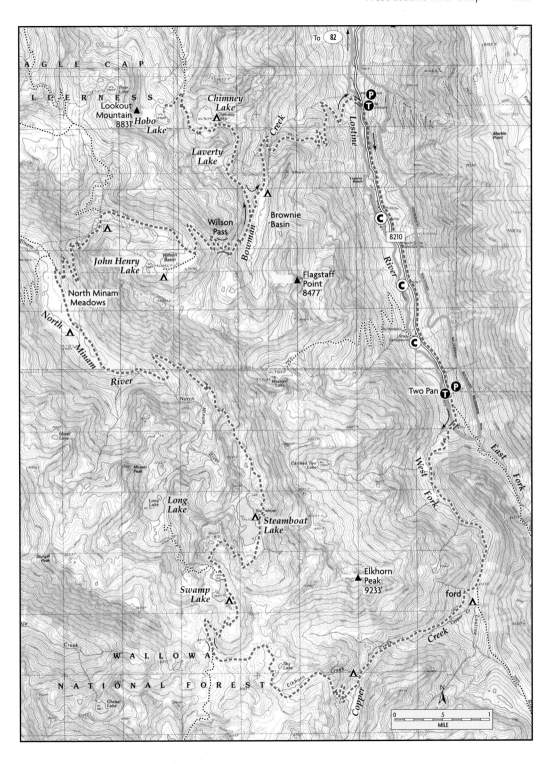

Swamp Lake is much more beautiful than its name.

granite cliffs surrounding this basin.

From Swamp Lake the trail goes over a minor ridge, passes a cluster of ponds, then switchbacks down to impressively large, deep, and very scenic Steamboat Lake at 11 miles. Good (but popular) campsites are along the east shore. The lake's name comes from a rock formation that, with a lot of imagination, resembles a steamboat. After a brief climb away from the lake, it is all downhill on well-graded traverses and switchbacks into North Minam River's deep canyon. Once you reach the bottom, a pleasant, woodsy stroll leads to large North Minam Meadows. More than fifty years ago, Supreme Court Justice and conservationist William O. Douglas wrote that this spectacular, lush meadow was "coveted by every man who loves the mountains and has seen it." That description remains accurate today. The best campsites are by the meandering stream at the south end of the meadows.

At the north end of North Minam Meadows is a junction at 16.5 miles. Turn sharply right and climb numerous switchbacks to good viewpoints on the east canyon wall. The switchbacks end near a pretty meadow and campsite where you hop over a small creek. Just beyond this creek you pass a junction at 19 miles with Bear Creek Trail, then gently ascend for 1.2 miles to an unsigned junction where the trail turns sharply left. The spur trail to the right leads to marshy John Henry Lake. The main trail climbs to 7820-foot Wilson Pass, where you will have your last looks west to the beautiful North Minam country and your first views east to the red spires of Twin Peaks. From the pass, the trail switchbacks down to a junction at 22.5 miles a little above the inviting green meadow in Brownie Basin.

The exit trail goes right, but having come this far, it would be a shame to miss an excellent side trip. So bear left (uphill) and traverse a flower-covered hillside to the lovely greenish waters of lower Laverty Lake at 23.5 miles. Around the next minor ridge is deservedly popular Chimney Lake, with several excellent campsites, two picturesque islands, and views of the surrounding talus slopes and granite peaks. The trail continues beyond Chimney Lake, climbing gradually to a pass and a junction at 25 miles with the steep 0.4-mile spur trail to Hobo Lake in a rocky alpine cirque on the shoulder of Lookout Mountain.

From the Chimney Lake area, return to the junction south of Laverty Lake (now at 29 miles) and turn left (east). This trail passes the lower end of the meadow in Brownie Basin, then begins the long descent to the Lostine River. Six long switchbacks keep the grade gentle all the way to a concrete bridge over the river and the Bowman/Frances Lake trailhead at 33 miles. If you did not leave a car here, it is a 3.3-mile walk up FR 8210 to the Two Pan trailhead.

83 FRANCES LAKE

Distance: 18.4 miles round trip
Hiking time: 2–3 days
Elevation gain: 4500 feet
Difficulty: Very strenuous
Season: July to October
Best: Mid-July and August
Map: Imus Geographics—Wallowa Mountains
Information: Wallowa Mountains Office, (541) 426-5546

Directions: From La Grande, drive Oregon Highway 82 east 55 miles to Lostine. Turn south, following signs to the Lostine River campgrounds, and proceed 14.9 miles on paved then gravel Forest Road 8210 to the Bowman/Frances Lake trailhead.

Hidden in a high basin along Hurricane Divide, Frances Lake is a delightful destination for fit hikers seeking a one- or two-night backpacking trip. The 30-acre lake sits in a spectacular bowl at the head of Lake Creek and is hemmed in on three sides by a ring of impressive 9000-foot peaks. Originally the lake was called Lost Lake, but this overused title was replaced with "Frances" to honor the friend of a group of locals who visited this location. Today, no one seems to know who "Frances" was, but judging by the lake named in her honor, she must have been beautiful. Start with full water bottles, because there is no reliable source until the destination.

The trail starts just below the west end of the parking lot, parallels FR 8210 for 200 yards, then makes the first of many switchbacks. The dense forest at this elevation is mostly grand firs, Douglas firs, and Engelmann spruces, with

Frances Lake

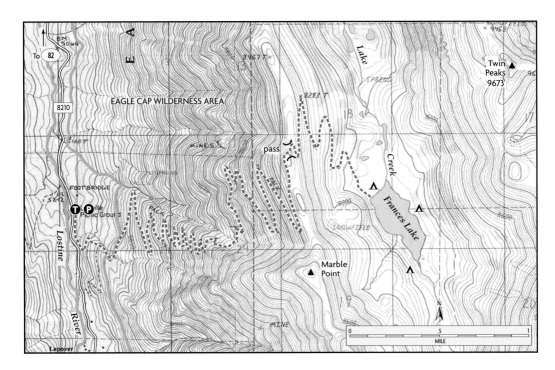

some western larches and quaking aspens. Wild-flowers are sparse, but a few stand tall amid the grasses, especially coneflower and grounsel. As you gain elevation, the forest changes to a mix of first lodgepole then white-bark pines along with subalpine firs.

The uphill is never steep, but it is relentless as switchback after long switchback takes you up the canyon wall to ever loftier viewpoints of the rugged peaks to the west. These viewpoints provide good opportunities to rest, something the trail's steady grade does not otherwise allow. Since this waterless slope is shady in the morning, the best plan is to camp along the Lostine River the night before, then get an early start. If you are bored or obsessed with numbers, you can spend your time counting switchbacks. There are about twenty-nine on the way up, depending on how you count the trail's first few twists and turns.

At 7.5 miles you finally top out at an 8600-foot pass, 3400 feet above the Lostine River and 900 feet above the basin holding Frances Lake. Views are superb, especially east to the sharp pinnacles of Twin Peaks. Since by now you would probably feel lost without switchbacks, the trail obliges with ten more that descend a rocky slope for 1.7 miles to the north shore of Frances Lake. There are few campsites near the lake, but those that do exist are wildly scenic. The best sites are above the east and southwest shores. Please do not camp in the fragile meadows that surround the lake, which would crush the colorful yarrow, onion, groundsel, and other wildflowers. The best fishing is usually in the string of ponds along the outlet creek.

For an easy exploration, wander up to the gorgeous meadow just south of Frances Lake. Here you will find great scenery, nesting water pipits alarmed by your intrusion, and numerous wild-flowers, especially cinquefoil, grass-of-Parnassus, and the two-foot-tall stalks of monument plant, which is uncommon in Oregon.

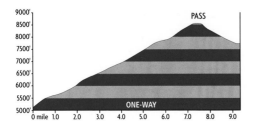

84 ICE LAKE

Distance: 15.6 miles round trip
Hiking time: 2–3 days
Elevation gain: 3500 feet
Difficulty: Strenuous (very strenuous with the side trip up the Matterhorn)
Season: Mid-July to October
Best: Late July and August
Maps: Imus Geographics—Wallowa Mountains
Information: Wallowa Mountains Office, (541) 426-5546

Directions: From La Grande, drive 70 miles east on Oregon Highway 82 to a junction in downtown Joseph. Go south on Main Street, following signs to Wallowa Lake, and continue 6 miles on the main road to Wallowa Lake State Park. Go straight at a campground turnoff and park in the huge signed lot at the south end of the state park.

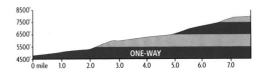

Most of the best things in life require effort, and hiking into Ice Lake certainly fits that rule. This is a long, tough climb. But the payoff is terrific: filled with fish and nestled in an alpine wonderland beneath bulky, multi-colored mountains, Ice Lake is close to the perfect mountain lake. Unfortunately, a significant number of other folks agree with this assessment, so despite the long access trail, the camps here are often crowded. For those with an extra day to spend exploring, the climb from Ice Lake up the Matterhorn is highly recommended and extremely rewarding.

Pick up the woodchip-covered trail beside the signboard at the southeast end of the parking lot and walk 75 yards to a fork. Bear right on West Fork Wallowa River Trail and gradually ascend for 0.3 mile past a noisy little power plant to a junction with Chief Joseph Mountain Trail. Turn left and ascend a dusty and heavily used trail in a forest of Engelmann spruce, lodgepole pine, ponderosa pine, western larch, and some cottonwood. On your right, cascading West Fork Wallowa River provides pleasant background music to your hike. The terrain gets increasingly brushy as you climb, with breaks in the forest

providing partial views of the surrounding peaks. In late August and September this section usually offers a lot of delicious thimbleberries for you to snack on.

At 2.9 miles is a junction where you bear right on Ice Lake Trail, which while still popular is not as heavily used as the West Fork Wallowa River Trail. The trail soon crosses the river on a substantial wooden bridge near a possible campsite.

Now begins a long, switchbacking climb that in 4.9 miles takes you all the way up to Ice Lake. It's a tiring and rather tedious haul, but the views improve as you ascend and you can enjoy the sight of the waterfalls on Adam Creek along the way. Aspen groves and wildflowers add to the scenery. After gaining 2300 feet, the trail finally tops out and makes a short, level traverse to the northeast end of large and very deep Ice Lake.

Filled with brook trout, this alpine gem perfectly reflects the Matterhorn, a hulking white mass of marble and limestone to the west. All around the lake are other summits, ranging in color from dark gray to reddish brown and even cream colored. The whole area is very photogenic and certainly worth all the sweat. An unofficial 1.7-mile trail goes around the irregularly shaped lake, passing numerous fine campsites

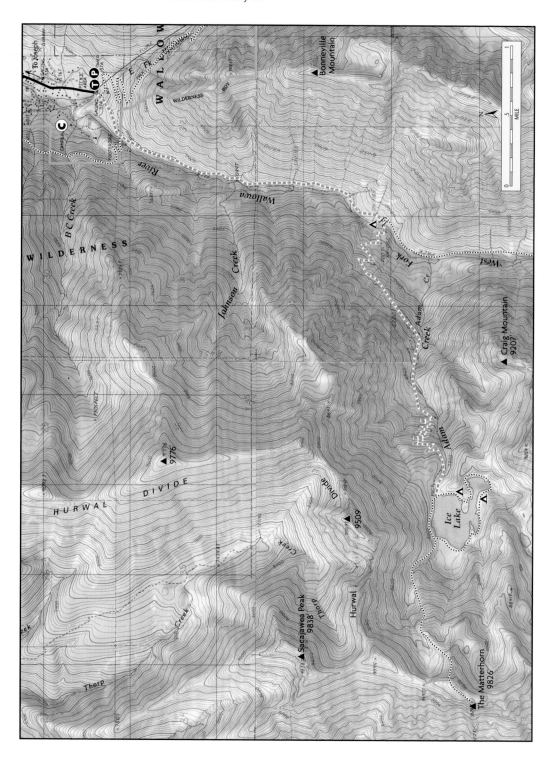

and fishing spots. Wildlife is common, especially mountain goats, which you can often spot on the nearby ridges. Both tree and ground squirrels are also common, and since these thieving rodents frequently steal hikers' food, you are well advised to take precautions.

At 9826 feet, the Matterhorn is the second-highest peak in the Wallowa Mountains, and energetic hikers often use Ice Lake as the starting point for climbing the mountain. The sometimes steep route is neither signed nor maintained, but the open terrain makes navigation reasonably easy. To make the attempt, hike the trail to the northwest end of Ice Lake and pick up an initially obvious but later intermittent boot path that goes west up an indistinct gully. The route is increasingly steep but wildly scenic with excellent views and a lot of wildflowers, most notably 3-foot-tall monument plants. Eventually the route climbs above the last of the contorted whitebark pines to a ridgeline, goes around a small cirque holding what appears to be a tiny remnant glacier (complete with crevasses and a little moraine), and makes a final very steep ascent over often sandy terrain to the cairn at the summit. Virtually every significant peak in the Wallowa Mountains is visible from this grandstand, while at your feet the frighteningly

Looking west across Ice Lake

steep west face of the Matterhorn drops a dizzying 3000 feet down to Hurricane Creek. On clear days you can also see much of the surrounding area's ranch and farm lands as well as the distant Elkhorn Mountains to the southwest and Idaho's Seven Devils Mountains to the east. Remember that this area is very exposed, so come prepared for stiff winds and cool temperatures, and be especially wary of thunderstorms, which often build in the afternoon.

85 BIG SHEEP BASIN AND BONNY LAKES

Distance: 5.2 miles round trip to Big Sheep Basin; 7.8 miles round trip to Bonny Lakes; 10.8 miles round trip to both
Hiking time: 3–7 hours (day hike or short backpack)
Elevation gain: 1400 feet to Big Sheep Basin; 1300 feet to Bonny Lakes; 2500 feet to both
Difficulty: Moderate
Season: July to October
Best: Late July
Map: Imus Geographics—Wallowa Mountains
Information: Wallowa Mountains Office, (541) 426-5546

Directions: From Joseph, at the end of Oregon Highway 82, drive 8.3 miles east toward Imnaha, then turn right on Wallowa Mountain Road (Forest Road 39). Go 12.8 miles, then turn right on rough FR 100 and proceed 3.2 miles to the road-end trailhead.

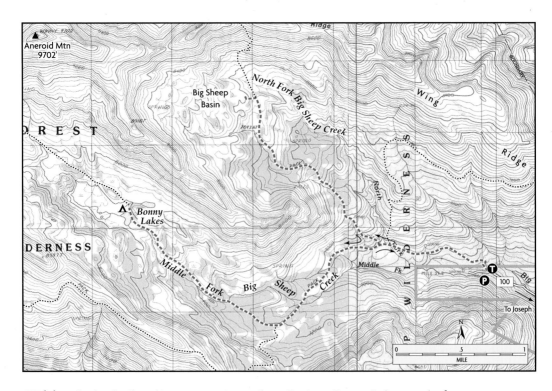

With hundreds of miles of interconnecting trails, thousands of idyllic campsites, and countless great destinations, the Wallowa Mountains are paradise for backpackers. Day hikers, however, are often frustrated, because most destinations lie beyond their reach. One of the few reasonable options is on the less-visited east side of the range, where the mountains are tinged with reddish rock rather than the usual white granite and, in late July, the meadows put on some of the best wildflower displays in Oregon. There are two superb destinations here, and they can be combined into a single outing if you are feeling ambitious.

The trail, which starts in a shadeless and rather desolate burn area, quickly drops to a ford of cascading Big Sheep Creek. Nearby logs across the flow allow you to keep your feet dry. After 0.4 mile the dusty, uphill trail leaves the burn zone and travels through open forest to a pair of junctions at 1.1 miles on either side of a hop-over crossing of North Fork Big Sheep Creek. Ignore the first junction; at the second one, decide whether you are going to Big Sheep Basin or Bonny Lakes—or both.

Turn right for the trail to Big Sheep Basin, which climbs steeply in forest and sloping meadows filled with bunchgrass, sagebrush, and wildflowers such as buckwheat, yarrow, lupine, and mariposa lily. After 0.7 mile you hop over a tributary of North Fork Big Sheep Creek, then climb intermittently another 0.5 mile to the meadows in the lower part of Big Sheep Basin. The trail is easy to lose from here as it goes from one rolling meadow to the next, especially since your attention is drawn away from the tread to the scenery. The best views are from any of several little knolls west of the trail at about 1.5 miles, where you will enjoy excellent perspectives of the rounded, reddish

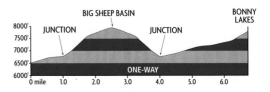

brown peaks and ridges to the north and west. Return as you came.

Back at the junction beside North Fork Big Sheep Creek, if the Bonny Lakes is your goal, go west, traverse for 0.5 mile, then make two rock-hop crossings, first of an unnamed tributary, then of Middle Fork Big Sheep Creek at 0.8 mile. Soon after these crossings the trail forks at 1.2 miles. Veer right and travel through dense forest to another crossing of Middle Fork Big Sheep Creek at 1.6 miles. Follow this lovely, flower-banked creek into more open terrain, then up a steep, rocky hill to the first meadow-rimmed Bonny Lake at 2.7 miles. Good campsites are near this shallow pool, which has superb views across its waters northwest to Aneroid Mountain and west to an unnamed, pyramid-shaped butte. To find the second lake, follow the trail around the east shore of the first lake, then go about 0.1 mile cross-country up a marshy inlet creek. Mosquitoes are numerous at both lakes until mid-August. Return to the junction and then to the trailhead the way you came.

Aneroid Mountain from above Bonny Lakes

86   EAGLE CREEK–WEST EAGLE LOOP

Distance: 35-mile loop (including side trip to Eagle Lake)
Hiking time: 3–5 days
Elevation gain: 8100 feet
Difficulty: Strenuous
Season: July to October
Best: Mid-July to mid-August
Map: Imus Geographics—Wallowa Mountains
Information: Wallowa Mountains Office, (541) 426-5546

Directions: From La Grande drive Oregon Highway 203 southeast 31 miles to Medical Springs. Turn left (southeast) on Eagle Creek Drive and go 1.7 miles to an intersection. Turn left on Big Creek Road (Forest Road 67) and drive 13 miles to a junction immediately after a bridge over West Fork Eagle Creek. Turn left on FR 77, go 0.7 mile, then go straight on

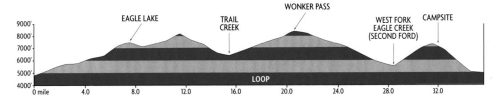

Looking toward Wonker Pass from a trail west of Trail Creek

FR 7755 and proceed 3.6 miles to the road-end trailhead.

The southern Wallowa Mountains are harder to reach than the northern part of the range, but once you get there you will have no doubt that it was worth it. Dozens of stunningly beautiful mountain lakes sparkle beneath towering peaks of scenic white granite. Elk browse in the meadows, deer visit your camp at night, and trout rise from lake waters, leaving distinctive circular ripples that disturb the classic reflections on a calm morning. This is mountain hiking at its best and with plenty of solitude, at least during midweek. Expect mosquitoes in July.

The wide trail gradually ascends through an open forest of mixed conifers for 0.6 mile to a bridge over Eagle Creek just below a cascading waterfall. From here, five switchbacks and an extended uphill lead through a brushy area filled with tall wildflowers, especially sweet-smelling horsemint, to a second creek crossing at 2.6 miles. You then make an easy ford of Copper Creek a little below veil-like Copper Creek Falls, which requires an off-trail scramble to see properly. At a junction 0.2 mile past the falls, bear right and traverse a hillside to lovely Eagle Creek Meadow at 4.4 miles. Here you will find good campsites and

access to the Bear Lake Trail (which fords Eagle Creek, then steeply climbs the east canyon wall to Bear, Culver, and Lookingglass lakes—a good side trip from a camp at the meadow).

The main trail steadily ascends through avalanche chutes, then switchbacks up an open slope to a junction at 6.2 miles. Take the dead-end trail to the right 1.1 miles to dramatic Eagle Lake, set in a deep bowl of 9000-foot peaks. A rock dam despoils the scene, but the lake is still worth a visit. Return to the Eagle Lake junction (now at 8.4 miles) and go right (west) as the trail climbs through flower-covered meadows to good campsites near enchanting Cached Lake at 9.5 miles. This gorgeous pool is backed by a scenic talus slope on one side and surrounded by lush meadows on the others. The meadows are filled with the blossoms of pussy toes, Cusick's speedwells, shooting stars, and other wildflowers throughout the summer. Pyramid-shaped Needle Point rises to the northeast, making this tiny gem one of Oregon's most photogenic lakes.

The trail climbs away from Cached Lake, passing through a small upper basin to a windy pass amid an intrusion of dark brown rock. Views are excellent here with serrated peaks and forested valleys visible in all directions. The trail now makes a switchbacking downhill to a

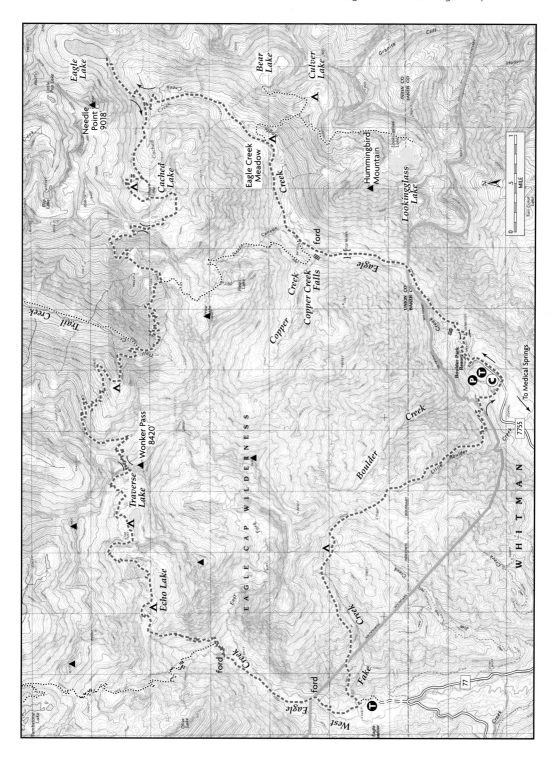

junction at 13 miles, where you bear right (the trail to the left returns to Copper Creek Falls for a shorter loop option) and descend several more switchbacks to a junction at 15 miles beside tumbling Trail Creek. Turn left, splash across the creek, then settle into a steady pace for a long climb. The first six switchbacks lead in less than a mile to a creek crossing and a scenic campsite (nearly all campsites in the Wallowas are scenic) in a small meadow. From here, thirty-six more switchbacks slowly take you into higher and more open terrain with terrific views and acres of alpine wildflowers. The long climb finally ends at 8420-foot Wonker Pass at 21 miles. From this rocky notch there are terrific views west to nearby Traverse and Echo lakes and to the distant Elkhorn Range.

The trail winds gradually downhill from Wonker Pass about 1.5 miles to spectacular Traverse Lake. This 19-acre wonder has numerous good campsites, which allow you to fully savor the evening view of an impressive, triangle-shaped granite pinnacle to the east. The trail descends 500 feet from this lake 1.6 miles to large Echo Lake, where delightful campsites offer stunning views of a serrated ridge to the south. More downhill (much more) goes through a meadow to a hop-over creek crossing, then descends a rocky slope on hundreds of short switchbacks

(well, maybe not hundreds, but a lot) to a junction at 26.5 miles. Bear left and descend to an easy ford of West Fork Eagle Creek.

Now in gentler terrain, the trail winds gradually downhill through forest and meadows to an ankle-deep ford of West Fork Eagle Creek, then goes through a soggy meadow and reaches a junction at 29 miles. Straight ahead a few hundred yards is a trailhead on FR 77, a possible way to shorten the trip if you have two cars.

To do the loop, turn left at the junction onto the irregularly maintained Fake Creek Trail, soon hop over its namesake creek, and make a very steep climb of a forested hillside (you will miss those earlier monotonous but gentle switchbacks). After quickly gaining 1600 feet, the grade eases as you traverse open country then hop over the bubbling headwaters of Fake Creek. A final steep incline takes you past a spring to a lush meadow with a good campsite at 32 miles. The obscure trail then tops an open ridge and disappears. As you go south along the ridge, you will eventually see the trail in a sloping, grassy basin on your left. Make your way down to the trail, then go steeply downhill in meadows and forest. Finish the trip by switchbacking down an abandoned jeep trail, pass several A-frame buildings, and at 35 miles reach FR 7755 about 0.3 mile from your car.

87 SOUTHEAST WALLOWAS LOOP

Distance: 44-mile loop (including 3.4-mile side trip to Hidden Lake and 2.6-mile side trip to Eagle Cap)
Hiking time: 4–6 days
Elevation gain: 10,100 feet
Difficulty: Strenuous
Season: Mid-July to October
Best: Mid-July to August
Map: Imus Geographics—Wallowa Mountains
Information: Wallowa Mountains Office, (541) 426-5546

Directions: From La Grande drive Oregon Highway 203 southeast 31 miles to Medical Springs. Turn left (southeast) on Eagle Creek Drive, and drive 1.7 miles to an intersection.

Turn east, following signs to Tamarack Campground, and drive 1.7 miles to an intersection. Turn left on Forest Road 67 and drive 13 miles to a junction just after a bridge

Glacier Peak over Glacier Lake

over Eagle Creek. Turn right, go 6 miles, then turn left on FR 7745, following signs to East Eagle trailhead, and drive 5.3 miles to the well-signed trailhead.

The Wallowa Mountains have almost 500 miles of trails, and every foot of every trail is worth taking. In all those magnificent miles, this loop may be the best. Here, before your awestruck eyes, the Wallowa Mountains present the perfect combination of sparkling lakes, clear streams, crashing waterfalls, deep canyons, high passes, wildflower meadows . . . it is almost impossible to take it all in. When asked to select my all-time favorite long hike in Oregon, this usually tops the list. Amazingly, even with all these scenic glories, the loop is relatively uncrowded. Although you briefly visit the heavily used Lakes Basin, by starting your hike from the south you avoid the overcrowded and dusty trails around Wallowa Lake.

The trail travels 0.5 mile through an old-growth forest of ponderosa pines, grand firs, and western larches to a junction with Little Kettle Trail and the start of the loop. A clockwise tour provides for a more gradual approach, so go straight and descend to the end of a gravel road at an old trailhead. From here, the trail heads north up the canyon of East Fork Eagle Creek, where steep walls rise as much as 4000 feet to the heights above. Small waterfalls streak down these slopes, feeding into the cascading creek. That creek has falls of its own, most notably an impressive cataract at about the 3-mile point, where the water twists and roars into a narrow gorge below the trail.

In the following 4 miles, the trail's up-and-down course goes through meadow openings and past a couple of mediocre campsites to a possibly unsigned junction with the trail to Hidden Lake. This side trip is very worthwhile, because

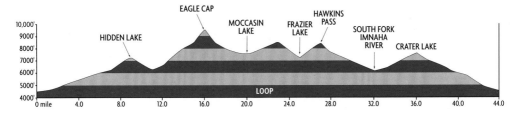

this large, meadow-rimmed lake has a spectacular setting and excellent campsites along its trailless north shore, 1.7 miles from the main trail.

From Hidden Lake, return to the main trail (now at 11 miles) and go straight; you soon pass a waterfall high above you on Knight Creek, then come to a usually unsigned junction with the Frazier Pass Trail. Bear right and make the long, rocky climb out of the creek's headwall basin to Horton Pass at 15 miles. Large snowfields linger here well into August. A trail to the right, the start of which is often buried under snow,

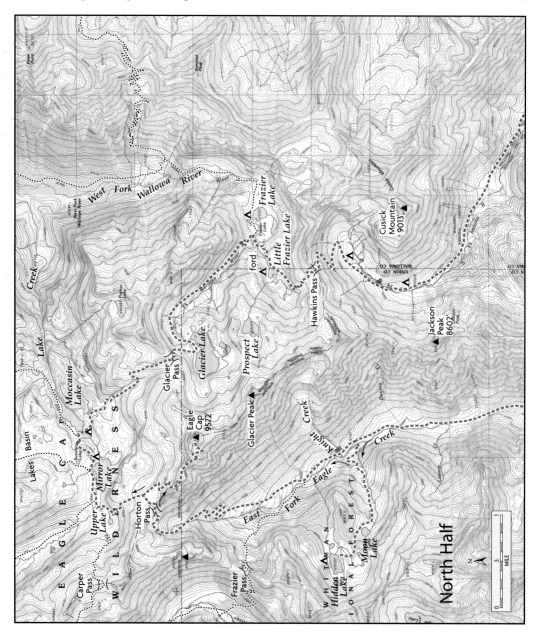

departs from here for the top of Eagle Cap in 1.3 miles. Weather permitting, this is a great side trip, because the peak serves as the hub of several radiating glacial canyons and provides the best viewpoint in the range.

Return to Horton Pass (now at 17.5 miles),

and turn right (north) on the loop trail as it leads down to a junction near tiny Upper Lake, which sits (appropriately enough) at the upper end of popular Lakes Basin. Turn right here and right again at a second junction just 100 yards later, then come to large Mirror Lake at 19 miles,

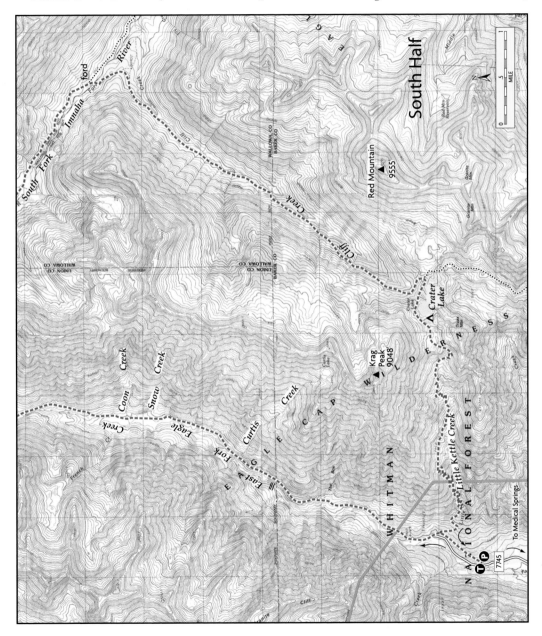

which, as the name implies, provides outstanding reflections of towering Eagle Cap to the south. Very popular campsites abound at Mirror Lake and at equally beautiful Moccasin Lake, 0.8 mile east.

Several very scenic lakes fill the lower part of Lakes Basin, but the loop trip turns right (south) at Moccasin Lake and makes a long climb out of the basin to view-packed Glacier Pass at 22 miles. From there, you drop to spectacular Glacier Lake, in a high basin beneath the white granite towers and permanent snowfields of Glacier Peak and Eagle Cap. Camping here is not recommended due to the fragile environment and the often cold, windy weather.

The trail makes a long downhill traverse southeast of Glacier Lake to a junction at 24.5 miles just above Frazier Lake (campsites a short distance to the left), where you turn right and soon make a chilly ford of West Fork Wallowa River. From here, a short climb leads to beautiful Little Frazier Lake (campsites), then a much longer, switchbacking ascent takes you to windswept Hawkins Pass at 27 miles. The best view here is southeast down the spectacular U-shaped canyon of South Fork Imnaha River—your next goal.

Reaching that goal entails descending the canyon's steep headwall past a complex mix of contorted rocks and talus slopes. Once it reaches the meadowy headwall basin, the trail goes downstream past campsites and a lovely waterfall, crosses the South Fork Imnaha River (only a creek here), then begins a gentle descent into the increasingly forested canyon. About 5 miles from Hawkins Pass is a junction, where you bear right and come to a chilly, calf-deep ford of South Fork Imnaha River. The next 4 miles are a steady uphill through a mix of forests and open slopes above Cliff Creek, with nice views of Red Mountain to the east. At the top of the climb is a junction in a wide saddle. Turn right and at 37 miles reach scenic Crater Lake, which has fish and the last good campsites of the trip.

From Crater Lake, you face a long (make that a very long) 6.5-mile descent on the Little Kettle Trail. In fact, the unpleasant prospect of going up this trail explains why this loop should not be done counterclockwise. The switchbacking descent crosses numerous rockslides and brushy avalanche chutes as it loses more than 3000 feet to the junction with East Fork Eagle Trail, where you go left to close the loop.

88 IMNAHA RIVER TRAIL

Distance: 9 miles round trip
Hiking time: 4 hours (day hike or backpack)
Elevation gain: 300 feet
Difficulty: Moderate
Season: Late March to November (avoid midsummer heat)
Best: Early to mid-May
Map: USFS Hells Canyon National Recreation Area
Information: Hells Canyon National Recreation Area, (541) 426-5546

Directions: From Joseph, at the end of Oregon Highway 82, drive 30 miles northeast to Imnaha. From Imnaha, turn north and drive 6.5 miles to Fence Creek Ranch, where the road abruptly changes to rough dirt. The road (Forest Road 4260) to the trailhead is one of the most scenic drives in Oregon, but it is also steep, narrow, and rough, so passenger cars must take it slow. Although the road can be treacherous when wet, the canyon scenery is superb. The trailhead is 14 miles from Fence Creek Ranch just before a bridge over the Imnaha River. The parking lot is on private property, so please be respectful of the landowner, who generously allows hikers to use this area.

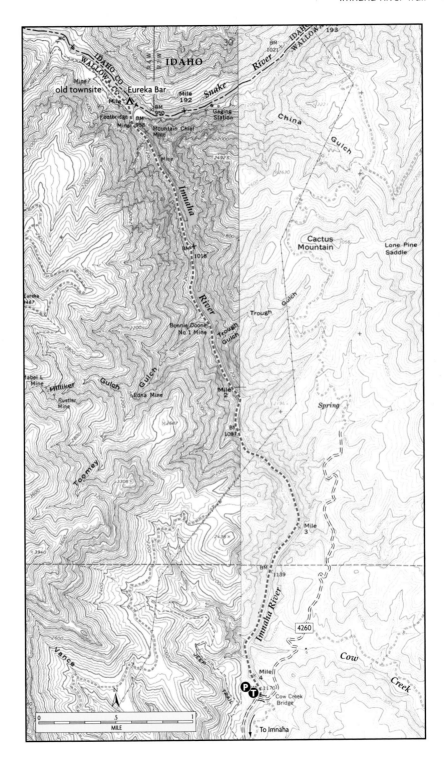

old townsite

Eureka Bar

IDAHO

China Gulch

Cactus Mountain

Lone Pine Saddle

Trough Gulch

Spring

Cow Creek

Imnaha River

4260

Mile 4

Cow Creek Bridge

To Imnaha

0   .5   1
MILE

Along the Imnaha River Trail

The Imnaha River rises in the snowfields of the Wallowa Mountains and quickly descends from the high country into an impressive, 5000-foot-deep, semi-arid canyon. In fact, were it not for Hells Canyon next door, this chasm would rank as one of the natural wonders of North America. The river's last 4 miles lead through an incredibly rugged defile to Eureka Bar, at the remote confluence of the Imnaha and Snake rivers, where the remains of an old mining town add a bit of history to the neck-craning scenery. For a few weeks in 1899, this boomtown had a population of 2000 hardy miners, but as often happened with such communities, the precious ores did not last, so by 1906 the place was a ghost town. Although you will be tempted to spend all of your time looking *up* at the rugged, reddish brown cliffs enclosing this chasm, don't forget to look *down* as well. Two potential boot-level hazards will demand your attention: rattlesnakes, which are fairly common here, and poison ivy, which crowds the trail and forces those who are particularly allergic to skip this hike.

The surprisingly gentle trail closely follows the cascading river through a narrow, steep-walled canyon for 4.1 miles to where the canyon abruptly opens at gravel-strewn Eureka Bar, where the Imnaha River empties into the much larger Snake River. It is fun to explore 0.4 mile north to a nice but shadeless campsite and the remains of the old mill and stoneworks of Eureka.

89   SOMERS POINT

Distance: 27 miles round trip
Hiking time: 2–4 days
Elevation gain: 2600 feet
Difficulty: Strenuous
Season: Mid-June to October
Best: Early to mid-June
Map: USFS Hells Canyon National Recreation Area
Information: Hells Canyon National Recreation Area, (541) 426-5546

Directions: From Joseph, at the end of Oregon Highway 82, drive 30 miles northeast to Imnaha. At a four-way junction in the middle of town, go straight (east) and start the long, very scenic drive on Forest Road 4240 to Hat Point. The road's surface is good gravel (with potholes), but some drivers may be unnerved by the steep drop-offs and relentless uphill. After 22 miles reach a junction with the road to Hat Point Lookout. Go straight, drive 1.7 miles to the end of gravel, then slowly go another 2.6 miles on an increasingly lousy dirt road to the Warnock Corral trailhead. An extremely rough jeep track continues beyond this point, but it qualifies as a "road" in name only. In fact, this road has been periodically closed to motor vehicles due to an ongoing debate about its legal status. For the time being, the "road" doubles as a wide trail and gets very little traffic.

On any list of Oregon's best viewpoints, Somers Point ranks near the top. From this remarkable grandstand you can look down on the raging Snake River, almost a vertical mile below, and east to the high peaks of Idaho. If that does not get you excited, then spend your time enjoying the tremendous variety of wildflowers that bloom here, including phlox, lomatium, skyrocket gilia, asters, and daisies. Although the flower show peaks in early June, the trailhead usually is not accessible until mid-June. Fortunately, the views are great at any time of year.

The Western Rim "Summit" Trail follows the jeep track as it gradually winds downhill through a rather monotonous ghost forest of silvery snags that were burned in a 1989 fire. The regrowing lodgepole pines do not provide much shade, so it can get uncomfortably hot on sunny days. After 1.8 miles you pass a trail to Sleepy Ridge on the left; stay straight, then leave the burned area for a greener and more attractive landscape. The trail/road drops to a saddle (the first of many along this ridge), then arrives at a junction at 3.3 miles with a jeep road that veers left to Windy Ridge. Go straight and climb a short distance to well-named Grassy Knoll. This location provides wonderful views east of the rugged Temperance Creek canyon and into the depths of Hells Canyon.

The rocky, up-and-down jeep track continues north, dropping through a monoculture of even-age lodgepole pines for 2 miles to a fence, where the vegetation abruptly changes to a more diverse mix of meadows and high-elevation

The view to Pittsburg Landing from Somers Point

forests. You then drop steeply to Indian Grave Saddle at 6.3 miles, which features a historic old gravesite, piped spring water, and good campsites. From here, the trail makes a short, steep climb through another burn area, goes over a hill, then drops to Ninemile Saddle at 7.4 miles. You soon pass an unsigned track to the left that leads to an old cabin and small spring, then gently ascend to a junction at 8.9 miles on a flower-covered hilltop with the wonderful title of Parliament. It is fun to pretend you are the "prime minister" of the government here, espe-

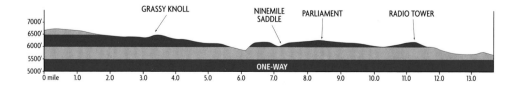

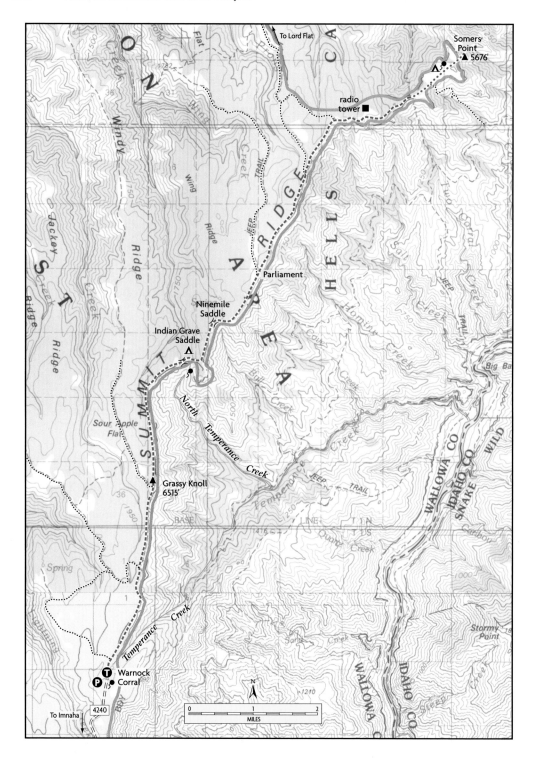

cially when you see the grandeur of your realm. Be prepared to share power with a herd of elk.

For the next 1.8 miles the Summit Trail/road gradually descends through open forest and past more viewpoints to a fork at 10.7 miles. The main "road" goes left to Lord Flat, but you bear right. After 200 yards, the route narrows to a trail and heads northeast for a little over 1 mile to a junction near a radio tower at 11.8 miles. Go right, descend a forested hillside, then ramble across a wide, meadowy ridge with outstanding wildflower displays and great views. Little-used trails branch left, then right, but your focus remains straight ahead, and in another 1.9 miles you reach the glorious view from Somers

Point. Actually, "glorious" hardly does the scene justice, but the English language lacks a grand enough adjective. You have to see this place for yourself.

For an overnight stay, camp in a strip of trees near a spring on the north side of the ridge about 0.2 mile west of Somers Point. In addition to flowers and jaw-dropping views, you can expect to see wildlife. Especially recommended is to spend the evening at Somers Point enjoying the changing shadows in Hells Canyon. Just remember to hang your food first, because black bears have been known to wander through camp checking out anything that smells interesting.

90 GRAND HELLS CANYON LOOP

Distance: 74-mile loop
Hiking time: 6–10 days
Elevation gain: 13,500 feet
Difficulty: Very strenuous
Season: Late March to late June; September to November (avoid midsummer heat)
Best: Early to mid-May
Map: USFS Hells Canyon National Recreation Area
Information: Hells Canyon National Recreation Area, (541) 426-5546

Directions: From Joseph, at the end of Oregon Highway 82, drive 30 miles northeast to Imnaha, turn south, and drive 13 miles to a junction just before a bridge over the Imnaha River. Turn left onto narrow gravel Forest Road 4230, following signs toward Saddle Creek Trail, and drive 3 miles to the Freezeout trailhead.

This long and difficult trip is the ultimate Hells Canyon hiking experience. The loop connects portions of two long trails: the Snake River Trail, which closely follows the rampaging river at the bottom of the canyon, and the Bench Trail, which follows a course about halfway up the canyon walls. Although "breathtaking" is the best word available, it is woefully inadequate to describe

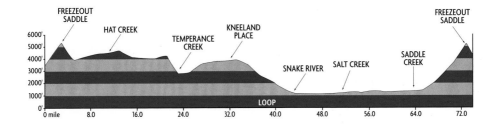

the eye-popping scenery. Stunning views are almost constant, both into the depths of the canyon and across to the snowcapped peaks of Idaho's Seven Devils Mountains. And even though it is easy to be distracted by all the great scenery, you should also see plenty of wildlife. In fact, if you do not see elk almost every day, then you're just not paying attention. Amazingly, even with the incredible scenery, crowds are nonexistent. You may run into a few horse packers or hunters, but backpackers are rare, kept away by the long distances from major metropolitan areas and the difficulty of the trails. The steep, difficult terrain makes for a lot of tiring up-and-down hiking, but it is worth it.

The trail's first 2.2 miles are a good intro-

duction to this difficult hike as several long, moderately steep switchbacks take you 1700 feet up a grassy hillside to a four-way junction at Freezeout Saddle. Go straight and descend a partly burned hillside to a junction at the start of the loop at 4.2 miles. There is no significant advantage to either direction, but for a clockwise circuit, bear left on the Bench Trail, which is often signed as the "High" Trail, and head northeast.

The trail goes gently up and down, zigging into side canyons, zagging out to small ridgelines, and crossing meadowy benches covered with a wealth of wildflowers. The vegetation follows a predictable pattern, with the wetter north-facing slopes covered with forests of Douglas firs and ponderosa pines and the sunnier

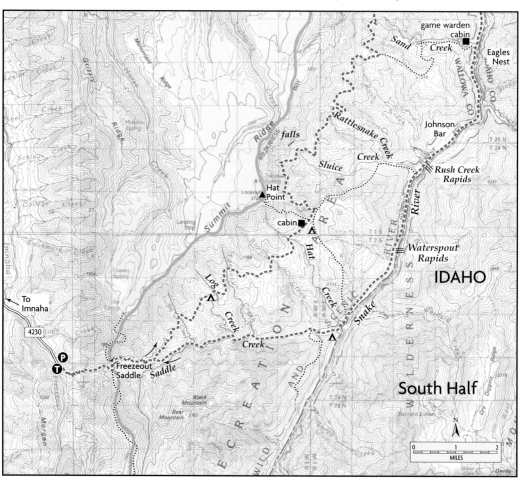

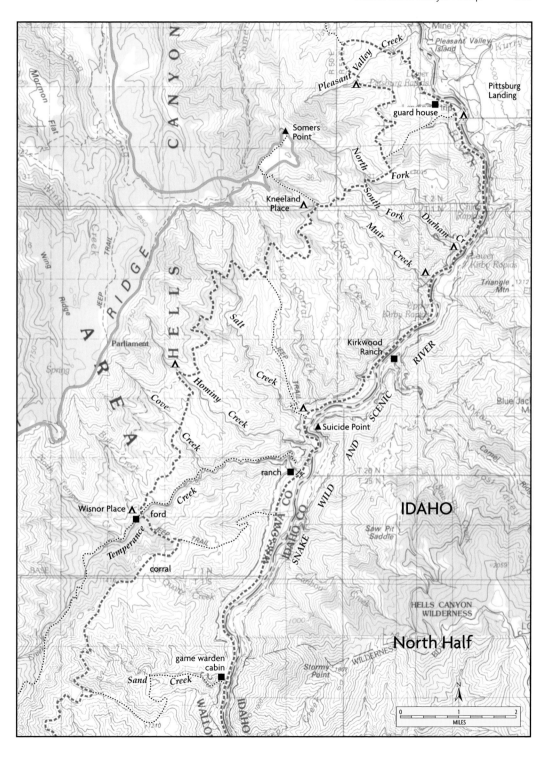

Along Bench Trail in Pleasant Valley

south-facing slopes featuring rocks, bunchgrass, and flowers. The zigzagging pattern and the alternating vegetation zones continue for the entire length of the Bench Trail. At the crossing of Log Creek at 7 miles is the first possible campsite, but a better one comes at Hat Creek at 11.5 miles, where there is an old sheepherder's cabin and a meadowy bench with enough room for even large horse parties.

Stick with the Bench Trail at two junctions just north of Hat Creek, then travel beneath steep walls to a waterfall at the crossing of Sluice Creek. From here, you cross ominously titled Rattlesnake Creek and come to a junction with the sketchy trail down Sand Creek. Go straight and ramble through burn areas and across bunchgrass-covered slopes to the top of the wide ridge separating Temperance Creek from the main canyon of the Snake River. The trail passes a fenced corral along this ridge, then rounds a knoll to a junction. Go left and descend very steeply to a ford of rushing Temperance Creek just before reaching the Wisnor Place at 22 miles. Excellent campsites are near this old wooden homestead.

The Bench Trail goes up and down to a crossing of Cove Creek, where poison ivy is common,

then climbs steeply to Hominy Saddle and possible campsites at Hominy Creek. This difficult section is followed by a glorious and relatively easy hike over view-packed slopes that takes you to the next good campsite, at the former site of Kneeland Place at 32.5 miles. (A side trail climbs steeply from here to Somers Point, Hike 89, which may still have snowdrifts in early May but compensates with some of the best views in the state.)

The going gets more rugged as you descend steeply to crossings of the two branches of Durham Creek, then go around a ridge and drop to a junction. Go straight on the Bench Trail, drop to some good campsites at aptly named Pleasant Valley (watch for bears), then gently ascend through sloping meadows to a junction with the Snake River Trail at 39 miles. This is where you begin the long return leg of this loop.

Turn right and descend this steep, rocky trail to a river-level bench with campsites and views of the boat launch and campground across the river at Pittsburg Landing. You soon pass Pittsburg Guard Station and come to a junction beside often-dry Robertson Gulch. South of here the canyon narrows considerably, forcing the trail onto very steep hillsides where the tread is blasted into the rock.

The rugged terrain compels the trail to make many small ups and downs, but the scenery remains outstanding with neck-craning views of the canyon rim several thousand feet above. You pass nice campsites at Durham Creek and Muir Creek at 45 miles, then hug the rampaging river's banks past the museum and historic buildings of Kirkwood Ranch in Idaho. The way now alternates between crossing steep, rocky hillsides and gentler benches near the mouths of small creeks, often taking you past rocks used by rattlesnakes to sun themselves in the morning and dense, difficult-to-avoid patches of poison ivy. At Salt Creek at 49 miles is a junction near campsites and an old cabin amid a tangle of riparian vegetation. You then round a bend across from the massive ramparts of Idaho's Suicide Point and reach a junction just before the bridge over Temperance Creek.

The trail passes an outfitter's ranch beside Temperance Creek, then skirts the west side of a fenced pasture. About 3.5 miles later you come to the tiny game warden's cabin at Sand Creek at 55 miles. Just beyond this is Eagles Nest, where trail crews used dynamite to blast a tall, open-sided cavern into the rock. This impressive cavern is large enough for even horseback riders to comfortably make it through. You pass a possible campsite beside often-dry Yreka Creek, then round a bend and cross large Johnson Bar. At the southwest end of this landmark is the class 4 whitewater of Rush Creek Rapids, where it is fun to watch rafters struggle to remain upright. After passing a campsite near the junction with Sluice Creek Trail at 59 miles, you go through a narrow section of the canyon that necessitates more up-and-down hiking beside Waterspout Rapids. Just south of this is an excellent campsite a little below the trail at the mouth of Saddle Creek canyon at 64 miles.

The trail turns inland here and begins the long, often-tiring climb out of Hells Canyon. First you ascend the canyon of Saddle Creek for 1 mile to a junction. The Snake River Trail turns left, but to complete the loop, go straight and steadily climb beside Saddle Creek, crossing its flow several times to the junction with the Bench Trail. Go straight and close the loop by returning over Freezeout Saddle to the trailhead.

91 SUMMIT TRAIL TO BEAR MOUNTAIN

Distance: 21 miles round trip
Hiking time: 2 days
Elevation gain: 3500 feet
Difficulty: Moderate
Season: Late May to November
Best: Early to mid-June
Map: USFS Hells Canyon National Recreation Area
Information: Hells Canyon National Recreation Area, (541) 426-5546

Directions: From Joseph, at the end of Oregon Highway 82, drive 8.3 miles east toward Imnaha, then turn right on Wallowa Mountain Road (Forest Road 39). Go 34.5 miles on this winding paved road, then turn left (east) on paved FR 3965, following signs to Hells Canyon Overlook. (From the south, head east from Baker City on Hwy 86 to FR 39, turn left/north, and drive 19.5 miles to the junction with FR 3965.) Drive 2.8 miles on FR 3965 to a developed viewpoint and the end of pavement. Go straight and drive 10.2 miles on a bumpy gravel road to a gate and the PO Saddle trailhead. This gate is open from mid-June to mid-September, allowing traffic to continue another 2.4 extremely rough miles to Saulsberry Saddle, where a berm blocks further travel.

Seven Devils Mountains from near PO Saddle

The Western Rim "Summit" Trail traces a scenic, up-and-down course along the top of Summit Ridge, the high divide that forms the western edge of Hells Canyon. The route is a continuous joy that passes a string of jaw-dropping view-points from which you can look down thousands of feet into the desertlike canyon. This hike follows the southern third of this national recreation trail past great wildflower displays and small springs. The hike ends by following

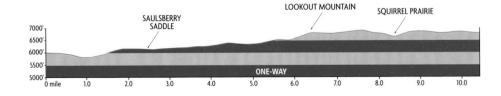

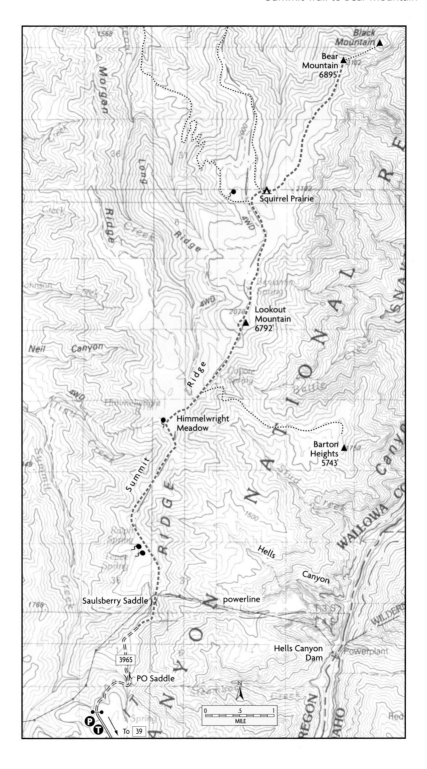

Black Mountain ▲

Bear Mountain 6895' ▲

Morgan Creek

Long Creek Ridge

Creek Ridge

4WD

Squirrel Prairie ▲

Buzzard Spring

4WD

Lookout Mountain 6792' ▲

Johnson Creek

Neil Canyon

Ridge

Coyote Spring

Rattle

N A T I O N A L

Himmelwright Meadow ●

Barton Heights 5743' ▲

Summit

Ridge

4WD

Himmelwright

RIDGE

Ralph Spring

Stud Creek

Hells

1500

Canyon

Canyon

WALLOWA CO.

Saulsberry Saddle

powerline

WILDERNESS

1768

Hells Canyon Dam

Powerplant

3965

PO Saddle

Spring

Spring Creek

OREGON

IDAHO

N

0   .5   1
MILE

P **T**
To 39

a terrific side trail to Bear Mountain, one of the best viewpoints in Hells Canyon.

Begin by walking or driving 2.4 miles to Saulsberry Saddle, where the jeep road goes under a set of powerlines. Bear right on an unsigned trail and go up and down through forests and wildflower meadows to a reunion with the closed road near the top of a gully. From here, the route flattens out on a wide ridge and travels mostly through dense forests to the marshy meadow at Himmelwright Spring at 4.7 miles. Although this meadow is trampled by cattle and smells of bovine pies, the wildflower displays are outstanding in early to mid-June. Of particular note are the large white blossoms of wyethia, which add colorful foregrounds to distant views of the snowy Wallowa Mountains.

The jeep track winds downhill from Himmelwright Spring, then climbs to a junction in 0.5 mile with Battle Creek Trail on the right. The Summit Trail goes straight and climbs gradually through dense forest to the top of Lookout Mountain at 6.3 miles, a wide spot in the ridge with partially obstructed views and nice wildflower displays.

The Summit Trail narrows here as it descends 1.8 miles to a junction, where you veer right and drop to Squirrel Prairie, a sloping meadow often badly trampled by elk and cattle. A spring here feeds the headwaters of Saddle Creek, and there are reasonably good campsites near the edge of the meadow. As is true throughout Hells Canyon, bears are common at Squirrel Prairie. Although they are all black bears, that name is deceiving, because the bears of Hells Canyon are light brown in color.

At a junction in Squirrel Prairie, the Summit Trail continues straight (north); go right (east) on the Bear Mountain Trail as it goes up and down through meadows and burn areas for 2 miles, then climbs to the top of 6895-foot Bear Mountain. The views east into the gaping depths of Hells Canyon and to the snowy crags of Idaho's Seven Devils Mountains are breath-taking.

If you want to explore even further, follow the rough trail another mile northeast to the top of Black Mountain before returning the way you came.

SOUTHEASTERN OREGON

Owyhee River Canyon below Lambert Rocks (Hike 99)

The seemingly endless sagebrush plains of southeastern Oregon remain little known to the majority of Oregonians, who only see this region when passing through on their way to someplace else. But the treasures hidden in this desert realm deserve to be considered destinations in their own right. Here, for example, is spectacular Steens Mountain, a towering fault-block ridge with some of North America's most outstanding glacial gorges. Further exploration leads you to the canyonlands of the Owyhee River, where colorful red, tan, and orange pinnacles and cliffs remind many visitors of southern Utah.

To the west, in the transition zone between the deserts and the Cascade Range, is a mountainous region covered by magnificent stands of ponderosa pines and quaking aspens. And in the vast tracts of desert in between, hikers who get claustrophobic in the dense forests of western Oregon delight in the wide-open expanses of sagebrush and alkali flats.

Wildlife lovers appreciate the chance to observe huge waterfowl migrations at Summer Lake and Malheur National Wildlife Refuge or to see pronghorn, bighorn sheep, badgers, wild horses, and other desert species. Southeastern Oregon is literally "where the deer and the antelope play," and it deserves to be the playground of hikers as well.

92 GEARHART MOUNTAIN

Distance: 11.2 miles round trip
Hiking time: 6 hours (day hike or backpack)
Elevation gain: 1900 feet
Difficulty: Moderate
Season: Late June to October
Best: July
Map: USFS Gearhart Mountain Wilderness
Information: Fremont-Winema National Forest—Bly Ranger District, (541) 353-2427

Directions: From Bly, on Oregon Highway 140 at 51 miles east of Klamath Falls or 43 miles west of Lakeview, go 1.5 miles east on Hwy 140, turn left (north) onto Campbell Road, and go 0.6 mile to a junction marked with a tiny green Gearhart Mountain Wilderness sign. Turn right (east) onto a single-lane paved road that becomes Forest Road 34 and proceed 14.9 miles to a junction. Turn left on Forest Road 012, following signs to Corral Creek Campground, and drive 1.5 miles to the trailhead. The last 0.5 mile of this narrow gravel road is quite rough, but it remains drivable in a passenger car.

The Dome

Most Oregonians have never heard of Gearhart Mountain, an ancient shield volcano that rises in a long, sloping curve above the rolling pine forests of south-central Oregon. This is a shame, because the small wilderness here hides a wealth of interesting sights. Marshy meadows are home to thousands of croaking frogs, a small lake is filled with hungry trout, and a hillside hosts an army of oddly shaped rock pinnacles. But the main attraction is Gearhart Mountain, especially the towering cliffs on the mountain's east face. This hike takes you to the base of those cliffs and along the way visits many of the wilderness' best features.

The well-maintained trail climbs steadily through open, parklike stands of ponderosa pines, lodgepole pines, white firs, and quaking aspens. The tread is loose and sandy, so getting traction is a bit difficult, especially when going uphill. After 1 mile you reach The Palisades, a fascinating area of eroded volcanic pillars that jut out of an open hillside.

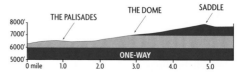

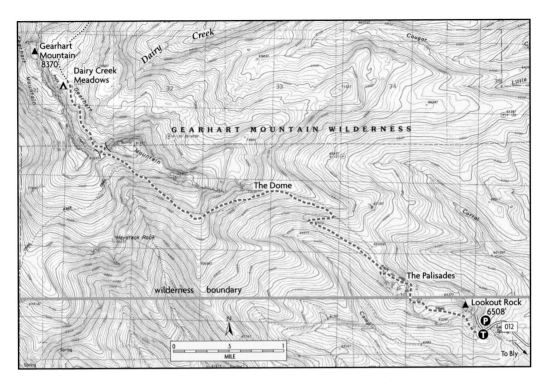

After traveling through The Palisades, the trail switchbacks downhill about 100 feet, then gently ascends past a small spring to The Dome at 3 miles, an impressive rock formation on top of the ridge. At 4.7 miles you reach a ridge-top saddle with terrific views north over the Dairy Creek Basin to the cliffs of Gearhart Mountain.

From here, the trail rapidly loses about 200 feet, then contours 0.9 mile to gorgeous little Dairy Creek Meadows directly beneath the imposing cliffs of Gearhart Mountain. Trickling Dairy Creek provides water for a good campsite, which allows backpackers to savor this outstanding scenery at leisure. This meadow is the logical turnaround point.

93 CRANE MOUNTAIN

Distance: 4.8 miles round trip (including 0.4-mile side trip to Willow Point)
Hiking time: 3 hours
Elevation gain: 1500 feet
Difficulty: Moderate
Season: Late June to October
Best: July
Map: USGS Crane Mountain
Information: Fremont-Winema National Forest—Lakeview Ranger District, (541) 947-3334

Directions: From the junction of US 395 and Oregon Highway 140, 4.5 miles north of Lakeview, go 8.1 miles east on Hwy 140, then turn right (south) on Forest Road 3915, following signs to Willow Creek Campground. After 5.6 miles, the pavement ends at a four-way junction beside the Rogger Meadow trailhead (an alternate exit point). Go straight, still on FR 3915, for 6.7 miles, turn right on FR 4011, then proceed 2.4 miles to an unsigned fork. Bear right, go 1.3 miles, then park where the gravel road abruptly ends. A jeep road continues to the summit, but it is too rough for passenger cars.

Since Crane Mountain is the highest point in south-central Oregon, you might assume that great views are the principal attraction of this hike—and you would be right. The panoramic vista from the summit, especially of enormous Goose Lake and the adjacent Lakeview Valley, is amazing. But in addition to offering views, the hike travels through attractive forests, features numerous wildflowers, and provides a good but not exhausting workout. Unfortunately, you have to share the trail with noisy motors—but nothing is perfect.

Follow the jeep road steadily but not steeply uphill through a cool forest of white firs and ponderosa, lodgepole, and western white pines. Views are infrequent but flowers, including lomatium, balsamroot, wallflower, and phlox, are common in late June and July. Unfortunately, this is also bug season. Although the mosquitoes are slow and easy to swat, they have such an enormous advantage in numbers that their strategy seems to be to continue the attack despite heavy losses.

After 0.9 mile the jeep road forks at a saddle. Take the 0.2-mile route to the right to Willow Point, a rocky overlook with a good view of Crane Mountain. Return to the main route, which goes right (west) and ascends a series of rounded switchbacks. At the seventh switchback, the northbound Crane Mountain Trail departs to the right at about 2 miles. (With a car shuttle you can turn this into a very scenic one-way hike by going 10 miles north on this trail to the Rogger Meadow trailhead; blessedly, this trail is closed to motorized vehicles.) You go left.

Still on the jeep road, climb a few more switchbacks, then partway up the final leg meet the southbound Crane Mountain Trail to the left at 2.4 miles. (For a slightly higher viewpoint, you can walk 0.8 mile south on this trail, then scramble up a 8456-foot knoll where whitebark pines frame great views in all directions.) For this hike, go straight and soon reach the summit.

Four concrete foundation posts are all that remain of the fire lookout that once stood on Crane Mountain, but the views are still outstanding. To the south runs the rugged spine of the Warner Mountains, while to the north and east are pyramid-shaped Drake Peak and the distant hump of Hart Mountain. Most impressive is the view southwest of huge Goose Lake.

Crane Mountain over Willow Creek

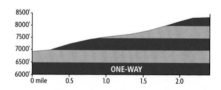

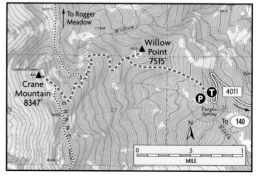

94

BIG INDIAN GORGE

Distance: 17 miles round trip
Hiking time: 9 hours (day hike or backpack)
Elevation gain: 1900 feet
Difficulty: Strenuous
Season: June to October
Best: Mid- to late June; late September and early October
Maps: USGS Fish Lake, Wildhorse Lake
Information: Bureau of Land Management—Burns District, (541) 573-4400

Directions: From Burns, drive Oregon Highway 205 south 70 miles (10.1 miles past Frenchglen) to a junction with the gravel Steens Mountain Loop Road. Turn left (east), following signs to Upper Blitzen River, and drive 19.1 miles to South Steens Campground. Turn into the Family Camping Area and park in a gravel lot at the southeast end of the loop road.

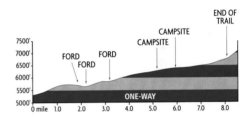

During the last ice age, the climate of southeastern Oregon was wetter than it is today, so much more snow fell on places like Steens Mountain. This snowfall compacted into huge glaciers that carved deep, U-shaped gorges into the mountain's flanks. Although this process took place on other mountains, Steens Mountain may be the best place in the country to observe the ice's handiwork, because there are no forests here to hide the evidence. Looking down these enormous gorges from above is awe-inspiring, but to truly appreciate these geologic marvels you

have to hike along the bottom. Of the mountain's seven glacial gorges, the most accessible and dramatic is Big Indian Gorge. **Note:** In June, call ahead to check on the feasibility of three major stream crossings.

The route begins as an abandoned jeep track that steadily climbs through a western juniper woodland then up a grassy slope. After topping a rise, the trail descends to a ford of Indian Creek at 1.9 miles. In early summer this crossing may be too dangerous for hikers, so look for a log about 100 yards downstream. The trail then climbs

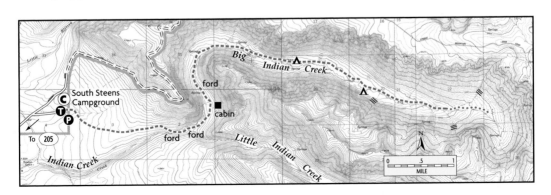

Big Indian Gorge near the second campsite

0.3 mile to a much easier ford of Little Indian Creek and curves north past a broken-down log cabin. As the elevation gradually increases, the junipers are joined by quaking aspens and mountain mahoganies, with some large cottonwoods beside the creek. In June, wildflowers are abundant, with geranium, balsamroot, lupine, and larkspur among the showier species.

The next obstacle is a ford at 3.1 miles of Big Indian Creek, which as the name suggests is more challenging than Little Indian Creek. Bring wading shoes for traction and a walking stick for a "third leg." Above this ford the trail is easy and joyous, gaining elevation steadily but slowly with increasingly spectacular scenery that draws you along. Tough-limbed sagebrush often crowds the path, but it is easy to push through if you wear long pants. As the canyon curves east, the walls tower ever higher and become more spectacular.

At about 5.2 miles is a good campsite in a grove of cottonwoods. Above this camp the trail crosses numerous small side creeks and wet meadows, but most of your time is spent gazing in awe at the stupendous scenery. At a little over 6 miles is an exceptional campsite in a grove of cottonwoods, near the first of several waterfalls that tumble down the south wall. This is a good base for further explorations.

The trail becomes sketchy above this campsite, but the scenery is even more impressive. Tall waterfalls, large aspen groves that turn gold in the fall, 2400-foot-high canyon walls—adjectives fail to convey the grandeur of the surroundings. You have to see this place for yourself. The trail disappears at about 8 miles, where the creek forks beneath the gorge's enormous headwall. You can go about 0.5 mile farther before facing the uninviting prospect of a very steep scramble up the headwall, so after a suitable time for gawking, return the way you came.

95 WILDHORSE LAKE

Distance: 2.6 miles round trip
Hiking time: 2 hours
Elevation gain: 1100 feet
Difficulty: Strenuous
Season: Mid-July to October
Best: Late July to mid-August
Map: USGS Wildhorse Lake
Information: Bureau of Land Management—Burns District, (541) 573-4400

Directions: From Burns, drive Oregon Highway 205 south 60 miles to Frenchglen. Turn left (southeast) on Steens Mountain Loop and stay on this extremely scenic gravel road for 25.4 miles tc the summit ridge of Steens Mountain and a three-way junction. Take the middle road and proceed 2 miles to the trailhead.

One of the most beautiful mountain lakes in Oregon is, paradoxically, surrounded by desert. Sparkling Wildhorse Lake fills a dramatic glacial cirque below the summit of Steens Mountain, and although sagebrush-covered hills can be seen in every direction, the snowfields and alpine splendor of this lake set it well apart from that desolate landscape. A short but strenuous trail reaches this mountain gem, and the beauty is well worth the long drive and tiring climb back out. Be aware that with a trailhead at almost 9500 feet, the air is noticeably thinner here than on most Oregon hikes.

The trail goes southwest down a rocky roadbed for 0.2 mile to a stunning overlook of shimmering Wildhorse Lake and the cliff-lined canyon to the south. You can also look west down gaping Big Indian Gorge (Hike 94) or simply admire the dozens of alpine wildflowers that bloom in profusion from late July to mid-August. You could easily admire this view for hours, but bring a windbreaker, since a stiff breeze constantly blows at this altitude.

The sometimes obscure path turns sharply left at the overlook, contours across the top of a rock escarpment, then winds very steeply down a rocky slope to a small upper basin at 0.5 mile rimmed with cliffs. From here, more steep downhill reaches a spring-fed creek at 0.8 mile, which leads 0.5 mile to Wildhorse Lake. The wildflower displays near the lake are outstanding. Look for bistort, wild carrot, paintbrush, Lewis' monkeyflower, false hellebore, alumroot, Oregon sunshine, yarrow, cinquefoil, and countless other species. As for the views, they are so stupendous

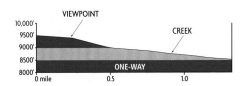

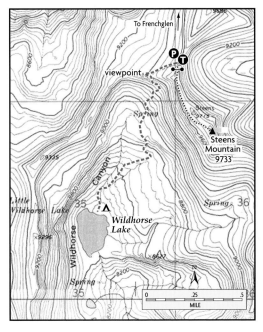

Wildflowers bloom near Wildhorse Lake.

the word "scenic" does not begin to adequately describe this place. See it for yourself and try to come up with something better. You can fish, study wildflowers, or just gaze in amazement for hours.

If you want to explore, check out a small tarn to the south of Wildhorse Lake, visit any of several cascading waterfalls to the east, scramble down the rugged canyon of Wildhorse Creek below the lake, or climb to the summit of Steens Mountain. That last goal is reachable from the trailhead by a closed 0.4-mile jeep road.

96 PIKE CREEK CANYON

Distance: 3.8 miles round trip to viewpoint; 6.5 miles round trip to Pike Knob
Hiking time: 2 hours to viewpoint; 5 hours to Pike Knob
Elevation gain: 1300 feet to viewpoint; 2000 feet to Pike Knob
Difficulty: Moderate to viewpoint; very strenuous to Pike Knob
Season: Mid-April to November
Best: May
Map: USGS Alvord Hot Springs
Information: Bureau of Land Management—Burns District, (541) 573-4400

Directions: From Burns, drive Oregon Highway 78 southeast 66 miles, then turn right (south) on a gravel county road, following signs to Fields. After 40 very scenic miles, exactly 3.7 miles past the turnoff to Alvord Ranch, turn right on an unsigned dirt road that immediately crosses a cattle guard. Follow this rough dirt road for 0.6 mile, carefully avoiding ominous rocks along the way, then park near rollicking Pike Creek.

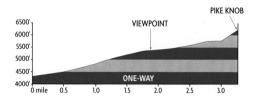

The rugged east face of Steens Mountain makes a precipitous, 5000-foot drop from alpine tundra to stark desert playa in just a few miles as the golden eagle flies. On a spring day, when the mountain is still covered with snow, looking up to those cliffs is one of the most dramatic sights in Oregon. Even better for avid pedestrians, this great wall is broken by several rugged canyons that invite exploration on foot. The most accessible of these is Pike Creek Canyon, which features a good trail and some of the most dramatic scenery in Oregon.

You immediately rock-hop Pike Creek, then find an old miners track that heads up the canyon. Towering above you to the right, left, and especially straight ahead are scenic pink and red-brown walls streaked with greenish yellow lichen. Above these walls is the snowy crest of Steens Mountain. In May, wildflowers are abundant. Look for balsamroot, larkspur, lomatium, desert parsley, prairie star, and lupine. Interestingly, the lupines change from the usual blue variety at the mouth of the canyon to a striking yellow color farther up. In the twisting canyon, splashing Pike Creek on your right supports a tangle of riparian trees and shrubs that form a strip of verdant greenery in the desert.

You pass a trail register box after 0.3 mile, where you enter the Steens Mountain Wilderness, then continue ascending. The increasingly narrow, rocky track is steep in places but easy to follow. At the 1-mile point, the trail dives briefly into the riparian shrubbery and crosses the creek. From here, you go around prominent Pike Point, climb a pair of fairly steep switchbacks, then traverse at a more modest grade.

Pike Point from the trail up Pike Creek Canyon

Just before a large boulder at 1.3 miles, the miners track heads downhill toward the creek, but you turn right onto a steep boot path. This path climbs over broken rockslides and sagebrush-covered hillsides for 0.6 mile to a stunning viewpoint at 1.9 miles of Pike Creek's upper canyon and the snow-streaked cliffs above. To the east you can see the Alvord Desert, which may or may not have water on it depending on precipitation levels and the time of year. The trail quickly disappears above this point, so most hikers turn around here.

Athletic types can scramble up another 1.4 miles, to the forks of Pike Creek and the top of Pike Knob, a 6102-foot knoll separating the two forks of Pike Creek.

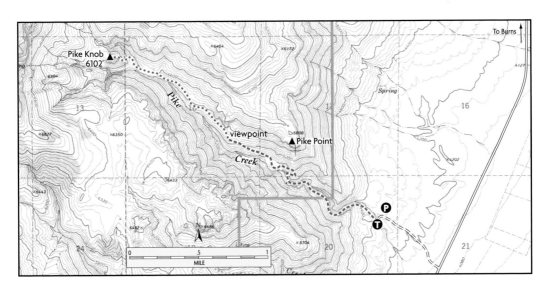

97

BIG SAND GAP

Distance: 11 miles round trip
Hiking time: 5 hours
Elevation gain: 300 feet
Difficulty: Moderate
Season: April to late June; September to November (avoid midsummer heat)
Best: May
Maps: USGS Miranda Flat SW, Tule Springs
Information: Bureau of Land Management—Burns District, (541) 573-4400

Directions: From Burns, drive Oregon Highway 78 southeast 66 miles, then turn right (south) on a gravel county road, following signs to Fields. After 31 very scenic miles, the road makes a 90-degree turn to the right. Turn left (east) on unsigned Bureau of Land Management (BLM) Road 7282-0-00, drive 2.5 miles, then turn right at another unsigned junction. Proceed 7.7 miles on this rough but passable dirt road across salt-desert scrub and sagebrush flats to a four-way junction. Park here.

If you are tired of Oregon's famous rain, then this is the hike for you. Like all of eastern Oregon, the Alvord Desert sits in the rain shadow of the Cascade Range. But in addition, this flat wasteland fills a basin immediately east of Steens Mountain, a huge fault-block mountain that effectively blocks what little water is left in

Steens Mountain stands in stark contrast to the Alvord Desert.

the clouds that make it this far east. As a result, the Alvord Desert is the driest place in the state of Oregon, with only seven inches of precipitation annually. The parched landscape has only limited plant life. The tallest living things are a few greasewood bushes along the edge of the playa. Since only the area's lizards consider this to constitute "shelter," hikers should bring a hat and wear plenty of sunscreen.

Some people enjoy hiking across the Alvord Desert, a unique experience but one that quickly saps the moisture out of your body. The trip described here is a better option, tracing the eastern edge of the desert to Big Sand Gap, a sand dune-filled break in the rimrock east of the desert, with great views of the snowy ridge of Steens Mountain. **Note:** There is no water in this desert environment. Carry at least two quarts per person and up to a gallon in hot weather.

Walk south on a rough jeep track (too rough for passenger cars) through a stark landscape of alkali flats and scattered clumps of black greasewood. Although the jeep track has many small ups and downs, it never strays more than a few feet in elevation from the starting point. On your left (east) is a tall basalt rim that shows evidence of the former shoreline of the ancestral lake that once filled this basin. On your right (west) is snowy Steens Mountain and the huge, flat expanse of the Alvord Desert. The tall landmark in the distance ahead of you (mostly south) is Pueblo Mountain (Hike 98).

The shadeless route continues south for 5 miles, crossing more salt scrub and dry washes to where the jeep track curves left (southeast) and goes uphill toward Big Sand Gap, a prominent break in the rim. When you get there, you discover that this gap is filled with sand dunes, thus giving the place its name. The jeep track disappears amid the rocks and sand at the base of Big Sand Gap, but it is fun to explore the dunes and climb to viewpoints on either side. While in the area, keep an eye out for lizards. This area hosts more species than anywhere else in Oregon. Herpetologists will love it.

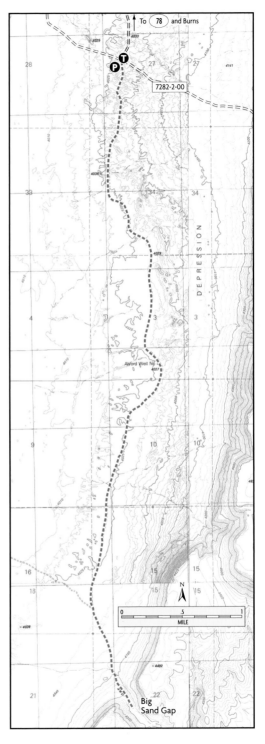

98 PUEBLO MOUNTAIN

Distance: 11 miles round trip
Hiking time: 7 hours (day hike or backpack)
Elevation gain: 3500 feet
Difficulty: Very strenuous
Season: Late May to October
Best: June
Maps: USGS Ladycomb Peak, Van Horn Basin
Information: Bureau of Land Management—Burns District, (541) 573-4400

Directions: From Burns, drive Oregon Highway 205 south 120 miles to Fields. Continue 9.4 miles south (0.9 mile beyond the Whitehorse Ranch Road), then turn right (west) on an unsigned dirt road. Climb this reasonably good road for 2.9 miles to a junction. Park here.

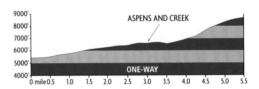

Rising to 8634 feet, Pueblo Mountain is the second-highest point in southeastern Oregon, and the view from the top meets or exceeds any expectations you may have when looking up from the bottom. Not only can you admire nearby features such as the main ridge of the Pueblo Mountains and the heart-shaped playa of Tum Tum Lake, but you can see snowcapped Steens Mountain to the north, Nevada's rugged Santa Rosa Range

Pueblo Ridge from Stergen Meadows

to the south, and rolling sagebrush-covered hills in every direction. Reaching this splendid viewpoint, however, requires stamina and plenty of sweat. It is a long way up, and since the only trees are a few mountain mahoganies and small groves of quaking aspens, shade is limited to the hat you carry with you. Fortunately, water is available from springs and small creeks.

Walk along the jeep road that goes right (west) across a sagebrush-covered slope with views north to Steens Mountain and south-southwest to rugged Pueblo Mountain. The jeep road curves left and climbs through the scenic upper canyon of Arizona Creek. Rock outcroppings are covered with colorful lichens, and wildflowers add more color in May and June.

At 1 mile you pass a spring in a little meadow that would be very attractive were it not so badly trampled by cattle. After this, the jeep road goes through a gate in a flimsy barbed-wire fence and comes to a saddle at about 1.7 miles, with your first views west to the serrated main ridge of the Pueblo Mountains. This impressive fault-block range usually has snow patches clinging to the undersides of its highest cliffs well into June.

From the saddle, your route turns south, then goes gradually uphill 0.5 mile to Stergen

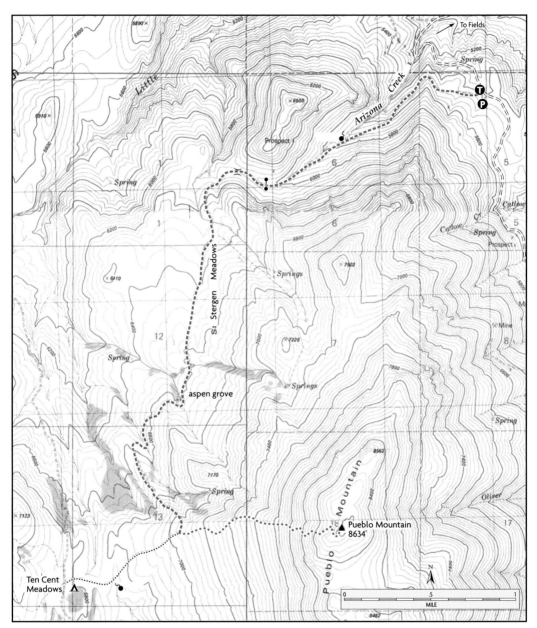

Meadows, a series of gently sloping, grassy areas with seasonal creeks and fine views of looming Pueblo Mountain. Wildlife is common here. Look for mule deer, coyotes, and badgers. You may even see bighorn sheep in the rocky areas to the southeast.

The steady uphill leads through the upper part of Stergen Meadows to a tiny creek and a small grove of quaking aspens at 3 miles. The road then climbs into higher terrain, with a few twisted mountain mahogany trees rarely more than 10 feet high. In 0.2 mile you top a small ridge, in another 0.3 mile descend to a small creek, then steeply ascend the spine of a second ridge to a high point at 4 miles, above the saddle separating Pueblo Mountain from the main ridge of the Pueblo Mountains. The large grassy area to the west 0.6 mile is Ten Cent Meadows, with springwater and possible campsites.

From the high point, your course leaves the jeep road and travels due east, initially on a very faint four-wheel-drive track, then cross-country toward the enormous hump of Pueblo Mountain.

For the first 0.5 mile the going is relatively easy over low sagebrush, wildflowers, and grasses, none of which grow more than a few inches tall in this high-elevation environment. The going then becomes more strenuous as the grade gets steeper and more rocky. Eventually you pick your way over rockslides and through boulder fields before finally reaching the summit. Your efforts are richly rewarded with outstanding views, complete solitude, and a strong sense of accomplishment from having scaled this huge mountain.

99   LAMBERT ROCKS AND CHALK BASIN LOOP

Distance: 11 miles round trip
Hiking time: 6 hours (day hike or backpack)
Elevation gain: 800 feet
Difficulty: Strenuous
Season: April to October (avoid midsummer heat)
Best: September
Map: USGS Lambert Rocks
Information: Bureau of Land Management—Vale District, (541) 473-3144

Directions: Begin from Rome, where US 95 crosses the Owyhee River. Just east of "downtown" Rome (the single store of the three buildings that make up this town), turn north onto an unsigned gravel road, drive 2.6 miles, then cross a bridge over the Owyhee River. The road then goes through a private ranch, turns right, and deteriorates into a rough and rocky track. The road is passable only when dry, and even then it is rough and extremely dusty. You need good ground clearance and plenty of nerve to reach the starting point. Stay on this miserable "road" for 14 miles to a four-way junction in the

middle of an indistinct dirt airstrip. Turn left and drive 0.6 mile to a fence across the road, where you have to get out to open the gate. Drive 2.4 very rough and dusty miles, then park beside a second fence shortly before the road drops off the end of a mesa.

This hike explores one of the most spectacularly beautiful places in the state of Oregon. The colorful badlands of Chalk Basin rise above the Owyhee River in a stunning display of eroded cliffs and spires. Enhancing this photographer's paradise are the nearby volcanic crags of the Lambert Rocks and the deep chasm of the Owyhee

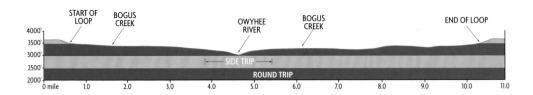

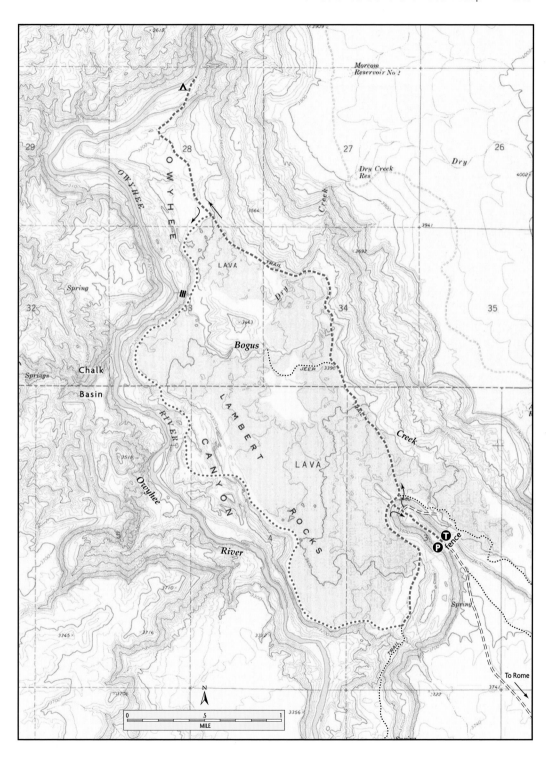

Butte in Chalk Basin across Owyhee River

River Canyon. But getting there is a challenge. More than any other trip in this book, the access road tests the limits of the rule that all hikes must be accessible in a typical passenger car. Not only that, the window of opportunity for visiting this area is small. Most people arrive on rafts in April and May, when the water is high enough for floaters on the Owyhee River. But the road then is usually muddy and impassable. By midsummer, temperatures soar above 100 degrees Fahrenheit, which is too hot for most hikers. That leaves September, after the temperatures cool and before winter rains turn the powdery dust into miles of mud. Fortunately, this is also when rabbitbrush and sunflowers add splashes of yellow to the desert's browns and grays.

Put on sturdy boots and steeply descend a rocky trail that drops off the end of the mesa. Do not follow the jeep road, which curves right and leads to private land. At the bottom of the steep drop-off at the base of the mesa is a jeep road. Turn right to begin the loop, walk a few yards, then bear left (north) onto a narrow jeep trail at 0.5 mile.

This trail crosses a generally flat plain through a stark landscape covered with dark volcanic rocks, sagebrush, and rabbitbrush. Immediately on your right is the meandering oasis of Bogus Creek, which supports marsh grasses, cattails, and abundant bird life. To your left are the lava flows forming Lambert Rocks. At a junction at the 1.5-mile point, turn right, then hop over trickling Bogus Creek. From here, the trail makes a scenic descent toward the grassy banks of the Owyhee River.

At about 3 miles you reach the northern edge of the sagebrush plain. Continue down for another mile or so to the river, where there are plenty of possible tent sites. Watch for poison ivy and rattlesnakes near the river. Just downstream from trail's end, the river enters a spectacular canyon, the entrance to which is worth investigating, although sheer cliffs block any extended foot travel in that direction.

To visit Chalk Basin, return to the edge of the sagebrush-covered plain (now at about 5 miles), then leave the trail and head right (southwest). The best course follows the cliffs above the river, so you can avoid walking over the jagged lava flow of Lambert Rocks on your left. In 0.7 mile cross Bogus Creek just above a seasonal waterfall, then walk past the increasingly spectacular spires and cliffs of Chalk Basin on the west side of the river. In several places you can scramble down and ford the river to get a closer look at the colorfully striated badlands.

About 3.5 miles after leaving the trail, at about 8.5 miles, you reach the southern end of Chalk Basin, across from a distinctive eroded butte with wide bands of light- and dark-colored rock. Turn east and follow sketchy game paths about 0.6 mile to the jeep road at the base of the mesa, then turn left and follow this track about 1.7 miles back to your starting point.

100   THREE FORKS TRAILS

Distance: 6.5 miles round trip on Wes Hawkins Trail; 4 miles round trip to hot springs; 2 miles round trip on military road; 12.5 miles total

Hiking time: 4 hours, Wes Hawkins Trail; 2 hours to hot springs; 2 hours on military road; 8 hours total

Elevation gain: 900 feet, Wes Hawkins Trail; 100 feet to hot springs; 800 feet on military grade; 1800 feet total

Difficulty: Moderate to strenuous

Season: April to October (avoid midsummer heat)

Best: September

Map: USGS Three Forks

Information: Bureau of Land Management—Vale District, (541) 473-3144

Directions: From Jordan Valley near the Idaho border, drive US 95 southwest to milepost 36. Turn left (south), following signs to Soldier Creek Wildlife Loop, and follow a remote gravel road that is normally fine for passenger cars, although the surface can be slippery after it rains. After 29 miles, turn right at the signed junction with the Three Forks Road. Continue south on the Three Forks Road; exactly 0.8 mile from the junction, park on the road shoulder where the unsigned Wes Hawkins Trail is on the right. To reach Three Forks, drive 2 miles farther south to the canyon rim; if your car has poor ground clearance or conditions are wet, park here. Otherwise, drive the steep and rocky road 1.3 miles to Three Forks junction beside a small corral at the bottom of the grade. Turn right and park near a raft launch site.

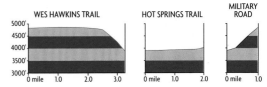

"Remote" hardly seems adequate to describe Three Forks. Hidden at the bottom of a precipitous canyon at the end of a lonely dirt road, this little-known site is the definition of isolated. But solitude is only one good reason to visit this place. The best reason is the scenery, highlighted by the meandering Owyhee River and its spectacular, 1000-foot-deep canyon of dark basalt and lighter-colored rhyolite. The list of reasons also includes abundant wildlife such as pronghorn, golden eagles, and coyotes. The final reason is that Three Forks has one of the best thermal springs in the Pacific Northwest.

The first recommended hike follows the Wes Hawkins Trail, which departs from the Three Forks Road and follows a sketchy jeep track that angles southwest. After 250 yards, climb over a fenceline, then walk 0.2 mile to a junction. Turn right (west) and walk across a gently rolling sagebrush plain where you are likely to see pronghorn, black-tailed jackrabbits, and, less pleasantly, cattle, which are drawn to the barrels of salt sometimes put out along this jeep track.

The jeep track ends after 2.5 miles, shortly before the steep drop-off of the Owyhee River Canyon. The canyon views are excellent and more than compensate for your efforts so far. If you are adventurous, continue your hike all the way down to the river. To find the way, head due west from the end of the jeep track to a large rock cairn on the canyon rim. From here, the somewhat overgrown but obvious Wes Hawkins Trail switchbacks 0.7 mile down to the river, where there are possible campsites. Return the way you came.

The other trails both start at Three Forks. The

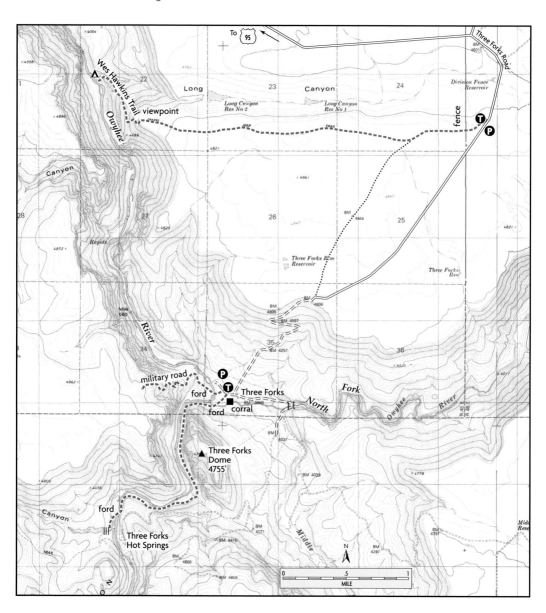

most popular destination is the hot springs. To reach it, ford the shallow North Fork Owyhee River, then follow an old wagon road along the east bank of the main stem Owyhee River. This winding route takes you around the base of the towering cliffs of Three Forks Dome in about a mile, then through native grasslands that peter out just before the hot springs. There are bathing areas on both sides of the river, but the most interesting and attractive sites are on the west bank, where the warm (calling it "hot" would be an overstatement) water drops over a scenic waterfall. The springs are on private property, but the landowner allows public access. Please do not abuse this privilege, so

Military Road offers spectacular views of Owyhee River Canyon.

the landowner's policy can continue in the future.

The last recommended hike follows a historic military road that switchbacks up the canyon wall west of Three Forks. To reach the road, from Three Forks ford the Owyhee River (usually possible by mid-June), then bushwhack northwest along the river to the base of the old wagon road and follow it up the canyon wall. The 1-mile route gains 750 feet to the western canyon rim, where views of the steep-walled canyon are breathtaking.

APPENDIX A:
LAND MANAGEMENT AGENCIES
AND INFORMATION SOURCES

Natural Resources Conservation Service
(snow survey data)
(503) 414-3200
www.nrcs.usda.gov/wps/portal/nrcs/main
/or/snow

Bureau of Land Management
Burns District
28910 US Highway 20 W
Hines, OR 97738
(541) 573-4400
www.blm.gov/or/districts/burns

Eugene District
3106 Pierce Parkway, Suite E
Springfield, OR 97477
(541) 683-6600

Roseburg District
777 NW Garden Valley Blvd
Roseburg, OR 97471
(541) 440-4930

Vale District
100 Oregon Street
Vale, OR 97918
(541) 473-3144
www.blm.gov/or/districts/vale

National Parks, Monuments, and Recreation or
Scenic Areas
Columbia River Gorge National Scenic Area
902 Wasco Avenue, Suite 200
Hood River, OR 97031
(541) 308-1700
www.fs.usda.gov/crgnsa

Crater Lake National Park
P.O. Box 7
Crater Lake, OR 97604
(541) 594-3000
www.nps.gov/crla/

Hells Canyon National Recreation Area
201 E Second Street
PO Box 905
Joseph, OR 97845
(541) 426-5546
www.fs.usda.gov/detail/wallowa-whitman
/specialplaces

John Day Fossil Beds National Monument
32651 Oregon Highway 19
Kimberly, OR 97848
(541) 987-2333
www.nps.gov/joda/

Oregon Dunes National Recreation Area
855 Highway Avenue
Reedsport, OR 97467
(541) 271-6000
www.fs.usda.gov/recarea/siuslaw/recreation
/recarea

National Forests
Deschutes National Forest
www.fs.usda.gov/deschutes

Bend/Fort Rock Ranger District
63095 Deschutes Market Road
Bend, OR 97701
(541) 383-4000

Crescent Ranger District
P.O. Box 208
Crescent, OR 97733
(541) 433-3200

Sisters Ranger District
P.O. Box 249
Sisters, OR 97759
(541) 549-7700

Fremont-Winema National Forest
www.fs.usda.gov/fremont-winema

Bly Ranger District
61100 Highway 140 East
Bly, OR 97622
(541) 353-2427

Klamath Falls Ranger District
2819 Dahlia Street
Klamath Falls, OR 97601
(541) 883-6714

Lakeview Ranger District
18049 US Highway 395 N
Lakeview, OR 97630
(541) 947-3334

Malheur National Forest
www.fs.usda.gov/r6/malheur

Blue Mountain Ranger District
P.O. Box 909
431 Patterson Bridge Road
John Day, OR 97845
(541) 575-3000

Prairie City Ranger District
P.O. Box 337
Prairie City, OR 97869
(541) 820-3800

Mount Hood National Forest
www.fs.usda.gov/mthood

Barlow Ranger District
780 NE Court Street
Dufur, OR 97021
(541) 467-2291

Clackamas River Ranger District
595 NW Industrial Way
Estacada, OR 97023
(503) 630-6861

Hood River Ranger District
6780 Oregon Highway 35
Parkdale, OR 97041
(541) 352-6002

Mount Hood Information Center
65000 E US Highway 26
Welches, OR 97067
(503) 622-4822

Zigzag Ranger District
70220 E US Highway 26
Zigzag, OR 97049
(503) 622-3191

Ochoco National Forest
www.fs.usda.gov/ochoco
3160 NE Third Street
Prineville, OR 97754
(541) 416-6500

Rogue River–Siskiyou National Forest
www.fs.usda.gov/rogue-siskiyou

Gold Beach Ranger District
29279 Ellensberg Road
Gold Beach, OR 97444
(541) 247-3600

Powers Ranger District
42861 Highway 242
Powers, OR 97466
(541) 439-6200

Siskiyou Mountains Ranger District
6941 Upper Applegate Road
Jacksonville, OR 97530-9314
(541) 899-3800

Siuslaw National Forest
www.fs.usda.gov/siuslaw

Central Coast Ranger District/Waldport Office
1130 Forestry Lane
PO Box 400
Waldport, OR 97394
(541) 563-8400

Hebo Ranger District
PO Box 235
31525 Oregon Highway 22
Hebo,OR 97122
(503) 392-5100

Umatilla National Forest
www.fs.usda.gov/umatilla

Pomeroy Ranger District
71 W Main Street
Pomeroy, WA 99347
(509) 843-1891

Walla Walla Ranger District
1415 W Rose Street
Walla Walla, WA 99362
(509) 522-6290

Umpqua National Forest
www.fs.usda.gov/umpqua

Diamond Lake Ranger District
2020 Toketee RS Road
Idleyld Park, OR 97447
(541) 498-2531

Tiller Ranger District
27812 Tiller Trail Highway
Tiller, OR 97484
(541) 825-3100

Wallowa-Whitman National Forest
www.fs.usda.gov/wallowa-whitman

Wallowa Mountains Office
201 E Second Street
PO Box 905
Joseph, OR 97846
(541) 426-5546

Whitman Ranger District
1550 Dewey Avenue, Suite A
Baker City, OR 97814
(541) 523-6391

Willamette National Forest
www.fs.usda.gov/willamette

Detroit Ranger District
HC 73, Box 320
Mill City, OR 97360
(503) 854-3366

McKenzie River Ranger District
57600 McKenzie Highway
McKenzie Bridge, OR 97413
(541) 822-3381

Middle Fork Ranger District
46375 Oregon Highway 58
Westfir, OR 97492
(541) 782-2283

Sweet Home Ranger District
4431 US Highway 20
Sweet Home, OR 97386
(541) 367-5168

Oregon State Parks
www.oregonstateparks.org
725 Sumner Street NE, Suite C
Salem, OR 97301
(503) 986-0707 or (800) 551-6949

Ecola State Park
(503) 436-2844

Floras Lake State Natural Area
(541) 888-8867, ext. 26

Guy W. Talbot State Park
(503) 695-2261

Oswald West State Park
(503) 368-3575

Saddle Mountain State Natural Area
(503) 368-5943

Samuel H. Boardman State Park
(541) 469-2021

Shore Acres State Park
(541) 888-3732

Silver Falls State Park
(503) 873-8681

Smith Rock State Park
(541) 548-7501

Tryon Creek State Natural Area
(503) 636-9886

Vinzenz Lausmann Memorial State
Natural Area
(541) 374-8811

Other Agencies
Linn County Parks
3010 Fetty Street SW
Albany, OR 97321
(541) 967-3917
www.linnparks.com

Portland Parks and Recreation
1120 SW Fifth Avenue, Suite 1302
Portland, OR 97204
(503) 823-7529
www.portlandoregon.gov/parks

Tillamook State Forest
Forest Grove District
801 Gales Creek Road
Forest Grove, OR 97116
(503) 357-2191
www.oregon.gov/ODF

APPENDIX B: SELECTED CONSERVATION AND HIKING GROUPS

Chemeketans
P.O. Box 864
Salem, OR 97308
www.chemeketans.org

The Freshwater Trust
65 SW Yamhill Street
Portland, OR 97204
(503) 222-9091
www.thefreshwatertrust.org

Friends of the Columbia Gorge
522 SW Fifth Avenue, Suite 720
Portland, OR 97204
(503) 241-3762
www.gorgefriends.org

Hells Canyon Preservation Council
P.O. Box 2768
La Grande, OR 97850
(541) 963-3950
www.hellscanyon.org

The Mazamas
527 SE 43rd Avenue
Portland, OR 97215
(503) 227-2345
www.mazamas.org

The Nature Conservancy of Oregon
821 SE Fourteenth Avenue
Portland, OR 97214
(503) 802-8100
www.nature.org/states/oregon

Obsidians
P.O. Box 322
Eugene, OR 97440
www.obsidians.org

Oregon Chapter Sierra Club
1821 SE Ankeny Street
Portland, OR 97214
(503) 238-0442
www.oregon.sierraclub.org

Oregon Natural Desert Association
33 NW Irving Avenue
Bend, OR 97701
(541) 330-2638
www.onda.org

Oregon Wild
5825 N Greeley Ave.
Portland, OR 97217-4145
(503) 283-6343
www.oregonwild.org

Portland Audubon Society
5151 Cornell Road
Portland, OR 97210
(503) 292-6855
www.audubonportland.org

Trails Club of Oregon
P.O. Box 1243
Portland, OR 97207
(503) 233-2740
www.trailsclub.org

INDEX

ABOUT THE AUTHOR

Doug Lorain has been obsessively exploring the trails and backcountry of Oregon for over 40 years. Over the years, he has hiked more than

eighteen thousand miles through every corner of Oregon and many thousands more in other western states and Canadian provinces. Despite a history that includes being charged by grizzly bears (twice!), bitten by a rattlesnake, and shot at by a hunter—and donating countless gallons of blood to mosquitoes—he claims that he would not trade one moment of it, because he has also been blessed to see some of the most beautiful scenery on Earth.

He is the author of *Backpacking Oregon, Backpacking Washington, Backpacking Idaho, Backpacking Wyoming, One Night Wilderness: Portland,* and *Afoot & Afield: Portland/Vancouver.*

THE MOUNTAINEERS, founded in 1906, is a nonprofit outdoor activity and conservation organization, whose mission is "to explore, study, preserve, and enjoy the natural beauty of the outdoors. . . ." The organization sponsors many classes and year-round outdoor activities in the Pacific Northwest, and supports environmental causes through educational activities, sponsoring legislation and presenting educational programs. The Mountaineers Books supports the organization's mission by publishing travel and natural

history guides, instructional texts, and works on conservation and history.

Visit www.mountaineersbooks.org to find details about all our titles and the latest author events.

The Mountaineers Books
1001 SW Klickitat Way, Suite 201
Seattle, WA 98134
800-553-4453
mbooks@mountaineersbooks.org

The Mountaineers Books is proud to be a corporate sponsor of The Leave No Trace Center for Outdoor Ethics, whose mission is to promote and inspire responsible outdoor recreation through education, research, and partnerships. The Leave No Trace program is focused specifically on human-powered (nonmotorized) recreation.

Leave No Trace strives to educate visitors about the nature of their recreational impacts, and offers techniques to prevent and minimize such impacts. Leave No Trace is best understood as an educational and ethical program, not as a set of rules and regulations.

For more information, visit www.lnt.org, or call 800-332-4100.